Carnegie Endowment for International Peace

DIVISION OF ECONOMICS AND HISTORY

JOHN BATES CLARK, DIRECTOR

PRELIMINARY ECONOMIC STUDIES OF THE WAR

EDITED BY

DAVID KINLEY

Professor of Political Economy, University of Illinois
Member of Committee of Research of the Endowment

No. 14

BRITISH LABOR CONDITIONS AND LEGISLATION DURING THE WAR

BY

M. B. HAMMOND

Professor of Economics, Ohio State University
Representative of U. S. Food Administration on the
War Labor Policies Board

NEW YORK

OXFORD UNIVERSITY PRESS

AMERICAN BRANCH: 35 West 32nd Street
LONDON, TORONTO, MELBOURNE, AND BOMBAY

1919

EDITOR'S PREFACE

The subject of this monograph is one of wide public interest. Perhaps no one subject connected with the war, aside from those having immediately to do with direct military operations, has aroused a greater interest in the minds of the public than have changes induced in the labor situation. The editor requested Professor Hammond to take up the subject, believing that his years of study of labor questions, and his familiarity with innovations in Australia and elsewhere, would enable him more quickly to understand and more justly to appreciate the importance of such radical changes as the war induced in the conditions of employment and life of the workers of the world. His treatment has justified this confidence.

Aside from contributing to our information on the condition of labor in the war, Professor Hammond's discussion will help the public to juster conclusions on many matters commonly described as a dispute between labor and capital, though more correctly described as between the systems of economic liberalism and social control of capital. Many of the critics of economic liberalism seem to show by their comments that their familiarity with the doctrines of liberalism are second hand. As in their theology they are presbyterians, perhaps, because their fathers and mothers were, so they are solidarists and critics of liberalism because their teachers were so. They bitterly assail Ricardianism, but have never read Ricardo. Many of the prophets fail to see, or seeing fail to admit, that the aim of the individual system of economic philosophy is precisely the same as that of the system of so-called social solidarity, the improvement of the economic life of the individual human being. Economic liberalism, as a system, has contributed, as shown by men like Hermann Levy, very largely to the progress of humanity. Its adherents, like those of the " new " social philosophy, believe that the earth belongs to us all. It bade each of us to go in and get his share in the belief, which was more or less justified under conditions of a century ago, that each would be able to get his share. Now that the field of competition is more crowded, and, therefore, men must jostle one another in the race, more complex "rules of the game" must be laid down. We can not now assume that each will get his share by his own strength. We must find some means of assuring him a share proportional in equity to his contribution to the general welfare. We are bound, moreover, to inquire into the legitimacy of unusual gains by individuals and to take such measures as are necessary to prevent the exploitation of one by another. Yet these necessities of the situation involve no new social, juridical, or philosophical principles. That private property is a public trust is a thought imbedded in the juridical system of the English-speaking peoples; that the community can compel the observance of this principle is a fact that has always been recognized among those peoples. Sometimes they have thought that a minimum of intervention secured the end. At other times, among them the present time, they have thought a maximum of intervention necessary. But the aim and the principle have been the same. We need to remember this in these days when so many proposals of social reconstruction, not well thought out and not logically coherent, are being foisted on the public attention.

Professor Hammond's study shows that in the attempt to secure that welfare of the worker which has been the common aim of liberalism, as well as of other social systems, the existing conditions of industry justify, and, indeed, necessitate, a more complex regulation of the relations between the employer and the employed, a better protection of the economically weak, a renewed insistence on the principle that the welfare of each is in a true sense the business of all. The study shows that some of the measures necessary are a greater coordination of the efforts of the worker and the employer, and greater efficiency on the part of both, leading permanently to the higher wages necessary for better living conditions. We are familiar with such proposals. The duty as well as the self-interest of the public, which after all is simply the whole number of us or the majority of us in certain relations, makes necessary insistence on the provision of better physical conditions of living, better moral surroundings, wider educational opportunities, and a wider and deeper sense of mutual obligation. It is hopeless to think that these ends can be largely or permanently attained through the exercise of force by any one class over another. The lasting solution lies in the acceptance of better moral standards which lead us to recognize our mutual duties and to make our self-interest more enlightened.

I commend Professor Hammond's work to the earnest consideration of all students of the subject.

DAVID KINLEY,
Editor.

Urbana, Illinois, February 19, 1919.

CONTENTS

CHAPTER   PAGE

I   The Social Background 3

II   English Industry and Labor at the Outbreak of the
War 22

III   Industrial Panic and Readjustment 32

IV   The Government and the Trade Unions 68

V   The Munitions of War Acts 86

VI   The Supply and Distribution of Labor 113

VII   The Dilution of Labor 140

VIII   Wages, Cost of Living, Hours of Labor, Welfare
Work and Unemployment 185

IX   Industrial Unrest 230

X   Industrial Reconstruction 269

         Index 329

CHAPTER I

The Social Background

The coming into power of the Liberal government in 1905 marks for England the beginning of a new era not only in politics but in social legislation. For a decade or more there had been signs of industrial unrest and of a growing discontent among the working classes. In spite of the wonderful expansion of industry and of trade during the preceding half century, and of an enormous increase of wealth whose rate of growth far exceeded that of the population, it can not be said that this prosperity had been shared by all classes or that either Parliament or party leaders showed any marked disposition to favor measures which tended to promote a better distribution of wealth or to raise the standard of living of the working classes. Imperialism, home rule, colonial federation and fiscal reforms were the questions which chiefly occupied the attention of the politicians, and even Mr. Chamberlain's advocacy of old age pensions was coupled with, and subordinated to, his desire to secure a protective tariff.

The struggle to secure factory legislation which had marked the first half of the nineteenth century found no counterpart during the second half, although the laws themselves were codified and improved in details. The legislative movement in behalf of shorter hours had apparently come to an end, and such later progress as had been made in that direction had come mainly through the trade unions.

The trade unions themselves had made continuous, if not steady, progress and in certain lines of industry had succeeded in securing for their members good wages and working conditions, but their influence was confined for the most part to the skilled trades and even in these trades their progress was by no means uniform. Among unskilled laborers low wages and irregularity of employment created a situation which bordered close upon dependency. The careful studies made by men like Charles Booth and B. S. Rowntree showed that in the larger English cities there was a considerable percentage of the population living close to the pauper line. Pauperism itself, while it showed a decline in most years, had been characterized by a rapidly diminishing rate of decrease in later years, in spite of a rapid increase of public expenditures for poor relief. The report of the Poor Law Commission published in 1909 said: " the country is maintaining a multitude of paupers not far short of the number maintained in 1871-72, and is spending more than double the amount upon each individual."

Recognition of these tendencies had begun to create uneasiness in both the leading political parties even prior to the incoming of the Liberal government in 1905, but neither the Liberals under Gladstone nor the Conservatives under Salisbury and Balfour· were ready to propose any very radical changes in the way of social legislation. Even of the changes proposed by the Balfour government in 1905, only one—the Unemployed Workmen Bill —secured parliamentary approval, and that in a form which left little hope of its practical success.

Meanwhile a new party (Labor) was being formed, composed of representatives of the trade unions and of the socialist societies, and this party succeeded at the election of 1906 in electing 29 members of Parliament from its own nominees, besides 24 others who were more or less identified with the labor movement. These added to 378 Liberals elected at the same time and pledged to labor reforms created a strong majority in the Commons in favor of the Liberal-Labor measures and left little doubt that the Parliament which assembled in 1906 would carry out a program of social reform of a far reaching character. What some of these reforms would be had already been indicated in the course of the campaign and in the resolutions adopted by political and labor bodies, but more substantial arguments were furnished for some of them, and the necessity of other reforms made evident, by the investigations and report of the Poor Law Commission, which was appointed in December, 1905, and which completed its work early in 1909.

FINDINGS AND RECOMMENDATIONS OF THE POOR LAW COMMISSION

Much of the work of the commission had to do with the history and administration of the existing poor laws, with statistics of the numbers, ages and distribution of paupers, with the costs of relief and with the work of private charities, but here and there in the report and the appendices are discussions of the causes of pauperism, which show that much of the prevalent poverty and distress was due to the social environment in which the laboring classes were living and to the failure of society to adopt preventive measures which are everywhere called for by the present mode of industrial organization.

Of the causes of pauperism, the commission placed chief emphasis upon the following: [1]

1. *Old age,* " when combined with, or following upon, other causes, such as low earning power, drink or shiftlessness." The relation of this cause to the industrial situation is seen in the significant statement that the commission " found a very general opinion that the development of industry is such as to make increasing demands upon the worker, and thus cause him to drop out of the industrial ranks at an earlier age." The obvious solution of the old age problem was a system of old age insurance or old age pensions and Parliament had already taken this step before the Poor Law Commission made its final report, by the adoption of the Old Age Pensions Act, 1908. As regards the reluctance of employers to engage old men, the commission said that this tendency to pauperism was beyond the influence of the poor law administrators, but that the remedy was to be found partly in a willingness of trade unions to allow older men to work for a lower wage than that paid to younger men, and partly in a system of insurance against unemployment.

[1] A summary of this part of the Poor Law Report is to be found in Helen Bosanquet's *The Poor Law Report of 1909,* pp. 24-42.

2. *Drink* as a factor in the creation of pauperism was shown to possess great importance by the evidence submitted to the commission. Especially in the case of inmates of workhouses and infirmaries, drink was held to be one of the chief causes of dependency. Not only the drinker himself but other members of his family were kept in poverty, if not reduced to a state of dependency by this cause. The commission suggested no radical remedy for this evil, believing that it must be found "in the greater self-control of the people themselves," but they did recommend that provision be made for the compulsory detention of inebriates in certain cases. Parliament had made some effort to deal with the drink question by means of the Licensing Bill of 1908, which was adopted in the Commons by a large majority, but was rejected by the House of Lords. No further legislation in the way of abatement of the drink evil seems to have been attempted prior to the war.

3. *Sickness* was a cause which contributed largely to pauperism, according to the report of the commission. "Any form of illness which is severe and prolonged tends to exhaust the resources of the family, especially when it is the wage earner who suffers." The specific diseases which the commission found most productive of pauperism were the venereal diseases and consumption, and the effects of these diseases were greatly aggravated by the living conditions amongst the very poor. The recommendations of the commission called for an entire change in the modes of furnishing medical relief, placed great emphasis on preventive measures and recommended that in certain cases, especially when dealing with the above mentioned diseases, power of compulsory removal to, and detention in, an institution should be given to the authorities under proper safeguards. As we shall presently see, the question of providing adequate medical assistance was dealt with by Parliament in a thoroughgoing fashion by Part I of the National Insurance Act, 1911.

4. *Bad housing conditions and bad sanitation*, as they induce sickness and loss of vitality, were among the causes of pauperism as stated by the Poor Law Commission. Especial emphasis was laid upon the influence of the unregulated or insufficiently regu-

lated common lodging houses and furnished rooms. The government undertook to deal with the housing problem by the Housing, Town Planning, etc., Act, 1909.

5. Amongst industrial causes of pauperism, the commission declared that *irregularity of employment* stood foremost. To a certain extent casual labor itself was found to be a result of the demoralization of the work people by other causes, but there was little doubt in the minds of the commission that if regularity of employment could be secured for those able and willing to work, pauperism of the worst type would be greatly reduced. "Take away casual labor and drink and you can shut up three quarters of the workhouses," is one of the strong statements in the report to which the commission apparently lent its approval. In this connection the commission called attention to the extent to which the casual labor force was recruited from the ranks of boys turned out from the elementary schools without having any industrial training.

The recommendations of the commission that a system of labor exchanges throughout the United Kingdom be established, that in connection with these exchanges and with the schools there should be created committees or agencies prepared to advise children and their parents in regard to the child's future work, and that a system of unemployment insurance be established, at first among the well organized trades, but gradually extended to others, were carried out in Parliament by the passage of the Labor Exchanges Act, 1909, and by the adoption of Part II (Unemployment) of the National Insurance Act, 1911.

6. *Low earnings* in certain occupations are mentioned by the commission as another cause of pauperism, but less emphasis is placed upon this than upon some of the others above mentioned. If, however, we substitute the word *poverty* for that of pauperism we should doubtless find low earnings occupying a much more important place among the contributing causes. By the Trade Boards Act, 1909, Parliament endeavored to furnish a means of combating the evil of low wages in the sweated trades.

The above mentioned do not exhaust the list of the factors contributing directly or indirectly to a state of dependency, as revealed by the investigation of the Poor Law Commission of 1905-1909. They do, however, constitute the most important causes there mentioned and they are the ones to which Parliament primarily directed its attention during the years which intervened between the incoming of the Liberal ministry and the outbreak of the war.

It would perhaps be a mistake to conclude that the investigations and report of the Poor Law Commission were mainly responsible for the adoption of the program of social legislation enacted by Parliament during these years. Many of these reforms had been urged for years by social reformers, who based their demands largely upon the results obtained through such legislation in other countries, particularly in Germany and the Australasian colonies of Great Britain. Furthermore, the recommendations of the Poor Law Commission were frequently disregarded by Parliament when it came to legislate on these matters. The commission itself was not a unit in its recommendation of reforms. A minority of four members were dissatisfied with the program of reforms submitted by the fourteen members who constituted the majority, and this minority submitted a demand for more radical changes than those advocated by the majority commissioners.[1] The great services of the investigation and report made by the Poor Law Commission were that they made clear the conditions existing among the poorer classes in the United Kingdom in 1909; that they revealed the tendencies towards degradation among laborers still living above the pauper line, and that, in some cases, they pointed out the direction which reform legislation should take.

THE TRADE DISPUTES ACT

The first important labor measure which, having been introduced and discussed in the House of Commons under the control of the Liberals, ran the gauntlet of the House of Lords and

[1] A discussion of the entire subject from the standpoint of the minority members is found in *English Poor Law Policy* by Sidney and Beatrice Webb. (London, 1910.)

received the royal assent was the Trade Disputes Act, 1906 (6 Edw. 7, c. 47).

Trade unions in Great Britain, which during the early years of the nineteenth century were deemed to be unlawful associations and their members prosecuted under the conspiracy laws for having united in restraint of trade, were legalized in 1824 and their position made more secure by the Trade Union Acts, 1871 and 1876. It was generally assumed that these acts, which held that trade unions were not unlawful combinations, even though they restrained trade, and which relieved from prosecution for criminal conspiracy members of such unions who acted in agreement or combination to further a trade dispute, had also relieved the unions of liability for damages suffered as a result of a trade dispute fostered or supported by the union or its agents. In 1900, however, as a result of a strike on the Taff Vale Railway, the railway company brought suit against the strikers for breach of contract and also claimed damages from their union (The Amalgamated Society of Railway Servants), which, although it had discountenanced the strike, had nevertheless given the men financial support. Mr. Justice Farwell, in the High Court of Justice, awarded damages against the union which, though neither a corporation nor a partnership, was, he said, an association of individuals vested by the legislature with a capacity for owning property and acting by agents and which, in the absence of express enactment to the contrary, must be held to possess liability to the extent of such property for the acts and defaults of its agents. This judgment was disallowed by the Court of Appeals, but was subsequently sustained by the House of Lords, the highest British court, to which the case had been carried on appeal.

The danger to the trade unions which this judgment threatened caused an active agitation by the unions and their friends to secure legislation relieving unions of financial responsibility for acts done in furtherance of a trade dispute. More than anything else this agitation was responsible for that crystalization of radical opinions which resulted in the creation of the Labor party. Even the Conservative government under the leadership of Mr. Balfour had attempted such legislation in 1905, but the bill introduced by the government was so mutilated in the course of its consideration in committee that it was withdrawn. Under Liberal leadership the Trade Disputes Act, 1906, was brought forward early in the next session, was amended by the adoption of a clause taken from a more radical bill introduced by the Labor members and, as amended, finally became law, as hitherto stated.

The act legalized peaceful picketing, removed liability for acts done in furtherance of a trade dispute, on the ground only that they induced other persons to break a contract of employment or that they interfered with the business or employment of some other person, and forbade any court to entertain an action against a trade union in respect to any tortious act alleged to have been committed by it or on its behalf. The enactment of this measure was probably largely responsible for the growth of trade unions in Great Britain, whose aggregate membership increased from 2,113,806 in 1906 to 3,987,115 in 1913.

WORKMEN'S COMPENSATION

Another important piece of labor legislation enacted at the 1906 session of Parliament was the Workmen's Compensation Act, 1906 (6 Edw. 7, c. 58). The principle of workmen's compensation as opposed to that of employers' liability, had been accepted by the British Parliament in 1897, but the 1897 act had limited the right to claim compensation to workmen engaged in the most dangerous occupations and had made the payment of compensation compulsory only upon employers in these trades who were solvent or who had insured themselves against the risks to their workmen. In 1900 the act had been extended to cover laborers engaged in agriculture and gardening, occupations not generally believed to be dangerous callings. In 1906 the government proposed further to extend the principle of workmen's compensation to all industrial callings, but excluded from its operation police-constables, clerks, shop assistants, domestic servants and employes of employers, other than those engaged in agriculture, whose workmen did not exceed five in number. Parliament refused to make these exceptions and the act as passed covered workmen in all occupations except clerks and salaried employes in receipt of salaries of £250 or over. Small as well as large employers were made liable, but insurance by employers was not made compulsory. A certain degree of protection was afforded to workmen whose employers might become bankrupt. The act classed certain occupational diseases as accidents, for which compensation was made payable, and provided that the Secretary of State might make orders extending this section of the act to other diseases due to the nature of the employment. It was estimated that the act of 1897 had afforded protection to 6,000,000 workmen, that another 1,000,000 engaged in agriculture were covered by the 1900 amendment and that the act of 1906 brought another 6,000,000 people—13,000,000 in all—under the provisions of the workmen's compensation law. Further amendments to the act were made in 1917 by the Workmen's Compensation (War Additions) Act.[1]

Old Age Pensions

Parliament next turned its attention to the subject of old age pensions. As already stated, the agitation for old age pensions had begun while the Unionists were in control of Parliament, but it had then been coupled with certain proposals for fiscal reform which Parliament was unwilling to accept. When the Liberals came into power, Labor members pressed for consideration of the question of furnishing old age pensions from the public funds. The government at that time lacked the necessary funds, but agreed to deal with the matter later. In the early part of 1908 the government introduced its bill for old age pensions. Opponents of the measure sought delay, claiming that Parliament should wait until the Poor Law Commission had made its report and, when this request was refused, they sought to make the measure unpopular by moving amendments which, if adopted, would add greatly to the cost of the government's plan. The Liberals resisted all efforts to weaken their measure and the bill became a law (8 Edw. 7, c. 40) on the first day of August,

[1] *Labour Gazette*, 1917, p. 313.

1908, the House of Lords, although not friendly to the measure, having accepted it as good party tactics.

The act allowed a pension to be paid from the public funds to every British subject resident within the United Kingdom for at least twenty years who had reached the age of 70 years and whose annual income did not exceed £31, 10s. The amount of the pension allowed varied according to the yearly means of the recipient, but might be not more than 5s. per week. No person was entitled to a pension (1) who was at the time of his application in receipt of poor relief; (2) who had received poor relief at any time between the dates of January 1, 1908, and December 31, 1910; (3) who had " habitually failed to work according to his ability, opportunity and need for the maintenance or benefit of himself and those legally dependent upon him "; (4) who was being detained in a lunatic asylum or in any place as a pauper or criminal lunatic; or (5) who was disqualified for registration as a parliamentary elector in consequence of conviction for an offense. A person might also be refused a pension while he was being detained in prison or for a period of ten years after his release, and the same disqualification might be applied to any person convicted and liable to a detention order under the Inebriates Act, 1908.

It was estimated in advance that the number of persons applying for a pension in 1909 and found entitled thereto would be about 386,000 and that this number would increase to 626,000 in 1912, chiefly as a result of the expiration of the poor relief disqualification at the end of 1910. Even these large estimates were far below the figures which experience showed to represent the persons entitled to this mode of assistance. The number of pensioners was 667,000 in 1909 and 942,000 in 1912. About three-fourths of the population over 70 years of age receive old age pensions under the act of 1908.[1]

The rapid rise in prices during the war bore with especial severity on the old age pensioners, and during the year 1916 the government decided to make an additional allowance (not to exceed 2s. 6d. a week) to any old age pensioner whose total in-

[1] Rubinow: *Social Insurance*, pp. 378-379.

come, including his pension, does not exceed 12s. 6d. a week. The additional allowance is for the period of the war only. The exact amount of the addition in the case of any individual is left to local pension committees or subcommittees to determine.[1]

MINIMUM WAGE LEGISLATION

The evil of low earnings in the sweated trades was dealt with by Parliament, as we have already observed, by the Trade Boards Act, 1909 (9 Edw. 7, c. 22). In 1907 the Home Office had sent a commissioner, Mr. Ernest Aves, to Australia and New Zealand, to investigate and report on the Australasian legislation for dealing with this problem and a bill, intended to establish wages boards along Australian lines, which should fix a minimum wage for workers in each one of certain sweated trades, had been introduced in Parliament in 1908 and after discussion had been referred to the Select Committee on Home Work.

On March 24, 1909, Mr. Winston Churchill introduced the government measure which provided for the establishment of a Trade Board composed of representatives of the employers and employes in the trade, in equal numbers, and of a lesser number of appointed members to look after the public interests involved, in each of four trades, ready made and wholesale bespoke tailoring, paper box making, machine made lace making and hammered and dollied or tommied chain making. These trades were among those in which large numbers of women were employed and in which investigations had shown that very low wages, long hours and bad working conditions generally prevailed. The Trade Board was to fix a minimum rate of wages for the trade which it represented and might also fix minimum rates of wages for piece work, and these minimum wages and rates when made obligatory by an order of the Board of Trade were to be binding on all employers in that trade. In order that all localities in which the trade in question was being carried on might have their peculiar circumstances considered by the board, any board was author-

[1] *Monthly Review of the U. S. Bureau of Labor Statistics*, July, 1917, pp. 34-35.

ized to establish district trade committees, constituted in the same manner as the board itself, to consider these peculiar circumstances and to recommend local variations in the general minimum wage adopted by the board. The minimum wage and piece rates were to be paid to home workers as well as to those employed in factories and heavy fines were provided for employers who failed to pay these minimum rates. Provision was made for extending the operations of the act by order of the Board of Trade to any industry in which the prevailing rate of wages was " exceptionally low as compared to that in other employments." In 1913, accordingly, the act was extended to the following additional trades: sugar confectionery and food preserving, shirt making, hollow-ware making and cotton and linen embroidery. About 400,000 workers were employed in the trades covered by the original act and the extension order, and were directly or indirectly affected by the minimum rates of wages established.

Although the trades which have been selected for the operation of the minimum wage under the provisions of this act are those in which women constitute the majority of employes, the minimum wages and rates apply to men as well as to women workers. Furthermore, in order to settle a strike in the coal mines occurring in the spring of 1912, an act was passed that year which provided wages boards to fix minimum wages and working conditions in the coal mining industry.

A few months prior to the outbreak of the war in 1914, the Chancellor of the Exchequer, Mr. Lloyd George, had proposed the establishment of a commission to fix minimum rates of wages for agricultural laborers and had further stated that the government was considering the extension of the wages boards system to all the lower paid industries in the towns. Although the outbreak of the war postponed further consideration of these proposals, they indicate that the principle of a legal minimum wage had met with acceptance in government circles and this partly explains the willingness of the government to make use of this principle when later it was called upon to regulate the manufacture of munitions. As we shall later see, a minimum wage was provided for agricultural labor in 1917. The Trade Boards Act,

1918, gave authority to the Minister of Labor to extend the provisions of the act of 1909 to other low paid trades.

HOUSING LEGISLATION

When the census of 1901 was taken in Great Britain the Census Commissioners discovered that 2,867,000 or 8.2 per cent of the population of England and Wales were living in 392,000 overcrowded tenements. Two-thirds of the people of London were living in dwellings having not more than four rooms each. In Glasgow one-fifth of the population lived in one room dwellings and more than half of the people had houses of not more than two rooms each.[1] Every industrial city in the United Kingdom showed housing conditions differing from the above only in degree; conditions which were the product of the rapid growth of municipalities, high rents, land speculation and failure to realize the connection between bad living conditions and vice, crime and disease.

Some improvement in the housing situation in the large cities had been effected by the Housing of the Working Classes Act of 1890, but more drastic reforms were needed and these were attempted by the Housing, Town Planning, etc., Act, 1909 (9 Edw. 7, c. 44). This act made it compulsory upon local authorities to provide new houses when ordered to do so by the Local Government Board, authorized the local authorities to purchase land compulsorily for such purposes and provided for loans from the public funds to local authorities, at minimum rates of interest, in order to enable them to carry out the orders of the Local Government Board. It also provided that in any house, let at low or moderate rentals, an implied part of the contract should be a requirement on the part of the landlord to put the house in a condition " in all respects reasonably fit for human habitation," and to keep it in such condition during the period of the lease. The duty was placed upon the local authorities to prohibit the use for dwelling purposes of any house deemed by the local medical authorities to be so dangerous to health as to be

[1] Percy Alden: *Democratic England*, p. 170.

unfit for human habitation, and upon refusal of the local authority to act, an appeal might be taken to the Local Government
Board. Houses closed because of improper conditions, which
were not or could not be made fit for human habitation within
a reasonable length of time, might be ordered demolished by the
local authorities.

Precautions were taken to see that land needed for parks and
open spaces in towns was not used for building purposes and
every local authority included under the terms of the act was
required to adopt a town planning scheme which had the approval
of the Local Government Board and to see that further city or
town developments were carried out in accordance with this
scheme. Every County Council was required to appoint a medical officer of health, who was not to engage in private practice,
but who, under the supervision of the County Council and the
Local Government Board, was required to perform such duties as
were prescribed by order of the Local Government Board or
were assigned to him by the County Council. Every County
Council was also to have a public health and housing committee
to consider matters relating to public health and the housing of
the working classes and to exercise such authority as was delegated to them by the County Council. The erection of back to
back houses was prohibited unless such houses were so con-
structed and arranged as to secure effective ventilation of all
rooms and were so certified by the local officer of health.

Parliamentary leaders recognized that no housing reform which
concerned itself merely with matters of construction and sanitation could remedy the evils of overcrowding in the cities, so long
as the problem of land monopoly was unsolved. One must consider, therefore, as supplemental to the Housing, Town Planning,
etc., Act, 1909, those parts of the Finance Act, 1910 (10 Edw. 7,
c. 8), which deal with taxes on the increment value of land
and with the undeveloped land duties. These were intended, as
Mr. Lloyd George said in his budget speech of 1909, to force
urban land withheld from use or not put to the best use, into the
market where it could be sold for housing or industrial purposes.
The House of Lords rejected this budget when it was first pre-

sented in 1909, but when the appeal to the country in 1910 led to the return of the Liberals, the Lords yielded and the Finance Act became a law on April 29, 1910.

Little was accomplished in the way of providing better housing facilities for the laboring classes during the years 1909-1914, due, it is said, to the failure of the Local Government Board to exercise the powers conferred upon it. What little was done proved woefully insufficient to meet the needs of many municipalities, especially those in which the manufacture of munitions has been extensively carried on during the war. Further legislation has been found necessary and still further laws and governmental assistance may be necessary to solve the problem.

The Relief of Unemployment

Unemployment was the one cause of pauperism on which the majority report of the Poor Law Commission laid especial emphasis. Parliamentary legislation followed more closely the recommendations of the commission with respect to this evil than it did in other matters which we have considered. By the Labor Exchange Act, 1909 (9 Edw. 7, c. 7), the Board of Trade was authorized to establish and maintain labor exchanges throughout the United Kingdom in such numbers and at such places as in their judgment were needed to facilitate the securing of employment by those out of work and to furnish laborers to employers having need of them. Under this act the Board of Trade established several hundred exchanges, there being over four hundred in existence at the outbreak of the war. The entire management of these exchanges was placed in the hands of the Board of Trade (later under the Ministry of Labor), which was also authorized to make advances in the shape of loans towards meeting the expenses of laborers who were sent to distant places where employment had been found for them through a labor exchange. About three and one quarter millions of applications for employment were made by laborers to the exchanges in the year 1914 and employers notified the exchanges of 1,425,000 vacancies. The vacancies which were actually filled by the exchanges during this year were 1,076,575, which was 76 per cent of the vacancies notified by employers.

Especial efforts have been made by the Board of Trade under authority of the Labor Exchange Act to assist boys and girls in finding employment in occupations which will enable them to learn a useful trade, and the same effort has been made by educational authorities under the Education Act. Although the correlation of the work of these two branches of the government service leaves much to be desired, considerable progress has been made in the way of advising and assisting juvenile laborers to secure employment.

The third step in affording relief for the unemployed was taken in 1911. Part II of the National Insurance Act, 1911, provided for the compulsory insurance of workers in seven trades: (1) building, (2) construction of works, (3) shipbuilding, (4) mechanical engineering, (5) ironfounding, (6) construction of vehicles, and (7) sawmilling. These trades are generally well organized, but much unemployment exists because of seasonal and cyclical fluctuations. Under the act as adopted, unemployed benefits amounting to 7s. per week were allowed to those unemployed in these trades. These benefits could only be drawn when work could not be found for men through the labor exchanges and in no case could unemployed benefits be received by any man for a longer period than fifteen weeks in any one year. The benefits were paid from an insurance fund created by weekly contributions of 2½ d. from employers and 2½ d. from employes while they remained at work. In addition to these contributions the government contributed one-third of the combined contributions of employer and employe. The act provided that trade unions which paid out of work benefits to their members might continue to do this and could then claim repayment from the public funds up to the amount which the men would be entitled to draw had they applied for benefits to the labor exchange.

In addition to the regular labor exchanges provided by the act of 1909, which assist in the administration of the act, the act provided for a number of insurance offices so located that one would be within five miles of every considerable group of workers in the kingdom and the insured man out of work might leave his insurance book at the nearest office, in which case he was entitled to the payment of benefits during the period for which no work was found for him.

The benefits were intended to be sufficient to prevent actual suffering, but were purposely kept low in order not to deter the beneficiaries from seeking work. No benefits were paid under the act during the first week of unemployment. In order to be eligible to receive unemployed benefits a worker must be unable to find work at his trade and he must not refuse suitable work which was found for him by a labor exchange, but he was not compelled to take work where a trade dispute was in progress nor was he obliged to accept less than the current rate of wages for the community in which he was at work.

Under the operations of this act, in 1913 about two and one-half million workers were insured and nearly a half million pounds sterling were paid out in the way of benefits to those unemployed during portions of that year.

Although the compulsory features of this part of the National Insurance Act were made applicable for the time being only to workers in the trades indicated, it was the intention of the framers of the act that these provisions should be extended as rapidly as possible to workers in other trades, and in order that this might be done, the administrative authorities were authorized to extend the system whenever they found it needful and practicable to do so. As we shall later see, Parliament itself, in 1916, provided for the extension of the unemployment features of the act to workers in the munition trades and to certain other closely allied trades.

THE HEALTH INSURANCE ACT

The last of the important pieces of social legislation enacted by Parliament in the decade preceding the war to which we desire to call attention was the National Insurance Act, 1911. Part II of this act dealing with unemployed insurance we have just considered. Part I of the act provided for the compulsory insurance against sickness and invalidity of all manual laborers between the ages of 16 and 70 and for persons not employed at manual labor whose annual earnings were less than £160. The act even included casual workers and home workers. The benefits under the act in case of sickness included not only cash benefits but medical care. No cash benefits were to be paid for the first three days of illness and in no case were they to be paid for more than twenty-six weeks in any one year. The cash benefits allowed were 10s. a week for men and 7s. 6d. a week for women. Hospital care was provided for in cases where it should be found necessary. The invalidity benefits were to consist of weekly payments of 5s. a week during incapacity, but these benefits were to cease at the age of 70, when the beneficiaries would be entitled to old age pensions.

The cost of this extensive system of sickness and invalidity insurance was to be divided between employer, employes and the state. Except in the case of those workers who received unusually low wages, men employes were to pay 4d. and women employes 3d. per week. The employer was to pay 3d. and the state 2d. per week. For employes whose wages were less than 2s. 6d. a day the workers' contributions were to be lessened and those of the employer and the state increased. Special benefits were to be paid under this act both to insured women and to the wives of insured men at times of childbirth. The benefits granted to the wives of insured men were 30s., and in case of women wage earners, an additional 30s. might be paid. These benefits were intended to make it possible for the beneficiaries to refrain from work for several weeks during confinement. Nearly 14,000,000 persons in the United Kingdom were insured under the terms of this act during the first year of its operation, 1912-13.

Effect of Social Legislation upon Problems of the War

This rapid sketch of important social legislation enacted in Great Britain during the ten years preceding the outbreak of war will suffice to show that, however poorly prepared for war the country may have been from a military point of view, it had enacted legislation which had the effect of providing a considerable measure of protection to the working classes, and this legislation has unquestionably made easier the task of meeting the domestic problems which have arisen during the war. It is true that the laws have been too recently enacted to have exerted any considerable effect in building up the health, strength and vitality of the existing generation of workers so as to fit them for military service, as has been the case in Germany, where laws of a similar character have been in operation for nearly a generation. Nevertheless, the English social legislation can not be overlooked as an important factor in helping to solve the social problems which have grown out of the war. The evils which the laws were intended to overcome were not of course those originating in military operations, but since those laws made it easier for the country to adjust itself to a war basis and to prevent or relieve distress growing out of the unusual activities of the war period, they must be considered in any attempt to describe the social conditions which have prevailed during the war. Some of them, like the workmen's compensation and the unemployment insurance laws, have been modified to meet the new conditions growing out of the war. All of these laws will doubtless show themselves to be of even greater use in that period when the country changes from a war to a peace basis, and when the problems of industrial readjustment will be unusually difficult to meet.

CHAPTER II

English Industry and Labor at the Outbreak of the War

Unemployment Statistics

The outbreak of the war found most British industries in a highly prosperous condition. Employment had been good for three and a half years, having attained its maximum during the first half of 1913. Although there had been a contraction after that time, conditions were still good at the end of July, 1914. Trade unions, having a net membership of 988,946 in July, reported that only 28,013 or 2.8 per cent of their members were unemployed at the end of that month.[1] This is to be compared with a mean percentage of four for the month of July for fifteen years, and, with the exception of the years 1912 (2.6 per cent) and 1913 (1.9 per cent), it is lower than for the same month in any year since 1900.[2]

In coal mining 710,453 persons were employed in July, working an average of 5.06 days a week. This, after allowing for the July holidays, is a record which compares favorably with the high level of 1913, when the average number of days worked per week was 5.58, "the highest yearly average recorded."[3] As compared to July, 1913, when an average of 5.26 days were worked, the reduction was only two-tenths of one per cent.[4]

In what are known as the "insured trades" (those in which, under Part II of the National Insurance Act, 1911, benefits are paid to unemployed workers), where the number of insured workmen amounted to 2,325,598 in July, 1914, the unemployed at the end of that month amounted to only 83,412 or 3.6 per cent,

[1] *Labour Gazette*, 1914, p. 281.
[2] *Seventeenth Abstract of Labour Statistics of the United Kingdom*, 1915, p. 6.
[3] *Labour Gazette*, 1914, pp. 3, 282.
[4] *Ibid.*, p. 282; *Seventeenth Abstract of Labour Statistics*, 1915, p. 10.

which is just about the mean per cent for the eighteen months ending in July [1]—a very prosperous period for these trades.

The most notable exception to the generally good conditions of employment was that of the textile trades. The very incomplete returns from the firms which report to the Board of Trade showed a decline in the number of work people employed on July 25, 1914, amounting to 1.8 per cent of those employed the closing week of July, 1913.[1] All of these trades, with the exception of hosiery, participated in this decline which, while not remarkable in itself, owes its significance to the fact that these trades (excepting woolen and hosiery) were the ones which were chiefly affected by the industrial depression which accompanied the outbreak of the war. Unemployment due to the war was therefore superimposed upon a certain degree of involuntary idleness which had already existed in these trades during times of peace.

The figures relating to employment are not the only ones which tend to show the prosperous conditions of labor and industry during the years and months immediately preceding the outbreak of the war.

PRODUCTION OF LEADING COMMODITIES

The production in Great Britain of coal, iron ore, salt, tin ore, steel ingots and puddled iron bars, measured in tons, was greater in 1913 than for any previous year,[2] and the same is true of the tonnage of merchant ships launched.[3] Foreign trade statistics, which are always considered a barometer of English industrial conditions, showed that the total value of imports into the United Kingdom for 1913 was £769,034,000, which represented an increase of 3.3 per cent over the figures for 1912 and 13.1 per cent over those for 1911.[4]

The total value of British and Irish exports was £525,461,000 for 1913, which was an increase over those for 1912 of 7.8 per

[1] *Labour Gazette,* 1914, p. 282.
[2] *Seventeenth Abstract of Labour Statistics of the United Kingdom,* pp. 30-36.
[3] *Ibid.,* p. 37.
[4] *Labour Gazette,* 1914, p. 35.

cent and over those for 1911 of 15.7 per cent.[1] Although the year
1914 did not maintain this record, the decline during the seven
months preceding the outbreak of the war was not considerable,
amounting in the case of imports to only 1.2 per cent of the
imports for the corresponding months of 1913, and in the case
of exports to 1.4 per cent of the amount exported during the first
seven months of 1913.[2]

WHOLESALE AND RETAIL PRICES

This prosperous state of affairs in industry was quickly reflected in both the wholesale and the retail prices of commodities.
The index numbers of wholesale prices contained in the report
on Cost of Living of the Working Classes and continued by the
Department of Labor Statistics of the Board of Trade applies
to 47 commodities, weighted in accordance with their estimated
consumption representing all classes of production. The year
1900 was taken as the basis-100. The weighted index number
for the forty-seven commodities considered collectively showed
a steady increase after 1908 and in 1913 amounted to 116.5.[3]
Retail prices showed a similar advance. The index numbers of
twenty-three articles, widely used by the laboring classes, were
obtained by weighing the percentage for these articles in accordance with the average expenditure on these articles by working
class families in 1904. Measured in this way, prices were 114.8
per cent in 1913 and 116.8 per cent in 1914, as compared to 100
per cent in 1900. The advance was even greater than this in the
case of bread, flour and the cereals, for imported meats and also
for eggs and cheese.[4]

CHANGES IN WAGES AND COST OF LIVING

If we turn now to consider the changes which had taken place
in wages during these years of advancing prices, we shall see
that the British working classes had not shared to the full extent

[1] *Labour Gazette*, 1914, p. 35.
[2] *Ibid.*, pp. 315-316.
[3] *Seventeenth Abstract of Labour Statistics*, 1915, p. 88.
[4] *Ibid.*, p. 102.

in the prosperity which had overtaken industry. The index number for wages of skilled or semi-skilled workers in various trades and for agricultural laborers shows an advance from the base 100 in 1900 to 106.5 for 1913, when all groups of workers are considered collectively. For agricultural workers the corresponding numbers for these years are 100-111.2; for textile workers, 100-111.6; for workers in the engineering trades, 100-105; for those in the building trades, 100-104.4 and for coal miners, 100-100.1.[1] When these advances are compared with the greater increase in the retail prices of most commodities consumed by the laboring classes, it will be seen that wages measured in purchasing power had actually declined during these years. Such a statement, however, takes no account of the greater steadiness of employment during prosperous years and it would probably not be true to state that the average earnings of the British laborer, measured either in money or in commodities, were less in 1913 or the first half of 1914 than they were during the early years of the century. Some further compensation for the failure of wages to rise as rapidly as prices is also found in the fact that in all trades and industries the number of hours worked per week shows a steady, though by no means a uniform, reduction.[2]

According to calculations made for the report on the Cost of Living of the Working Classes, rents of working class dwellings in London had declined in London by percentages varying from 2 to 6 according to the location, and had increased in other towns and cities by percentages varying from 0.7 to 4.3, according to the county.[3] When rents and retail prices of food and coal were combined, the mean percentage increase in the cost of living, between 1905 and 1912, measured in this way varied from about 8 in London and the southern counties to 2.9 in Wales and Monmouthshire, 10.9 in Scotland and 12.2 in Ireland.[3]

Other tests of the prosperity of the working classes, frequently applied, although not entirely satisfactory, are found in the statis-

[1] *Seventeenth Abstract of Labour Statistics*, 1915, p. 66.
[2] *Ibid.*, pp. 79-82.
[3] *Ibid.*, p. 122.

tics of savings bank deposits and of the number of pauper dependents. For the United Kingdom there had been a steady increase in the deposits in the post office savings banks since 1899, when they amounted to £130,118,605. By 1913 they had reached a total of £187,248,167. The corresponding figures for the trustee savings banks were £51,404,929 in 1899 and £54,258,861 in 1913.[1] Possibly a better test of the extent to which the population in general shared in these deposits is found in the number of accounts open, which in the case of the post office savings banks were 8,046,680 in 1899 and 13,198,609 in 1913, and in the case of trustee savings banks were 1,601,485 in 1899 and 1,912,816 in 1913.[2]

REDUCTION OF PAUPERISM

The statistics of paupers show that, exclusive of vagrants and insane persons, the mean number of indoor and outdoor paupers in England and Wales had reached its maximum in 1909, when it was 793,851, being a ratio of 22.6 per 10,000 of the estimated population. By 1914 the mean number [3] had fallen to 617,128, a ratio of 16.7 per 10,000. To a slight extent this reduction of number is due to the fact that in 1911 a number of paupers ceased to be dependent on poor relief in consequence of the partial removal of the pauper disqualification from old age pensioners.[4]

Much more indicative of the changes which had taken place for the better in the condition of the wage earners is the falling off in the work of the local distress committees which under the Unemployed Workmen Act, 1905, are " empowered to provide or contribute to the provision of work for unemployed persons." [5]

During the industrial depression of 1908-09, when unemployment had reached a stage of intensity not since attained (except for a very brief period in 1912), these distress committees in Great Britain were very busy in receiving and acting on

[1] *Seventeenth Abstract of Labour Statistics*, pp. 326-327.
[2] *Ibid.*, p. 328.
[3] As the mean number is the mean of the numbers relieved on January 1 of the year given and of July 1 preceding, it is clear that the 1914 figures are unaffected by war.
[4] *Seventeenth Abstract of Labour Statistics*, p. 331.
[5] *The Labour Year Book*, 1916, p. 31.

applications for relief by working men who were temporarily out of work. The following table [1] offers a comparison of the work of these committees for 1908-09 and for 1913-14, during which period there had been a steady decline in the work and relief found necessary by them. The figures are given for England, Wales and Scotland considered collectively, although the dates returns were made are not the same for all these countries:

WORK OF DISTRESS COMMITTEES

	1908-09	1913-14
Number of committees who received applications at some time during the year	138	62
Number of applications received	230,807	25,343
Number of applications considered eligible	159,303	17,205
Number of applicants provided with work	104,344	10,389
Number of persons assisted to emigrate	11,142	1,950
Number of persons assisted to move to another area	457	131
Cost of work provided	£324,779	£75,220
Total expenditure	£419,081	£124,380

LABOR AND INDUSTRIAL ORGANIZATIONS

One other set of facts needs to be given to complete the picture of industrial and labor conditions in Great Britain at the outbreak of the war. This relates to the growth and strength of the trade union movement. It is a well known fact that trade unions increase in numbers and financial strength during years of industrial prosperity and generally show a diminution in the number of members in good standing during years of industrial depression and unemployment. The membership of British trade unions had with few fluctuations shown a steady increase during the fifteen years ending with 1913.

In 1899 the number of trade unions, exclusive of a few unimportant ones for which the figures were not available, was 1,310 and their combined membership was 1,860,913. By 1913 the number of unions had fallen to 1,135, chiefly as a result of amalgamation, but the total membership had more than doubled,

[1] Compiled from the annual reports on distress committees issued by the local government boards for England and Wales and for Scotland. *Abstract of Labour Statistics for United Kingdom*, 16th (1913), p. 36; 17th (1915), p. 28.

being 3,993,769 at the close of that year.[1] This was an increase
of 21.5 per cent over the membership for 1912. " This membership," said a writer in the *Labour Gazette*,[2] " is greatly in excess
of any hitherto recorded, and the rate of increase is little below
the high rate of 1911 (23.4 per cent). The expansion in membership was common to practically all trades, but was especially
marked in the transport and general labor groups. Some of the
increase is attributable to trade union activity in connection with
the National Insurance Act."

" The total membership," the writer goes on to say, " of all
trade unions in 1913 increased by 109 per cent compared
with 1904 and by 175.1 per cent compared with 1895, when the
membership was lower than at any time during the period 1892-
1913, for which the Department has comparable statistics." [3]

One of the most remarkable facts connected with this movement was the increase in the number of female members. Their
numbers had grown from 129,084 in 1904 to 318,607 in 1913,
an increase of 176.4 per cent. " Nearly three quarters (258,732)
of the total female membership were engaged in the textile trades,
the cotton industry accounting for 212,534 or 60 per cent." [3]

In discussing the strength of trade unionism at the outbreak of
the war, mention should be made of the Triple Alliance of trade
unions formed in 1914 between the Miners' Federation, representing 800,000 workers, the National Union of Railway Men,
with a membership of 300,000, and the Transport Workers'
Federation, comprising 250,000 workers. The purpose of
the alliance was to take joint action on matters of a national
character or those vitally affecting a principle which necessitated
combined action.

The significance of the federation lay in the fact that all three
of these powerful organizations are formed along industrial lines,
that they represent the workers in industries in which the public
is vitally affected and that syndicalist views have permeated more
or less the rank and file of the membership.

[1] *Seventeenth Abstract of Labour Statistics*, 1915, p. 197.
[2] *Labour Gazette*, 1914, p. 282.
[3] *Ibid.*, 1914, p. 283.

Plans for the formation of the Triple Alliance had been laid before the war was dreamt of, but were not completed until December, 1914. The alliance has already taken steps to secure compliance with the government promise that trade union practices and customs will be restored with the coming of peace and that demobilization shall take place in such a way as to prevent a period of unemployment and low wages.[1]

The organization activities among the working classes had found its counterpart among their employers. How large a proportion of the employers were organized at the outbreak of the war we do not know, but in 1914 there were 1,558 organizations of employers, of which ninety-eight were federations or national associations and 1,460 were local associations. These numbers include only those organizations which deal directly with industrial relations. Employers were for the most part organized in the same trades and along the same lines as were their employes. Thus 496 associations of employers were in the building trades and 246 were in the metal, engineering and shipbuilding trades.

That these organizations of employers and of their work people existed for the most part to deal on friendly terms with each other is shown by the fact that in 1910 an investigation made by the government showed that at least 1,696 trade agreements of one sort or another were in existence to govern the relations between employers and employes. The total number of workers affected by these agreements was estimated at 2,400,-000, of whom 900,000 were engaged in mining and quarrying, 500,000 in the transport trades, 460,000 in the textile trades, 230,000 in the metal, engineering and shipbuilding trades and 200,000 in the building trades.

INDUSTRIAL DISPUTES

It is perhaps to be expected that with a great increase in the number of trade unionists there should come an effort to make

[1] Leland Olds: *Railroad Transportation in British Industrial Experience During the War*, vol. 2, pp. 1155-1158.

the potential strength of the unions effective in securing increases in wages and improvements in working conditions. This expectation is fully realized when one consults the record of industrial disputes for the years preceding the war.

In its review of " Labor Disputes in 1913," the *Board of Trade Labour Gazette* of November, 1914, has this to say concerning conditions during these years:

> The year 1913 was the third of a series in which a considerable number of important disputes have occurred. Single years in the past have surpassed one or more of these years in respect of number of disputes, number of work people involved, or aggregate duration of disputes; but, so far as the available statistics show, there has never before been a series of three consecutive years marked as a whole by such widespread industrial unrest.[1]

A study of the strike statistics shows that practically all the main groups of trades were affected by the increase in the number of disputes or in the number of workers affected by them. In view of the general industrial prosperity and of the increase in the cost of living, it is to be expected that demands for advances in wages would be the cause for the majority of disputes during these years. Disputes over wages explain the suspension of industry by 46.1 per cent of the workers directly involved in trade disputes in 1911, 82.8 per cent in 1912 and 54.9 per cent in 1913.[2] In the great majority of cases the workers were at least partially successful in obtaining their demands.[3]

The period of intense industrial disturbances did not come to an end with the close of 1913, but continued into 1914 down to the very outbreak of the war. The number of disputes occurring during the seven months January-July, 1914 (772), was somewhat short of the number for the same months of 1913 (852), but the number of work people involved in 1914 (412,131) was only a trifle fewer than in 1913 (413,019), while the aggregate duration in working days of all disputes was much larger in 1914 (9,107,800) than in 1913 (6,339,400).[4]

[1] *Labour Gazette*, 1914, p. 398.
[2] *Seventeenth Abstract of Labour Statistics*, 1915, p. 190.
[3] *Ibid.*, p. 191.
[4] *Labour Gazette*, 1914, p. 308.

The brief statistical survey of industrial and labor conditions in England during the months and years immediately preceding the outbreak of the war which we have just given is probably sufficient to show that it was on the whole a " merrie Englande " upon which the ravages of war began to fall in August, 1914. The country had been enjoying prosperous conditions for several years and while a retrograde movement had begun during the latter part of 1913, which had continued up to August, 1914, the decline had not been great and there was as yet no indication that it was to be a serious or prolonged industrial depression.

While it seems evident that the laboring classes had not shared in the prosperity of the industries to the same extent as had the shareholders, owing tó the fact that the retail prices of those commodities which enter most largely into the wage earner's consumption had risen more rapidly than had the laborer's wages, yet a full consideration of such matters as the regularity of employment, the reduction of hours of work and the growth of social insurance warrants the statement that laborer as well as capitalist had profited by the industrial prosperity of the years 1911-1914, even though they had profited in an unequal degree.

CHAPTER III

Industrial Panic and Readjustment

The first effect of the war on industry was the creation of a feeling of uncertainty. Mr. G. D. H. Cole in his book entitled *Labour in War Time* [1] well describes this uncertainty in the following terms:

> When war broke out, the workers, the capitalists, and the government seem to have been equally in the dark as to its probable effects upon industry. No one knew what would be its reaction upon the credit system and on external trade; no one knew how far the home demand was likely to suffer contraction; no one foresaw the scale on which the war would be carried on, or the immense demands it would make upon production. It was, of course, anticipated that a few industries ministering directly to military needs would be busy beyond their wont; but even here nothing like what has actually happened was expected in the early days of August. On every side people made up their minds that there was bound to be a very severe dislocation of the industrial machine, if not a complete collapse.

The way in which this uncertainty first communicated itself to trade was, of course, through the medium of retail prices, especially the prices of food. Food prices began to advance on August 1, but the sharp rise took place after August 3, which was a bank holiday. [2] By August 8 prices had attained their maximum for the month and were then on an average 15 or 16 per cent higher than the level for July. This advance was general, but by no means uniform for the various commodities, being only one per cent in the case of milk, whereas in the case of sugar it was 83 per cent in the towns of over 50,000 inhabitants and 86 per cent in the smaller towns. [2] After August 8 the prices of most foods began to recede and by the 29th of the month the percentage increase over the July level was 11 for

[1] Page 62.
[2] *Labour Gazette*, 1914, p. 323.

the larger and 9 for the smaller towns.[1] The only notable exceptions to this general decline were fish and, in the case of the larger towns, mutton. In the case of potatoes, the decline was so considerable that prices during the latter part of August and throughout the remainder of the year were actually lower than in July. This was, of course, mainly due to the coming to market of the new crop.

GROWTH OF UNEMPLOYMENT

The effect of war upon employment was not the same in the various industries and was further obscured by the fact that August is the dull season in certain industries as dressmaking,

[1] *Labour Gazette*, 1914, p. 323. What action, if any, taken by the government, had to do with this fall of prices seems a matter of doubt. Labor writers refer specifically to "maxima prices" being specifically "fixed" by the government and having assisted in the fall of food prices, following the August panic. Thus the *Labour Year Book*, 1916, after showing what changes in food prices took place said (p. 42): "How has this situation been dealt with by the government and by labor? After their first action in checking the purely panic rise of the first weeks of August by fixing maxima prices, the government retired from the scene." Likewise Cole (*Labour in War Time*, p. 119) said: "The 15 per cent increase during the first week of August was largely a panic increase which was checked partly by the government's action in fixing maximum prices, but still more by the natural evaporation of the panic."
A careful investigation of the war emergency legislation and governmental orders and proclamations has failed to reveal any action taken by the government in August, 1914, in the way of fixing maxima prices. On August 10, 1914, Parliament enacted the Unreasonable Withholding of Food Supplies Act, 1914, providing that "if the Board of Trade are of opinion that any foodstuff is being unreasonably withheld from the market, they may, if so authorized by His Majesty's Proclamation (made generally or as respects any particular kind of foodstuff) and in manner provided by the proclamation, take possession of any supplies of foodstuffs to which it relates, paying to the owners of the supplies such price as may in default of agreement be reasonable," etc. (4 & 5 Geo. 5, c. 51). No proclamation was ever made under this power. (*Manual of Emergency Legislation*, p. 17.) The act itself was repealed on August 28, its place being taken by the Articles of Commerce (Returns, etc.) Act, 1914, (4 & 5 Geo. 5, c. 65). This later act was put in force by Proclamation of September 17, 1914 (*Manual of Emergency Legislation*, p. 96), and it was apparently on its authority that the Board of Trade entered into an agreement with the leading sugar refiners to prevent speculation in this commodity and to keep its price within reasonable bounds. (*Foreign Food Prices as Affected by the War*, Bulletin of the U. S. Bureau of Labor Statistics, No. 170, p. 62.) In August and September, 1914, the Board of Trade published a list of so-called "maximum retail prices" for various food commodities which were recommended by advisory committees of retail traders as reasonable, (*Labour Gazette*, 1914, pp. 283, 323-324) but there appears to have been nothing but moral suasion to compel their adoption by retailers.

millinery, tailoring and the like.   In other industries, notably cotton, the adverse effects of the war were added to a trade decline, which had already been marked for some time.   In still other industries, especially in the north of England, employes were absent in August on their holiday vacation.[1]   Certain industries, or rather certain establishments, profited immediately on the outbreak of the war by government orders.   This was notably true of shipbuilding and of certain establishments in the engineering, saddlery and harness, boot and shoe, military clothing and hosiery trades, where some overtime was worked.[2]   Aside from these special establishments, however, it may be said that the general effect of the war during August was to lessen employment in nearly all industries.

Unemployment in the trade unions which make reports to the Board of Trade took a sudden upward leap from 2.8 per cent of the membership at the end of July to 7.1 per cent at the end of August.   At the end of August, 1913, only 2 per cent of the members had been unemployed.[1]

The total number of people remaining on the registers of the British labor exchanges for whom no work had been found was 194,580 on August 14, as compared with 112,622 on July 17, and with 89,049 in August, 1913.[3]

In the insured trades where the number of insured people was 2,341,508, 6.2 per cent of the workers were unemployed at the end of August, as compared with 2.6 per cent at the end of July, and 3.1 per cent at the end of August, 1913.[4]

The figures relating to unemployment do not begin to show the full effect of the crisis upon employment, however, since in many industries and establishments the workers were put on short time instead of being laid off.   This was especially true in the tin plate and steel sheet, engineering, printing, bookbinding, building, pottery and in all of the textile trades.   This resulted in a great decrease in the earnings of the workers.[2]   In the cotton manufacture, where conditions were especially bad, earnings during

[1] *Labour Gazette*, 1914, p. 321.
[2] *Ibid.*, pp. 328-342.
[3] *Ibid.*, p. 348.
[4] *Ibid.*, 1914, p. 322.

one week in August were 58.8 per cent less than in the corresponding week in July and 60.9 per cent less than for the corresponding week in August, 1913.[1]

METHODS OF AFFORDING PUBLIC RELIEF

Under the circumstances it is perhaps not surprising to find that there was an increase in the number of persons seeking relief. For workers in the seven " insured trades " there was, of course, the relief afforded by the payment of unemployment benefits, payable under the provisions of Part II (Unemployment) of the National Insurance Act, 1911. Claims for unemployment benefits amounting to 180,233 were made during the four weeks ending August 28, 1914, as compared with 103,730 claims made during the five weeks ending July 31, and the average weekly amount of benefits paid during August was £11,772 as compared with £8,793 in July.[2] There was a fall in the total number of claims made to 133,692 in September, but the average weekly amount of benefits paid rose to £19,734 during this month.[3] Conditions in these trades thereafter improved steadily.

For workers in other trades other methods of affording relief had to be provided. " At the end of August, 1914, 40 distress committees had their registers open, compared with sixteen at the end of July, 1914, and fifteen at the end of August, 1913. Of those operating at the end of August, 24 had opened their registers during the month owing to the disturbed state of employment caused by the war. In addition, numerous local organizations were set up for the relief of distress." [2] The number of persons receiving employment relief was 2,843 as compared with 589 in August, 1913, and in addition employment was provided for 180 persons by arrangement with employers and local authorities.[2]

The number of pauper dependents, which, as we have observed, had been steadily declining since 1909, took a sudden leap upward

[1] *Labour Gazette,* 1914, p. 322.
[2] *Ibid.,* p. 351.
[3] *Ibid.,* p. 387.

in August, showing an increase of 1.9 per cent in number, and of 4 in the rate per 10,000 of the total population. The increase was in thirty out of thirty-five of the urban districts, but was especially noticeable in the Leicester district and in East London.[1]

The distress produced by the sudden disturbance of industrial conditions due to the war was such that the War Office found it necessary in August to issue to the contractors working on army orders suggestions intended to minimize the evils of unemployment and a warning not to allow sweating conditions to enter into their subcontracts. The following are the words of the Memorandum sent out by the War Office:[2]

In order to assist as far as possible in minimizing the evils of unemployment which must in some districts arise as a result of the war, it is particularly desired that, in the execution of army orders, contractors shall act upon the following suggestions to such extent as they reasonably can, viz:—(1) Rapid delivery to be attained by employing extra hands in shifts or otherwise, in preference to overtime, subject always to the paramount necessity of effecting delivery within the times requisite for the needs of the army. (2) Subletting of portions of the work to other suitable manufacturers situated in districts where serious unemployment exists, although contrary to the usual conditions of army contracts, is admissible during the present crisis, and it is desired to encourage such subletting on the following conditions, viz:—(a) The main contractor to remain solely responsible for due execution of the contract as regards quality, dates for delivery and in every respect. (b) The fair wages clause to apply strictly with the exception of the passage prohibiting subletting. The main contractor to be responsible for subletting only to manufacturers who will undertake to observe the other provisions of the fair wages clause. (c) Names and addresses of all firms to whom it is proposed to sublet work to be submitted for approval before work is actually given out to them.

REDUCTION IN NUMBER OF TRADE DISPUTES

One of the important immediate effects of the outbreak of war was the great reduction—almost cessation—of labor disputes. In July, 1914, ninety-nine trade disputes had begun in

[1] *Labour Gazette*, 1914, p. 352.
[2] *Ibid.*, p. 322.

the United Kingdom involving, directly or indirectly, 49,370 persons. This, added to the number of persons involved in disputes which began before July but continued into August, gave a total of 98,112. The working days lost as a consequence of these disputes was 1,327,800 during the month.[1] In August the number of disputes begun during the month fell to fifteen and their relatively insignificant character is shown by the further statement that they involved, directly and indirectly, only 2,004 persons.

The decline in the number and seriousness of these disputes was not accidental, nor was it unpremeditated. It seems to have been the more or less instinctive feeling of both laborers and employers that a period of international war was not a time to press demands for changes in industrial relations. Accordingly, a period of industrial truce began and settlements were reached in most disputes then in progress even before the trade union leaders met in conference to suggest such settlements. It is said, however, that the disputes were "settled, generally without consultation of the rank and file" (of the unionists).[2] This was, in the main, true of the settlement of the London building trade dispute, where an agreement was reached on August 6 by the executives of the unions and of the employers' associations along the lines of a proposed agreement which had several times been rejected by a vote of the workers.[3]

On August 24, a conference called by the joint board of the Trades Union Congress, the General Federation of Trade Unions, and the Labor party adopted the following resolution:

That an immediate effort be made to terminate all existing trade disputes, whether strikes or lockouts, and whenever new points of difficulty arise during the war period a serious attempt should be made by all concerned to reach an amicable settlement before resorting to a strike or lockout.[4]

The net result of all these efforts to foster industrial peace was that the number of lost working days due to trade disputes

[1] *Labour Gazette*, 1914, p. 308.
[2] Cole: *Labour in War Time*, p. 43.
[3] *Labour Gazette*, 1914, p. 326.
[4] *The Labour Year Book*, 1916, p. 22.

fell from 1,327,800 in July to 526,900 in August, with a further decline to 229,800 in September.[1]

RAPID RECOVERY OF EMPLOYMENT CONDITIONS

The August panic soon passed and industrial readjustment took place rapidly in most trades, except those in which female laborers were largely employed.   Trade unions with 7.1 per cent of their members out of work at the end of August reported but 5.6 per cent unemployed at the end of September.   By the end of October this percentage had fallen to 4.4, in November to 2.9 and by the end of the year to 2.5, which was practically equivalent to conditions at the close of 1912 and 1913—the best previously reported conditions for December.[2]

In the insured trades the rate of recovery was even better, as is shown by the following table, which gives the percentage of unemployed to the total number of workers in these trades for the last six months of 1914.[3]

	Per cent
July	3.6
August	6.2
September	5.4
October	4.2
November	3.7
December	3.3

The reasons for this rapid recovery in the conditions of employment were, first, the placing of government contracts, which not only created a great demand for labor in those industries and establishments which received government orders, but tended to cause a shifting of labor from other establishments and industries, and, second, the recruiting campaign and the progress of voluntary enlistments, which depleted the industrial supplies of male labor and soon changed a labor surplus into a labor shortage in many trades.

[1] *Labour Gazette*, 1914, pp. 346, 382.
[2] *Ibid.*, pp. 357, 393, 429; 1915, pp. 1-2.
[3] *Ibid.*, 1914, pp. 282, 323, 358, 394, 429; 1915, p. 2.

The first trades to recover were, of course, those working on war material, such as the engineering, shipbuilding, saddlery, furniture, bit and stirrup, woolen, hosiery, leather and boot and shoe trades. Some establishments in these trades began to prosper even in August, but the recovery is much more marked in September, when statements like the following appear frequently in the Board of Trade reports for the various industries:

Employment was good, with much overtime on government work. . . . Many men were brought from other districts. (Engineering trades: London district.) [1] Employment was good, especially on government orders, much overtime being worked and men obtained from other districts. (Engineering trades: West Midlands district.) [1] There was a decline in employment on the south coast, though government work was brisk. (Shipbuilding trades.) [1] At Walsall there was a further improvement in the saddlery, furniture and bit and stirrup trades, due to army orders, and employment was very good. (Miscellaneous Metal Trades.) [2] Owing to the execution of government orders, employment during the month showed a very marked improvement. Of the total number of work people covered by the returns, under 20 per cent were working short time compared with 60 per cent a month ago. (Woolen trade.) [3] Employment showed a considerable improvement . . . due mainly to government contracts. (Hosiery trade.) [4] In Leicester . . . improvement was mainly with firms engaged on army and navy contracts, these were working double shifts and on Sundays. (Hosiery trade.) [4] Employment was good, with much overtime in districts engaged on government contracts. (Boot and Shoe trade.) [5] At Leeds . . . most of the firms were engaged on army and navy contracts, including orders for French army boots, and a great deal of overtime was worked. (Boot and Shoe trade.) [5] Owing to the execution of army contracts, employment on the whole was fairly good, and better than a month ago and a year ago. (Tailoring trade; Ready made and Wholesale Bespoke Branch.) [5]

It was not until a month or two later that this prosperity of the war times began to filter down into the other industries which furnished them with their materials. By October the iron and steel works had begun to receive government orders, [6] in the

[1] *Labour Gazette*, 1914, p. 367.
[2] *Ibid.*, p. 368.
[3] *Ibid.*, p. 369.
[4] *Ibid.*, p. 371.
[5] *Ibid.*, p. 373.
[6] *Ibid.*, p. 402.

worsted trade, " firms engaged on khaki yarn and clothes were very busy," [1] in the carpet trade, " some firms reported that they were turning their attention to blanket making," [2] and among carpenters " the number unemployed was reduced by more than half, large numbers of men being employed upon the erection of huts for the troops and upon other government work." [3]

The effect of military service in reducing the amount of unemployment was a little slower in its operation. It appears first as a notable influence in the agricultural districts where even in August it is said that " some temporary inconvenience was caused in certain districts through men being called to the colors," [4] and in the shipbuilding trades, where there was " some temporary dislocation on the outbreak of war through the calling up of reservists." [5] During the closing months of the year the influence of this cause was more marked, not only in agriculture,[6] but in such industries as coal mining,[7] iron and steel,[8] glass, cement,[9] and on the docks.[10] By February, 1915, unemployment in certain trades seems to have become an aid in the recruiting campaign, for in nearly all the depressed trades in which men are largely employed, such as the tin plate,[11] brick, pottery,[12] bleaching, printing and dyeing [13] industries, the fact is noted that unemployment is being reduced by enlistments.

The net effect of the operation of these combined forces— government contracts and voluntary enlistments—was that by the end of the year conditions in most trades had reached their prewar level of employment and in other industries, those largely engaged on government work, there was an extraordinary activity.

[1] *Labour Gazette*, 1914, p. 406.
[2] *Ibid.*, p. 408.
[3] *Ibid.*, p. 411.
[4] *Ibid.*, p. 341.
[5] *Ibid.*, p. 331.
[6] *Ibid.*, p. 377.
[7] *Ibid.*, p. 400.
[8] *Ibid.*, p. 402.
[9] *Ibid.*, p. 413.
[10] *Ibid.*, p. 415.
[11] [12] & [13] *Ibid.*, 1915, pp. 89, 99, 95.

These trades were, as a rule, working the maximum possible hours, many factories having double shifts, working day and night, and working on Sundays as well as week days; there was a general complaint of a shortage of work people in these trades, owing to enlistments.[1]

SLOW RECOVERY IN THE WOMEN'S TRADES

Those industries which did not soon recover their prewar prosperity were the cotton, linen, silk, lace, bespoke tailoring, dressmaking, millinery, hat, tin plate, brick and pottery manufactures and the fishing industry. It will be seen at once that most of these industries are those in which women are largely employed and there can be no doubt that the burden of unemployment during the first six months of the war fell with much greater severity upon the women than upon the men.

The loss of employment to the women was not alone due to the slow recovery of certain trades. Partly due to increased taxation and partly to economies voluntarily adopted, the spending power of the people was reduced and the reduction took the form of a lessened demand for luxuries. Dressmakers, milliners, silk weavers, collar workers, tailoresses and lacemakers found their services dispensed with. House and hotel servants were dismissed in many cases. Clerks and typists who had been employed by firms with a continental trade found no further demand for their services. Factories making candy and stationery closed their doors or ran on short time. Employment was bad in the high class branches of the jewelry manufacture, and in some towns even the laundry workers felt the effect of short work.[2]

The review of the work of the Board of Trade labor exchanges showed that in the case of both men and women the number of work people on the registers at the middle of each month, *i.e.*, those for whom no vacancies had been found, was larger during 1914 than during 1913 in every month from Febru-

---

[1] *Labour Gazette,* 1915, p. 3.
[2] "Unemployment Among Women in October, 1914." *Ibid.,* p. 395.

ary to October, inclusive. The percentage of increases or decreases for the remaining months were as follows:[1]

		Men	Women
Nov. 13, 1914	....	—11.7	+113.0
Dec. 11, 1914	....	—32.3	+107.1
Jan. 15, 1915	....	—47.9	+ 88.5

Government Efforts to Relieve Distress Due to Unemployment

Believing that a good deal of distress was likely to occur as a result of unemployment during the war, the Prime Minister on the very day war was declared (August 4) appointed a committee, whose chairman was Right Hon. Herbert Samuel, M.P., President of the Local Government Board, "to advise on the measures necessary to deal with any distress that might arise in consequence of the war." The report[2] of the committee made December 31, 1914, stated that they had made "the prevention of unemployment and distress their primary object throughout." In their circulars to local committees they urged that work people be continued in employment, so far as possible, in their local trades and that cooperation with the labor exchanges be established. They induced the principal spending departments of the government to spread their contracts, in order to secure the employment of the maximum amount of labor. They obtained the assistance of the Road Board and the Development Commission in promoting new work in districts where any exceptional amount of unemployment prevailed or was anticipated.

The committee found that "the fears of a widespread dislocation of trade which were entertained in some quarters at the beginning of the war have not been realized. Except in a few districts and in a few particular industries unemployment has proved to be much less serious than was anticipated, and, as previously stated, the policy of the committee has been to secure that, so far as possible, unemployed labor should be absorbed in

[1] *Labour Gazette*, 1915, p. 43.
[2] Report on the Special Work of the Local Government Board Arising out of the War. (Cd. 7763), December 31, 1914.

schemes of useful work, the cost of which is as a rule properly chargeable on local rate or on other public funds." [1]

The committee was able to report that it had not been necessary to make any very heavy demands upon the National Relief Fund for the assistance of cases of distress among the civilian population, and such grants as were made for this purpose were " applied in financing schemes of employment and training." The total amount of such grants up to December 31, 1914, was £158,266.

The committee further reported that " the effects of the war on employment have been more severely felt in the case of women than in the case of men." A Central Committee on Women's Employment was constituted, which not only gave assistance to local committees in formulation of schemes of work directly under the control of these committees but also established workrooms under its own immediate supervision and inaugurated schemes for the training of women and girls and for experiments in the creation of new industries. A special fund was collected for the purpose of coping with distress among women workers. [2]

The committee's mention of having secured the cooperation of the Road Board makes desirable the following statement of the efforts made by the Road Board to care for the unemployed.

At the outbreak of the war the board decided to suspend the distribution of grants made to local authorities on the ordinary lines and to make grants in case they should be necessary to relieve distress. The board arranged with the highway authorities of areas in which distress was reported to grant sums aggregating £209,259 in road construction or improvement.

In addition to these amounts the board made further arrangements with the highway authorities by which road construction and improvement, estimated to cost in the aggregate £2,115,824,

---

[1] Report on the Special Work, etc., p. 6.
[2] Ibid. For further information on this subject see the monograph in this series by Irene Osgood Andrews and Margaret A. Hobbs, entitled *Economic Effects of the War Upon Women and Children*, chapter iii.

" should be carried out in the event of the state of employment for labor rendering it desirable to do so, and towards which the board promised to contribute." [1]   " The works agreed upon," it was said, " are all useful works, the need for which has been established; and, though the board have not pledged themselves to make grants in respect thereof, except on the occurrence of distress arising from lack of employment, they will be prepared to consider applications made by highway authorities in respect of such works in the ordinary course, and upon their merits." [1]

Efforts to Furnish Work to Belgian Refugees

It was the Special Committee on the Prevention and Relief of Distress which also undertook to care for the Belgian refugees, to provide for their transportation to England, for their care on arrival and to secure work for those able to work. With regard to the matter of employment of these refugees, the committee reported that difficulties soon appeared. " Many of the refugees were skilled workmen and there was a demand for their services in several trades, while among the refugees themselves there was naturally a desire to find some useful occupation during their stay here. It was most desirable to secure that any occupation found for them should not interfere with the employment of British labor, and it was also desired to safeguard the refugees so that they did not suffer from improper conditions of employment." [2]

It was decided to appoint a special committee " to investigate these and other similar questions," and to make recommendations. This committee, of which Sir Ernest Hatch, Bart., was the chairman, was appointed at the end of October and made its first report [3] in December. The committee reported that out of about a million refugees—nearly a sixth of the population—

[1] *Labour Gazette,* 1915, 316. (Review of 5th Annual Report of the Road Board.)

[2] Report on Special Work, etc. (Cd. 7763), p. 6.

[3] First report of the departmental committee appointed by the President of the Local Government Board to consider and report on questions arising in connection with the reception and employment of the Belgian refugees in this country. (Cd. 7750.)

about 110,000 had arrived in England and arrangements were
being made to bring over more from Holland "to relieve the
excessive pressure there." Of the refugees in England information was secured by the Registrar General from about 100,000,
which showed that the number of men above 18 years of age was
approximately 32,000, of whom about 5,000 were estimated to be
of military age. The number of women above the age of 16 was
also approximately 32,000 and two-thirds of the women whose
marital condition was known were married.

The committee quite early in its deliberations received an
intimation from the Belgian government that it was desirable
that no employment should be given to unmarried men between
the ages of 18 and 30 who were in a fit condition for military
service. This class was accordingly excluded from the scope of
the committee's investigations.[1]

The registration of the workers according to their occupations
showed that they fell into three main groups: "(1) Workers
qualified to fill vacancies in industries in which a shortage of
British labor exists, such as armament workers, glass blowers,
woolen workers, miners, motor mechanics, and agricultural laborers. (2) Workers qualified for and in need of employment for
whom no opportunities in British industries exist, such as tailors,
ironmongers, jewelers, milliners, dressmakers, printers, book-
binders, fancy goods makers and cabinet makers. (3) Other
special classes, mainly of a professional character, such as government officials, employers, clerks, musicians, teachers, authors
and lawyers."[2]

The committee expressed the opinion that no great difficulty
would be found in securing employment for those in the first
group, that for those in the second group "special measures will
have to be devised if work is to be provided," and that for those
in the third group "practically no chance of employment exists."[3]

In considering what work could be found for the refugees and
under what conditions they should be employed the committee

[1] Report of Committee on Belgian Refugees (Cd. 7750), pp. 4-6.
[2] Ibid., p. 38.
[3] Ibid., pp. 38-39.

consulted with employers of labor, representatives of trade unions and government officials. "The representatives of the trade unions raised no objections to the employment of Belgians, but they all made the following stipulations:

(1) That no Belgian should be given any work for which British labor was available.

(2) That in respect of wages paid to Belgians and the conditions of their employment the trade union regulations should be observed.

(3) That in the event of the slackening of trade Belgian employes should make way for British workmen.

It was also considered desirable that all Belgians for whom work might be provided, should become members of British trade unions.[1]

The committee decided that the proper organization to undertake the task of finding employment for the refugees was the Labor Exchanges Department of the Board of Trade and it requested local refugee committees to cooperate with the local labor exchanges. It was ascertained that voluntary agencies had already sprung up to advertise for Belgians to fill vacancies in certain trades and that certain employers were taking steps to obtain the services of Belgian workmen. Investigation showed that in some instances refugees had obtained work for which they were receiving wages at lower rates than those paid to British workmen in the same occupation.

The policy which the committee recommended should be followed by the labor exchanges had as its two main principles the following:

(1) That no Belgian labor should be employed until every reasonable effort had been made to find British labor through the agency of the labor exchanges.

(2) That no Belgian labor should be employed at rates of wages lower, or on conditions less favorable, than those generally observed in the district concerned by agreement between the Association of Employers and of Workmen, or failing such agreement, than those generally recognized in such district by good employers.[2]

Although these conditions imposed upon the labor exchanges did not go as far as the trade union recommendations, it appears that they were sufficiently exacting to make it difficult for the

[1] Report on Belgian Refugees, p. 17.
[2] *Ibid.*, p. 9.

exchanges to place the refugees in positions which were deemed satisfactory. Up to November 30, the exchanges had received applications for Belgian laborers from 1,281 employers, only 1,099 of which could for various reasons be considered and dealt with. Excluding the requests of 239 employers who did not state the precise number of workers desired, the numbers requested were 3,775 men and 1,508 women or a total of 5,283.[1] Yet up to December 21 only 607 Belgians, of whom five were women, had been placed in employment by the labor exchanges. The reasons for so few placements were said to be that the local refugee committees did not take any steps to bring the vacancies advertised by the labor exchanges to the notice of the refugees and that the conditions imposed upon the exchanges by the Local Government Board, as just given, meant delay in placing refugees in some cases and made it impossible in others.[2] The committee went on to say that " there are many other agencies at work not subject to these conditions, and it is known that many refugees have obtained work independently of the exchanges without the security which employment through their agency affords. The fact that the conditions recommended by the committee must necessarily be satisfied before employment can be offered to Belgians through the agency of the exchanges, tends to divert the business from the exchanges to other agencies, which are under no obligation to see that those conditions are satisfied." [3]

" The committee fear that in some instances refugees have been employed on unsatisfactory terms and conditions, and it has been suggested that, with a view to preventing occurrences of this kind, which are greatly to be deplored, measures should be taken to make the employment of Belgians through the agency of the labor exchanges compulsory." [3]

The committee did not make this as a formal recommendation at the time of making its report, but announced that it was making further investigations with a view to making a definite recommendation. The committee found it difficult to make

[1] Report on Belgian Refugees, p. 11.
[2] Ibid., p. 36.
[3] Ibid., p. 39.

practicable suggestions concerning employment for workers in its second main group, those trained for occupations in which there was already a surplus of British workers. These were largely the luxury trades in which at the time there was much unemployment. The committee recommended that the Belgian refugees in these occupations be employed in making clothes, furniture and other articles for household use for the benefit of their own people when they should return to their own country at the close of the war. Several workshops had already been established having this purpose in view.[1]

The greatest difficulty in carrying out this plan, it was admitted, was the fact that the refugees were scattered throughout the country and it would be difficult to find enough workers in any one place who had sufficient knowledge of any one trade to conduct a workshop for the carrying on of that trade. The committee therefore recommended that the government undertake a redistribution of the refugees and that a central authority be formed to advise and assist local refugee committees in the organization of schemes for the establishment of such workshops.[2]

CRITICISM OF THE GOVERNMENT'S PLANS

The Local Government Board's plans and methods of preventing and relieving distress met with considerable criticism from "The Workers' National Committee" formed on August 6 by the Labor and Socialist Emergency Conference to protect working class interests during the war. The main grounds of criticism were (1) that "the problem of relieving distress should have been a charge on the nation, and should not have been handed over to a voluntary fund," and (2) that "the Local Representatives Committees were practically delivered over to the tender mercies of the 'social worker,' so that an atmosphere of 'pauperization' resulted."[3]

The Workers' National Committee formulated a program about the middle of October for relieving distress and preventing

[1] Report on Belgian Refugees, pp. 33-35.
[2] Ibid., pp. 40-41.
[3] Labour Year Book, 1916, p. 32.

unemployment and called upon " the entire Labor and Socialist movement to force these demands upon the government by an immediate national campaign." [1]   There were thirteen different proposals made in this program, which included among others demands that all war relief be merged together and be taken over and administered by the government, that there be labor representation on all national and local committees, provision of productive work at standard rates of wages for the unemployed, fixing of maxima prices for food and commandeering of food supplies by the nation where advisable, the inauguration of a comprehensive policy of municipal housing, and the continuance of national control over public utilities at the close of the war.

Although it is conceded by the friends of this program that " hardly any of its demands were granted, and of the more important none were fully conceded," [1] yet it is claimed that the Workers' National Committee did much " to prevent abuses and ameliorate the hardships to which the workers were subjected," and the further claim is made that:

> It is true to say that it was chiefly due to this emergency committee that at the outset the workers were not utterly crushed by the burden and novel hardships of the European War.[1]

EMERGENCY GRANTS

In line with the demands made by the Workers' National Committee, although apparently independent of these demands, since it was claimed by the committee that the government's action was entirely inadequate, was the announcement of the Board of Trade, acting under authority given by section 106 of the National Insurance Act, 1911 (1 and 2 Geo. 5, c. 55), and section 14 of the National Insurance (Part II, Amendment) Act, 1914 (4 and 5 Geo. 5, c. 57), that it was prepared to entertain applications from trade unions and other associations paying unemployed benefits to their members for the payment from the

[1] *Labour Year Book*, 1916, pp. 32-35.

Exchequer of emergency grants intended to supplement the funds of the unions used for these purposes.

These emergency grants were in addition to the refunds of one-sixth of the benefits paid by the unions as allowed under section 106 of the Original Insurance Act of 1911. The emergency grants were payable subject to the following conditions:

(1) The union or association must be one in which there was an abnormal amount of unemployment (at least double the normal for a period of years) and the Board of Trade must be satisfied of this fact.

(2) The union or association must agree to pay as unemployed benefits not more than 17s. weekly to any member (including the amount paid by the state).

(3) While receiving this emergency grant, the union or association must agree to impose upon its members who were fully employed weekly levies over and above the ordinary contributions made for this purpose.

(4) The union or association receiving the grants must furnish the Board of Trade with information, as required, as to the unemployment of their members.

The amount of the emergency grant was to vary according to the rate of levy and the rate of levy would vary according to the maximum benefit paid. Under no circumstances would the subsidy paid by the state (including the amount ordinarily obtainable under section 106) exceed one-half the unemployment benefits paid by the association. Thus, if an association decided to pay the maximum benefit of 17s. a week and in order to do this made a levy of 6d. per week upon its fully employed members, it would (subject to its fulfilling the other conditions) be entitled to an emergency grant of one-third its expenditure plus the ordinary grant of one-sixth, or a total allowance from the Exchequer of one-half the expenditure for unemployed benefits. If the levy was only 3d. per week, where the maximum benefit was paid, the emergency grant would be only one-sixth the expenditure (combined with the one-sixth under section 106), a total allowance of one-third the expenditure.

The emergency grants would ordinarily be given in respect of expenditures made after the application for a grant had been allowed, but, under certain conditions, might be made retroactive to a date not earlier than August 4, 1914 (the date on which war was declared).[1]

It may be well to follow here the history of these emergency grants, as they throw considerable light on the extent of unemployment during the early months of the war and indicate the trades affected thereby.

Up to the end of December, 1914, 156 unions had made application for the emergency grants. These unions had a total membership of 232,880 and the amounts paid to them were, up to that time, £41,775. Of this amount £37,437 went to 117 unions in the cotton industry, having a membership of 181,970. Other textile workers received £1,560 and four unions in the printing trades received £1,560. Small amounts were paid to unions in the metal, hatters, woodwork and other trades.[2] Emergency grants continued to be made in rapidly decreasing amounts during the succeeding months, but in May the Board of Trade announced that " in view of the complete change of conditions " it would pay no grants on expenditures incurred after the end of May.[3] As a matter of fact, very little was paid on expenditures incurred after April 30, 1915. The total results of this policy up to August 1, 1915, are shown in the following table:[4]

| Trade Group | APPLICATIONS GRANTED | | Amounts |
	No. of Associations	Membership	Paid
Building	1	61	£ 4
Metal	18	8,372	1,297
Cotton	135	221,413	70,566
Other textiles	7	5,402	2,285
Printing	6	23,260	5,491
Woodwork	8	17,302	2,148
Other trades	10	8,487	2,385
Total	185	284,297	£84,176

[1] *Manual of Emergency Legislation*, Supplement No. 1. (To Nov. 3, 1914), pp. 41-44.
[2] *Labour Gazette*, 1915, p. 8.
[3] *Ibid.*, p. 231.
[4] *Ibid.*, p. 307.

Any need for unusual measures to relieve distress or to prevent unemployment among male workers had disappeared by the end of 1914. A few trades, like the bespoke tailoring, hat and brick trades, were still dull, but the ordinary agencies for dealing with unemployment and distress were probably able to cope with the situation so far as men workers were concerned.

IMPROVED CONDITIONS AMONG WOMEN : INDUSTRIAL TRANSFERS

In the women's trades (textiles, dressmaking, millinery, etc.) improvement took place much more slowly. The February, 1915, *Labour Gazette* notes

that during the past four months there has been a gradual improvement owing to the demand for women's labor in connection with the equipment of the new army, especially as regards tailoring, shirts, boots and leather work.[1]

The establishment of workrooms where girls were taught new trades had relieved the situation somewhat in London, especially among dressmakers.[1]

Transference of female workers from one industry to another does not yet appear to have become frequent, although there were instances of such transfers having been made or attempted. Thus it is said that among the Lancashire cotton operatives,

over 200 women went either into Yorkshire or into the Rochdale woolen mills. But with the recent improvement in the cotton industry a large proportion of these workers have returned, and it seems improbable that anything more can now be done in the way of transferring workers from the one trade to the other.[2]

Other cases of transfers were corset factory workers in Bath and Portsmouth being put at work at making knapsacks for the army;[2] girls in Redditch employed in making fish hooks were " absorbed by the local development in the manufacture of hosiery

---

[1] *Labour Gazette*, 1915, p. 38.
[2] *Ibid.*, p. 39.

machine needles; " [1] dressmakers in Walsall were taken on in the lighter and less skilled branches of the leather industry; [1] in Kilbirnie (Scotland) the net makers went into the textile mills employed on government work,[1] and in the northern division the ammunition works absorbed large numbers of work people from other factories.[1]

Some efforts at transfer of workers to new industries failed. Thus in Basford an effort was made to use lace menders in the hosiery trade "but they were not found to be suitable for the work." [1] It was stated, however, that a new industry for the manufacture of tapes, braids, etc., would absorb an appreciable number of lace workers, " who are well adapted to their class of work." [1]

Further instances of these industrial transfers are noted in February. Dressmaking in London was still depressed, but many dressmakers were finding employment on army clothing, shirts, etc.[2] In the bootmaking trade, where a shifting had taken place from football boots to army boots, it was said that the fact that there was less work on an army boot had caused the dismissal of a certain number of the women.[2]

Still another factor in the unemployment situation is brought out in the following quotation:

The high wages earned by men have also to some extent reacted on the supply of women's labor. The women who were thrown out of work at the beginning of the war in certain colliery districts, for example, are comparatively indifferent whether they obtain fresh employment or not, as the men's contribution to the family income has compensated for their own lack of wages. Under such circumstances it is obviously difficult to induce the women to learn any new trade or to move to districts where their labor would be really needed.[2]

In the districts where soldiers were billeted, the effect of war conditions was seen in an increased demand for domestic help, without a corresponding increase in the supply.

[1] *Labour Gazette*, 1915, p. 39.
[2] *Ibid.*, p. 79.

Women who went out either for industrial or domestic help now find occupation at home; in many cases they even need help, and the two influences combined have in some districts resulted in the unusual state of affairs that the supply of charwomen is insufficient to meet the demand.[1]

DISAPPEARANCE OF UNEMPLOYMENT

A further recital of the improvement in labor conditions which took place during the first half of 1915 would only be in the nature of repetition. Among male laborers, the condition of labor surplus which existed in August and September had given way to a labor shortage by the early part of 1915. Unemployment among women workers diminished more slowly. The luxury trades continued depressed, but the transfer of workers from one industry to another and even from one district to another relieved the situation from the workers' standpoint.[2] In such trades as the textile, boot and shoe, and in agriculture, female labor was being substituted for males at a rapid rate.

Unemployment among trade unionists, as shown by returns made to the Board of Trade, had by April reached a percentage "lower than in any month during the last twenty-five years"[3] and every subsequent month in that year showed a further decrease.[4] By June the unemployed in the insured trades was less than one per cent.[5]

The *Labour Gazette* in its review of the employment situation since the outbreak of the war thus summarizes the situation at the close of the first year of the war period:[6]

Owing to the large number of enlistments the number of males available has greatly decreased. To meet this shortage of labor there has been a considerable transference from trades adversely affected by the war to other industries which were rendered abnormally active; in addition there has been, wherever possible, a growing movement in the direction of substituting female for male labor. The net result is that at the present time there is very little unemployment, except in a few luxury trades, while in a number of

[1] *Labour Gazette*, 1915, p. 79.
[2] *Ibid.*, p. 235.
[3] *Ibid.*, p. 155.
[4] *Ibid.*, p. 1.
[5] *Ibid.*, p. 265.
[6] *Ibid.*, p. 273.

industries, notably coal mining, engineering, shipbuilding, agriculture and transport, the demand for labor greatly exceeds the supply.

Government efforts of an unusual sort to relieve distress due to unemployment seem practically to have ceased by the end of 1914. This does not mean that such distress no longer existed, but that such agencies as existed at the outbreak of the war or had been created to meet the emergency were found to be able to cope with the situation.

The number of paupers, which had suddenly increased in August and September, 1914, showed a steady decline month by month thereafter. In June, 1915, the number in England and Wales was 584,580,

a smaller number than has been recorded for the end of June in any year since 1875 (the first year to which the return relates) in spite of the rise in population. The rate per thousand of the population was 15.8, as compared with 16.7 and 16.8 in June of the two previous years, and rates exceeding 20 per thousand in 1910 and every preceding year. The decline was common to all districts, and was shown in both indoor and outdoor pauperism.[1]

We have already noted the cessation of emergency grants to the trade unions in May, 1915. The number of persons who received employment relief through distress committees was 115 in August, 1915, as compared with 580 in July, 1914, and 2,843 in August of that year.[2]

RELIEF OF DISABLED SOLDIERS AND SAILORS

One form of government assistance in finding employment became increasingly necessary as the war continued. This had to do with disabled soldiers and sailors and presented in some respects a new problem. No systematic method of dealing with the situation was made until February, 1915, when the President of the Local Government Board appointed a " committee to consider and report upon the methods to be adopted for providing employment for soldiers and sailors disabled in the war." Sir

[1] *Labour Gazette*, 1915, p. 301.
[2] *Ibid.*, pp. 307, 346.

George Murray was made chairman. The committee made its report in May, 1915.

The committee, after declaring it to be the duty of the state to assume the care of the sailors and soldiers disabled by the war, stated that

> this duty should include (a) the restoration of the man's health, where practicable; (b) the provision of training facilities, if he desires to learn a new trade; (c) the finding of employment for him, when he stands in need of such assistance.[1]

To accomplish this work it was recommended that a central committee be appointed, to have the assistance of local subcommittees wherever needed, and empowered to act through existing agencies where practicable or independently, if need be.

> The functions of the committee would be: (a) to arrange for the care and treatment of all disabled sailors and soldiers, immediately on their discharge, with the view of restoring them to health, when possible, and enabling them to earn their own living; (b) to obtain early information of approaching discharges from hospital and to arrange for the registration of every disabled man, who was capable of work, with the labor exchange of the district to which he was going; (c) to communicate with public departments with the view of obtaining employment therein for such disabled men as could properly be appointed to vacancies; (d) to organize public or private appeals to employers in order to secure their good will in filling any vacancies which were suitable for disabled men; (e) to appoint local committees (where necessary), or local representatives, to assist the committee generally in the performance of its duties and especially in finding employment and negotiating with employers; (f) to organize and assist schemes for training men who were desirous of obtaining technical instruction to fit them for skilled occupations, and to arrange for their maintenance during the period of training; (g) to consider and deal with schemes for employing disabled men in agriculture and the industries allied with it; (h) to arrange for the emigration of men who were desirous of settling in other parts of the Empire.[2]

The committee discovered that between September 11 (the date of the earliest discharges from the army) and the date of

---

[1] Report of the committee appointed by the President of the Local Government Board upon the provision of employment for sailors and soldiers disabled in the war (Cd. 7915), p. 8.
[2] *Ibid.*, p. 6.

their report (May 4, 1915), a period of nearly eight months, 2,874 persons had been discharged on account of incapacity. This was at the rate of 360 a month. The rate of discharge at the time of making the report was about 1,000 per month. The committee admitted that there might be some increase in the number of incapacitated as the number of men engaged in hostilities increased.[1]

One important point covered by the committee's report related to the effect of the Workmen's Compensation Act in causing reluctance on the part of employers to accept the services of partially disabled men, because of the liability imposed upon employers by the act. The committee discovered that insurance companies did not, save in very exceptional cases, charge an additional premium on account of physical disability. The committee said:

We think, therefore, that no objection is likely to be taken on' this ground to the employment of a disabled man, except where the employer had refrained from covering his liability by insurance.[2]

EMIGRATION AND IMMIGRATION

Ordinarily the movements of emigration and immigration are closely related to employment conditions within a country. In normal years Great Britain loses a considerable number of her citizens to Canada, Australia, New Zealand and other of her colonies as well as to the United States and other countries. The number of persons of British nationality who leave Great Britain to take up their permanent residence in these countries is larger than the considerable number who return to Great Britain from the colonies and elsewhere to reside permanently in the mother country. In 1913 the excess of emigrants of this sort was 303,685 and 1913, it must be remembered, was a year of unusual prosperity in Great Britain, when the motive to migrate in order to better economic conditions would naturally be weak.

During the first seven months of 1914 industrial conditions in

[1] Report on Disabled Soldiers, pp. 2-3.
[2] Ibid., pp. 7-8.

Great Britain were still favorable, but were not so good as in 1913. In spite of this fact, however, we find an almost steady decline in the number of emigrants, due apparently to the fact that economic conditions in the United States and the British colonies were not such as to attract large numbers of immigrants.

The first effect of the war seems to have been to stimulate emigration from Great Britain, as we find that the number of emigrants suddenly increased from 18,960 in August to 21,542 in September. At the same time the number of immigrants declined from 8,993 in August to 5,954 in September.[1] There are indications that the explanation of this changed condition is to be found in a desire to escape military service, as the increase in emigration was mainly to the United States. After September, however, the tide changed and by November there was an excess of immigrants, amounting to 3,492. The change was chiefly due to the large homeward trend of Canadians who were apparently returning to the mother country to enlist in British regiments, although the increased demand for male labor may have attracted some. With the exception of the month of January, the excess of immigrants over emigrants continued throughout the whole of 1915.[2]

CHANGES IN RATE OF WAGES

One would naturally expect that the increased demand for labor in the closing months of 1914 would reflect itself not only in more steady employment but in higher rates of wages. No marked change of this sort took place, however, in 1914, if we consider the industries collectively.

During the first seven months of 1914 (the period before the war) the total number of people whose rates of wages decreased was larger than the total number of people whose rates of wages increased, but the explanation is found in the fact that the decreases took place in the mining, pig iron, and iron and steel industries, where wages were governed by a sliding scale and fell

[1] *Labour Gazette*, 1914, pp. 390, 425.
[2] *Ibid.*, 1916, p. 74.

with a decline in the selling prices of coal and iron.[1] In other industries wages showed an increase.

After the outbreak of the war an exact reversal of conditions took place. Prices of coal and iron began to rise and wages in these industries automatically advanced. Other industries, however, like the textile, clothing, printing, etc., suffered a more or less temporary decline in their prosperity and here rates of wages did not advance, but in some cases fell.

In consequence of these diverse movements, the net amount of the changes in rates of wages for the whole year was very small, being an increase of only £5,062 per week.[2]

Changes in hours of labor in 1914 affected 79,135 of whom 78,689 had their hours reduced.[3] For the first six months of the war changes in rates of wages were few,[4] but by February, 1915, a sharp upward tendency was noticeable. The increases generally took the form of bonuses granted for the duration of the war and were allowed on the ground that they were necessary to meet the rise in the cost of living.[5] Aside from increases made under the sliding scale in the iron and steel industries, the increases in January and February were most notable for the engineering, building, textile and transport workers.[6]

The increases which took place in March, 1915, were much more numerous and affected a much wider range of trades.

Not only was the number of increases or bonuses much above the average, but also the amounts were in most cases greater than those granted in previous periods of rising wages.[7]

No decreases were reported for this month and 446,267 persons shared in the increases, which were especially numerous in the engineering. shipbuilding, transport and textile trades. The increases frequently took the form of a 10 per cent increase in

[1] *Labour Gazette*, 1914, p. 309.
[2] *Ibid.*, 1915, p. 3.
[3] *Ibid.*, p. 4.
[4] "During the last five months of 1914 there were practically no important advances in wages." Cole: *Labour in War Time*, p. 143.
[5] *Labour Gazette*, 1915, p. 105.
[6] *Ibid.*, pp. 67, 105.
[7] *Ibid.*, p. 142.

piece rates or of war bonuses of from 5 to 12½ per cent, or from
1s. to 4s. a week for time workers.

Besides the changes given in the table, war bonuses and other
increases are mentioned as having been granted to government
employes, to railway servants, to seamen and to agricultural
laborers.[1] In April, there were further large increases in rates
of wages, but the upward movement was less marked than in
March.[2] In May, however, came another great upward movement. "The amount of the increase in weekly wages were [sic]
the largest ever recorded in a single month."[3] The increases
were chiefly in the coal mining industry, which had 823,900 out
of the 969,680 work people who received increases during this
month. The war bonuses in this industry were frequently as
much as 15½ per cent on the existing wages, which were in some
places 65 per cent higher than the basis rates of 1878 or 1879.[4]

Further increases in wages were made in June and July. The
Labour Gazette, in reviewing the changes made during the first
year of the war, said that the total number of work people whose
rates of wages were affected by the war was 2,336,700 and that
the net increases amounted to £12,585 per week. "These figures
are much in excess of those recorded for any previous year." At
first the increases, taking the form of war bonuses, were in those
industries concerned directly with the output of munitions. Later
they were extended to most of the industries of the country, "the
principal exceptions being the building, printing and furnishing
trades."[5] The increase of the earnings of the workers was
much greater than the increase in the rates of wages, since much
overtime was worked in some of the trades, and usually paid for
at higher rates than for ordinary day work.

CHANGES IN PRICES

Having observed the effect of the first year's war on wages let
us turn our attention to the changes in prices which took place

---

[1] *Labour Gazette,* 1915, pp. 142-143.
[2] *Ibid.,* p. 184.
[3] *Ibid.,* p. 223.
[4] *Ibid.,* pp. 223-224.
[5] *Ibid.,* p. 300.

and which were said to have been the cause of the more or less voluntary increase in the rates of wages.

The Board of Trade *Labour Gazette*, calculating its index numbers for forty-seven separate articles weighted according to estimated consumption, discovered that, compared with prices in 1913, the prices for the first seven months of 1914 were 2½ per cent below and for the last five months of 1914, 5.2 per cent above the 1913 level.[1] The advance was entirely in the food, drink and tobacco and miscellaneous groups: the coal and metals and the textile groups showed a decline in the price level. The greatest advances took place in the prices of sugar, wheat, oats and timber.[2]

We have already observed the effect of the August (1914) panic in sending upward the retail prices of food. Prices which on the 8th of the month were 15 or 16 per cent higher than in July receded after that date until at the end of the month they were about 10 per cent above the August level. From then on they advanced and the advance continued throughout the first year of the war. The percentages above so-called "normal prices" in July, 1914, on the first day of each month are as follows:[3]

	Per cent		Per cent
September, 1914	10	March, 1915	24
October, 1914	12	April, 1915	24
November, 1914	13	May, 1915	26
December, 1914	16	June, 1915	32
January, 1915	18	July, 1915	32½
February, 1915	22	August, 1915 (July 31)	34

The advances were greatest in the case of sugar, fish, flour and beef, lowest in the case of margarine, milk, bacon and butter. Although the Board of Trade has worked out no index number for wages during this period and a direct comparison between wages and food prices is therefore impossible, it is probable that

[1] *Labour Gazette*, 1915, p. 158.
[2] *Ibid.*, p. 159.
[3] *Ibid.*, p. 275.

the advance in wages during the first year of the war was not as great as the advance which took place in the retail prices of food. The *Labour Year Book*, 1916, claims that " the standard working class budget," which would have cost 22s. 6d. in the summer of 1904, and 25s. 8d. in 1914, would by July 1, 1915, have cost " something more than 33s." [1]

RECRUDESCENCE OF STRIKES

With the great increase in food prices and the apparent failure of wages to advance during the early months of the war, it is perhaps not surprising that trade unionists should begin to regret the implied promise made on their behalf by the conference of labor leaders on August 24, when it was agreed to make an effort to terminate existing trade disputes and to settle further difficulties arising during the war, if possible, by amicable means.[2]

Even at the time the " industrial truce " was declared, there were some among the labor writers who felt that a mistake had been made in declaring the truce unconditionally. This feeling grew as prices continued to advance during the closing months of 1914, and industry after industry began to prosper through government orders without any effort being made by the government to induce employers to advance wages.[3] Such steps as were taken by the Chief Industrial Commissioner on behalf of the government during these months were in the direction of discouraging disputes, in order that production might not be interfered with, and temporary settlements were arranged which usually took the form of maintaining the *status quo*.[4]

The number of industrial disputes, which as we have seen had fallen to as low a figure as fifteen in August, slowly increased after that month, being twenty-three for September, twenty-seven for October, twenty-five for November and seventeen for December. The increase is more apparent than real, however,

[1] *Labour Year Book*, 1916, p. 212.
[2] *Ibid.*, p. 22.
[3] Cole: *Labour in War Time*, pp. 44-45.
[4] " Railway Conciliation Scheme," *Labour Gazette*, 1914, p. 362.

for practically all of these disputes were of an insignificant character, involving directly or indirectly very few workers. Industrial peace was most nearly realized in December when the seventeen new disputes involved directly and indirectly only 1,192 workers and all disputes (old and new) in progress that month involved only 3,065 workers.

These causes (says Mr. Cole) combined to create a partial change of attitude on the part of trade unionists by the New Year. The first, but perhaps the least important, was the government's policy in its dealings with trade unionism; the second was the rise in the cost of living; the third, probably the greatest in its psychological effect, was the growing suspicion that the capitalists were making a good thing out of the war.[1]

Although the month of January, 1915, showed some increase in the number and importance of industrial disputes, the first really important breach in the " industrial truce " was not made until February. During that month the number of disputes begun during the month rose to forty-seven, involving directly and indirectly 29,000 workers. In February the railway servants who in November had agreed to suspend their demand for changed conditions made a demand upon the companies for increased wages. A settlement was made by which the companies agreed to pay a war bonus of 3s. a week to all men earning less than 30s., and of 2s. a week to all who were earning more than 30s.

This agreement was subject to considerable criticism by laborers in other industries and occupations. It served as a precedent among employers whenever demands were made for advances in wages due to war conditions. The amount of the advance was insufficient, it was claimed, to bring real wages to prewar conditions in view of the very considerable advance in the cost of living. The three shilling bonus allowed to workers receiving less than 30s. a week meant an advance in money wages of 10+ per cent. By February the percentage increase of retail food prices over prices for July, 1914, was from twenty to twenty-three and according to " the standard working class budget " worked out

[1] *Labour Gazette*, 1915, pp. 4, 25. Cole, *op. cit.*, p. 140.

by the Board of Trade in 1904, 66 per cent of family incomes between twenty-five and thirty shillings a week went for food.[1] The 2s. a week bonus allowed to employes receiving over 30s. a week took even less account of the advance in the cost of living.

The chief criticism of the railway agreement, however, pertained not to the amount but to the form of the increase of wages. The 2s.-3s. increase was a " war bonus," not a permanent increase of wages.

> When once a war bonus had been accepted in any great industry, it became difficult, if not impossible, for workers in other industries to secure permanent advances.[2]

The ground of the criticism of the war bonuses is briefly this: that at the end of the war, when industrial readjustment is taking place and labor is weakest in bargaining power, the bonuses will disappear and labor will have to enter into new agreements concerning standard rates. Under the circumstances, will laborers be able to retain any of the war increases?

Whether the trade unionists, had they refused the war bonuses, could have persuaded employers to make any considerable permanent advances in wages during the uncertainty prevailing in the first year of the war, may well be doubted, but it is probable that, in view of the government's desire to have the good will of organized labor, public opinion would have supported them in demanding that wage increases be made to fluctuate with changes in the cost of living, as measured by fluctuations in the prices of certain commodities; the extent of these fluctuations to be ascertained at certain regular intervals by the Board of Trade.

We are dealing, however, not with " what might have been," but with what actually took place. Believing that they were not bound by the terms of the " industrial truce," declared by their leaders and which had never been a stipulated agreement, the unionists resumed their stoppages of work early in 1915.

[1] *Labour Year Book*, 1916, p. 211.
[2] Cole, *op. cit.*, pp. 144-145.

THE CLYDE STRIKE

The first of these stoppages was that caused by the strike of the Amalgamated Society of Engineers employed in the Clyde shipyards. It began on February 16, 1915, and soon spread to nearly all the engineering shops on the Clyde, involving some 9,000 workers.[1] The three years' agreement entered into in 1912 had come to an end in January, 1915. In their negotiations for a renewal, the men were demanding an increase of 2d. an hour and this demand had been decided upon even before the outbreak of the war.[2] The employers made counter proposals and matters dragged on until February, when the employers offered an increase of $\frac{3}{4}$d. an hour, but offered it in the form of a war bonus. Its acceptance was recommended by the national executive of the Amalgamated Society of Engineers, but the men, not even waiting for the results of a ballot on the question of accepting it, ceased work. The ballot on the employers' proposal, when completed, showed that it had been rejected by a vote of 8,927 to 829.[3]

The government now decided to intervene. On February 4 there had been appointed a government Committee on Production in engineering and shipbuilding establishments, whose duties were

to inquire and report forthwith, after consultation with the representatives of employers and workmen, as to the best steps to be taken to insure that the productive power of the employes in engineering and shipbuilding establishments working for government purposes shall be made fully available so as to meet the needs of the nation in the present emergency.[4]

The chairman of this committee was Sir George Askwith, Chief Industrial Commissioner. He sent a letter on February 26 to both employers and workers in the Clyde dispute, which contained the following striking paragraphs:

I am instructed by the government that important munitions of war urgently required by the navy and army are being held up by the present

[1] Cole, op. cit., p. 147.
[2] Ibid., p. 148.
[3] Ibid., p. 151.
[4] Labour Year Book, 1916, p. 53.

cessation of work and that they must call for a resumption of work on Monday morning, March 1.

Immediately following resumption of work arrangements will be made for the representatives of the parties to meet the Committee on Production in engineering and shipbuilding establishments for the purpose of the matters in dispute being referred for settlement to a court of arbitration, who shall also have power to fix the date from which the settlement shall take effect.

The language of this communication clearly implies that the government then had the right to order a resumption of work. There is some doubt as to whether this is true, but the executive committee of the Amalgamated Society of Engineers urged the men to resume work. The Central Withdrawal of Labor Committee, on the other hand, advised the men to resume work on March 4, three days after the date set by the government's request. Work was actually resumed on March 3. Employers and employes being unable to agree on the terms of settlement, the matter was referred by request of the government to arbitration by the Committee on Production. The award of this committee gave the engineers an advance of 1d. an hour on existing wages. It gave this advance not as a permanent increase of wages, but it was

to be regarded as war wages and recognized as due to and dependent on the existence of the abnormal conditions now prevailing in consequence of the war.[1]

Thus the Committee on Production adopted at the outset the precedent set by the railway agreement of making wage increases take the form of war bonuses.

Upon what principle the advance was fixed at 1d. per hour does not appear. The laborers themselves complained bitterly that the advance was not sufficient to bring the standard rate up to the level in other parts of Great Britain or to cover the rise in the cost of living prior to the war, let alone the advance in such costs since the war began.[2]

Particular attention has been given to the Clyde strike because its settlement marks the beginning of a new policy of the govern-

[1] *Labour Year Book*, 1916, p. 52.
[2] *Ibid.*, pp. 52-53. Cole, *op. cit.*, pp. 153-154.

ment towards labor, a policy which developed through a period of several months and found its fruition in the enactment of " The Munitions of War Acts." Before tracing the course of the developments, however, we will notice the efforts made by employers and trade unions in the engineering trades to agree on a program of production during war times.

CHAPTER IV

The Government and the Trade Unions

DISAGREEMENT IN THE ENGINEERING TRADES

The engineering trades were among the first to experience a shortage of labor due to the war. This was due primarily to the unusual demands made upon them by the government to supply munitions of war. It is also said that ten thousand workers from this industry enlisted in the first few months of the war. From whatever cause, the shortage of labor made itself felt in this industry very soon and was acute by November, 1914.

In December the Engineering Employers' Federation proposed to the unions that they modify (practically abandon) their regulations as to skilled and unskilled, nonunion and female labor, the demarcation of work between trades and the limitation of overtime. They offered guarantees that the federated employers would resume the old conditions at the close of the war and that payment of the standard rates would be maintained.[1]

The unions would not agree to these propositions, basing their refusal on the following grounds:

(1) The proposals were only from the federated employers and could bind only members of the federation. Only the government's promise to enforce the guarantees could solve the difficulty.

(2) At the end of the war, when there was a surplus of labor, the employers would have the advantage and competition would have the effect of lowering wages, despite the guarantees.[2]

The unions on their part made counter proposals:

[1] *Labour Year Book*, 1916, p. 53.
[2] *Ibid.*, p. 54.

(1) Firms not engaged on war work to be given such work.

(2) Firms working short time to transfer their workers to firms engaged on government work.

(3) Employers and unionists jointly to request the government to pay subsistence allowance money to men working in places at a distance from their homes.

(4) That the government draft skilled engineers from the colonies.

(5) That skilled engineers who had enlisted be withdrawn from military service and be restored to industry.

The employers held that the proposals of the unions did not "provide any adequate remedy for the present difficulty of obtaining the necessary supply of work people." They also expressed their "disappointment that their proposals to assist the country should have met with no response." [1]

The men naturally resented the implication that they were unpatriotic, but further conferences failed to lead to an agreement. As to the practicability of the unions' suggestions, the authors of the *Labour Year Book* say: [2]

It is an interesting commentary on the bluff (sagacity) of the employers that practically all the workers' proposals have since been adopted by the government.

While the government's Committee on Production was still at work and before it had issued its report, Mr. H. J. Tennant, Under Secretary of War, made a speech in the House of Commons which met with much criticism from trade unionists and members of the Labor party. He asked the Labor members of Parliament to use their influence to get the unions to relax their rules, but did not indicate that the government was willing to protect the workers against the natural results of such relaxations or that the government would also ask employers to limit their profits in order that both sides might make sacrifices to assist in the prosecution of the war. The Labor members replied that this was a matter which the government should take up directly with the unions. The government eventually did so, but before this

[1] *Labour Year Book*, 1916, p. 54.
[2] *Ibid.*, p. 55.

took place an industrial dispute arose in the settlement of which the unionists obtained certain concessions which exercised much influence on subsequent negotiations between the government and the unions.

The dispute was in the Elswick works of Armstrong, Whitworth & Company, one of the largest engineering firms in Great Britain and one which was at the time working almost entirely on government work. The company had, contrary to trade union rules, engaged unskilled workers from "depressed industries, coppersmiths, lace makers, cotton operatives, silversmiths," and the like, and put them to work on skilled jobs. The engineers and shipbuilders objected and posted notices of a strike.

A conference between the management and delegates from each shop was called and at this conference an agreement was reached which was to become operative until the question could be referred to a central conference between the unions and the employers' federation. The important terms in this provisional agreement, most of which in one form or another later were incorporated in the Munitions Act, were as follows:

(1) That whatever the class of labor taken on, the district rate for the job must always be paid; (2) that the unions should inspect not only the credentials of the imported workers, but also the actual work done by them; (3) that the employers should furnish a complete return of all unskilled men taken on together with the name of their unions; (4) that the services of such workers should be dispensed with at the end of the war, and that copies of the list containing their names be sent to every member of the Engineering Employers' Federation, with the instructions that they should in no case be employed; (5) that for the present no further unskilled workers be set on skilled jobs, and that the unions be consulted on all doubtful cases.[1]

The subsequent national negotiations with the employers did not result in any agreement, but the provisional agreement with this large firm helped to put the workers in a strategical position when the government took up the matter of trade union rules.

[1] *Labour Year Book*, 1916, p. 55. Cole, *Labour in War Time*, pp. 174-175.

REPORTS OF THE COMMITTEE ON PRODUCTION

The Committee on Production issued four reports from February 16 to March 4 inclusive, dealing respectively with (1) " Irregular Time Keeping," (2) " Shells and Fuses and Avoidance of Stoppage of Work," (3) "Demarcation of Work," and (4) " Wages in Shipbuilding Trade."

The report on irregular time keeping in ship yards, issued February 16, dealt with the failure to attain the maximum output of work because of time lost by riveting squads. Riveting is carried on by "squads" or groups of workers. When any member of the squad was absent, his place was not filled but the whole squad remained idle. The committee did not indicate in any specific way how the difficulty was to be overcome, but urged that the parties directly concerned should make an effort to arrive at some satisfactory arrangement. If an agreement was not reached within ten days the committee recommended that any outstanding difference should be referred to the committee for immediate and final settlement.

The report on shells and fuses, issued on February 20, dealt with trade union rules which had the effect of limiting the output of munitions of war.

Restrictive rules or customs calculated to affect the production of munitions of war or to hamper or impede any reasonable steps to achieve a maximum output are under present circumstances seriously hurtful to the welfare of the country, and we think they should be suspended during the period of the war, with proper safeguards and adjustments to protect the interests of the work people and their trade unions.[1]

The committee recommended that the men making shells and fuses should relax their practice of confining their earnings on a piece rate basis to " time and half " or whatever the local standard might be. It recognized that the practice had been adopted to prevent cutting of piece rates, but pointed out that the government was the only consumer of shells and fuses and had no motive for cutting rates. It recommended that firms making shells and

[1] *Labour Gazette*, 1915, p. 83.

fuses for the government give an undertaking to the committee not to consider the earnings of the men as a factor in making new piece rates and not to cut existing rates, unless this was warranted by a change in machinery.

A second recommendation made by the committee was that female labor be more largely employed "under suitable and proper conditions in the production of shells and fuses." [1]

The second portion of the report issued on February 20 had to do with "Avoidance of Stoppage of Work." After expressing the opinion that, in establishments engaged on productive work, employers and workmen should, during the war, "under no circumstances allow their differences to result in a stoppage of work," the committee recommended that the government immediately publish the following recommendation and ask government contractors, subcontractors and trade unions to declare their adhesion to the recommendation:

Avoidance of stoppages of work for government purposes. With a view to preventing loss of production caused by disputes between employers and work people, no stoppage of work by strike or lockout should take place on work for government purposes. In the event of differences arising which fail to be settled by the parties directly concerned, or by their representatives, or under any existing agreements, the matter shall be referred to an impartial tribunal nominated by His Majesty's government for immediate investigation and report to the government with a view to a settlement.

In order to safeguard the position of the trade unions and of the work people, the committee recommended that firms contracting with the government be required to give an undertaking, to be held on behalf of the unions, in the following terms:

To His Majesty's Government

We hereby undertake that any departure during the war from the practice ruling in our workshops and shipyards prior to the war shall only be for the period of the war.

No change in practice made during the war shall be allowed to prejudice the position of the work people in our employment or of their trade unions in regard to the resumption and maintenance after the war of any rules or customs existing prior to the war.

In any readjustment of staff which may have to be effected after the war,

[1] *Labour Gazette*, 1915, p. 83.

priority of employment will be given to workmen in our employment at the beginning of the war who are serving with the colors or who are now in our employment.

Name of firm....................................

Date....................................[1]

The third report issued by the committee dealt with the subjects of demarcation of work and utilization of semi-skilled or un-skilled labor.

The committee urged that in government establishments where, apparently, demarcation restrictions were not numerous, they be at once suspended. In private engineering and shipbuilding establishments they also recommended the suspension of demar-cation restrictions on work required for government purposes during the continuance of the war, accompanied by the follow-ing safeguards:

(a) Men usually employed on the work to be given the prefer-ence.

(b) If suitable labor were not available locally men might be brought from a distance if the work were of sufficient magnitude to warrant the transfer and if the work would not be delayed by waiting for them.

(c) The customary rates should continue to be paid for the jobs.

(d) A record of the nature of the departures from the *statu quo* should be kept.

(e) Difficulties arising between the parties which they had not settled should be referred within seven days to the Board of Trade for speedy settlement and in the meantime there should be no stoppage of work.

(f) The same form of guarantee to work people prescribed in the Stoppage of Work report should be adopted.[1]

The second part of this report dealt with the utilization of semi-skilled or unskilled labor. The committee recommended the use of such labor whenever an employer working on govern-ment work was " unable to meet the requirements because of his

[1] *Labour Gazette*, 1915, pp. 83-84.

inability to secure the necessary labor customarily employed on the work," provided that the use of unskilled or semi-skilled labor was surrounded with "proper safeguards and adjustments to protect the interests of the work people and their trade unions." [1]

The success of the recommendations depended upon the willingness of the unions to accept them. The government therefore undertook to secure the acceptance by the unions of the principles underlying the recommendations. The government itself was quick to announce its concurrence in the committee's recommendation concerning the avoidance of stoppage of work and immediately named the Production Committee itself as the tribunal to settle disputes. It was apparently under this authority that the committee acted when it intervened in the Clyde strike and called for a resumption of work on March 1.

The fourth report made by the committee was issued on March 1 and contained the terms of settlement of the Clyde engineering strike, which have already been given.

AMENDMENT OF THE DEFENSE OF THE REALM ACT

The Defense of the Realm Consolidation Act, 1914 (5 Geo. 5, c. 8), enacted November 27, 1914, was amended on March 16, 1915, so that Subsection 3 of Section 1 read as follows:.

It shall be lawful for the Admiralty or Army Council or the Minister of Munitions (a) to require that there shall be placed at their disposal the whole or any part of the output of any factory or workshop of whatever sort or the plant thereof; (b) to take possession of and use for the purpose of His Majesty's naval or military service any factory or workshop or any plant thereof; (c) to require any work in any factory or workshop to be done in accordance with the directions of the Admiralty or Army Council or the Minister of Munitions, given with the object of making the factory or workshop, or the plant or labor therein, as useful as possible for the production of war material; and (d) to regulate or restrict the carrying on of any work in any factory, workshop or other premises, or the engagement or employment of any workmen or all or any classes of workmen therein, or to remove the plant therefrom, with a view to maintaining or increasing the production of munitions in other factories, workshops or premises, or to regulate and control the supply of metals and material that may be re-

[1] *Labour Gazette*, 1915, p. 84.

quired for any articles for use in war; and (e) to take possession of any unoccupied premises for the purpose of housing workmen employed in the production, storage, or transport of war material; and regulations under this act may be made accordingly.

It is hereby declared that when the fulfilment by any person or any contract is interfered with by the necessity on the part of himself or any other person of complying with any requirement, regulation or restriction of the Admiralty or the Army Council or the Minister of Munitions or the Food Controller under this act, or any regulations made thereunder that necessity is a good defense to any action or proceedings taken against that person in respect of the nonfulfilment of the contract so far as it is due to that interference.

In this subsection the expression "war material" includes arms, ammunition, warlike stores, and equipment and everything required for or in connection with the production thereof.[1]

The Treasury Conference

Armed with this persuasive measure the government, on the day following the passage of the above amendment, invited representatives of the Trades Union Congress, the General Federation of Trade Unions and of the principal unions in the industries producing commodities for government use to a conference with the Chancellor of Exchequer (Mr. Lloyd George) and the President of the Board of Trade (Mr. Runciman)

to consider the general position in reference to the urgent need of the country in regard to the large and a larger increase in the output of munitions of war, and the steps which the government propose to take to organize the industries of the country with a view to achieving that end.[2]

The invitation was pretty generally accepted. Besides representatives from the two federal bodies above mentioned, there were representatives from unions in the following industries: engineering, shipbuilding, iron and steel, other metal trades, wood workers, laborers, transport, woolen and boot and shoe. The Miners' Federation of Great Britain was represented on the first day, but its representatives withdrew because they were

[1] *Manuals of Emergency Legislation. Defense of the Realm Manual*, 3d enlarged edition revised to February 28, 1917, p. 3 (a).
[2] *Labour Year Book*, 1916, p. 59.

unwilling even to consider and discuss proposals for compulsory arbitration.[1]

Mr. Lloyd George explained to the conference the powers given to the government by the amended Defense of the Realm Act and said that it called for the full cooperation of employers and employed. He asked the unions to accept arbitration and to relax the trade union rules under adequate safeguards and proposed that this be accompanied by a limitation of profits, "because we see that it is very difficult for us to appeal to labor to relax restrictions and to put out the whole of its strength, unless some condition of this kind is imposed."

A subcommittee of seven was appointed to draw up, in consultation with Mr. Lloyd George and Mr. Runciman, proposals for submission to the conference. The proposals submitted the next day were along the lines proposed in the recommendations of the Committee on Production and contained: (1) an agreement that during the war there should be no stoppage of labor on work required for a satisfactory completion of the war, but that all industrial disputes which could not be settled by agreement of the parties should be made the subject of arbitration by one of the following:

(a) the Committee on Production;

(b) a single arbitrator agreed upon by the parties or appointed by the Board of Trade;

(c) a court of arbitration upon which labor is represented equally with the employers.

If none of these methods were acceptable to both parties, a settlement should be made by the Board of Trade. (2) A proposal that the government appoint an advisory committee representative of the organized workers to facilitate the carrying out of the recommendations. (3) An agreement to relax trade union practices and customs in order to accelerate the output of war munitions or equipment, provided that the government require all contractors and subcontractors engaged on war work (a) to give an undertaking to restore at the close of the war, without prejudice to the position of the work people or their unions,

[1] *Labour Year Book*, p. 78, note.

any practice ruling in their shops or yards at the beginning of
the war; (b) to give preference of employment to workmen in
their employ at the beginning of the war; (c) to pay semi-skilled
men called upon to perform work which had been done by skilled
workers the usual rates of the district for that work; (d) to keep
a record of the nature of the departure from conditions prevailing at the time of the agreement and to keep this record open to
inspection by the authorized representatives of the government;
(e) to give notices to the workmen, wherever practicable, of
changes in working conditions which it was proposed to introduce, and to furnish an opportunity for consultation with them
or their representatives; and (f) to settle disputes without stoppages of work by one of the methods above described.[1]

The representatives of all the unions represented at the conference, except the Amalgamated Society of Engineers, endorsed
the proposed agreement. It seems to have been generally understood that the agreement reached at this Treasury Conference
was an agreement entered into by the unions there represented,
but in form it was merely an agreement of the signers to " recommend to their members " the proposals submitted by the committee. Mr. Arthur Henderson, the Chairman of the Workers'
Representatives at the conference, said that the agreement had
no binding force until it had been submitted to the unions
concerned.[2]

The failure of the representatives of the Amalgamated Society
of Engineers to sign the agreement was considered by the government to be a serious omission, in view of the strength of that
union in the munitions factories. The representatives of the engineers felt that the agreement did not sufficiently safeguard their
members, and they were also dissatisfied because the agreement
did not express the government's declared intention to limit war
profits.

A further conference between Mr. Lloyd George and Mr. Runciman and the representatives of the Amalgamated Society of
Engineers was held on March 25, and the following important

---

[1] *Labour Year Book.* 1916, pp. 60-61.
[2] Cole, *op. cit.*, p. 185.

additions to the agreement were made, after which the engineers gave their signatures to the agreement.

1. That it is the intention of the government to conclude arrangements with all important firms engaged wholly or mainly upon engineering and shipbuilding work for war purposes, under which these profits will be limited with a view to securing that benefit resulting from the relaxation of trade restrictions or practices shall accrue to the state.

2. That the relaxation of trade practices contemplated in the agreement relates solely to work done for war purposes during the war period.

3. That in the case of the introduction of new inventions which were not in existence in the prewar period the class of workmen to be employed on this work after the war should be determined according to the practice prevailing before the war in the case of the class of work most nearly analogous.

4. That on demand by the workmen the government department concerned will be prepared to certify whether the work in question is needed for war purposes.

5. That the government will undertake to use its influence to secure the restoration of previous conditions in every case after the war.[1]

The government proceeded at once to appoint the advisory committee provided for in the agreement, naming as the members thereof the seven labor leaders [2] who had, as members of the subcommittee, presented the proposals to the union representatives at the Treasury Conference.

The Treasury Conference agreement was very favorably received by public and press throughout England. This much is admitted by Mr. Cole, who is throughout critical of the recommendations, the effect of which, he says, " was to weaken, rather than to strengthen, trade unionism." Mr. Lloyd George was very enthusiastic over the results of the conference and said that the " document that was signed on Friday night ought to be the great charter for labor." [3]

[1] *Labour Year Book*, 1916, p. 61. Cole, *op. cit.*, pp. 188-189.

[2] Mr. Arthur Henderson, M.P. (Ironfounders), Mr. C. W. Bowerman, M.P. (Parliamentary Committee), Mr. W. Moses (Pattern Makers), Mr. John Hill (Boiler Makers), Mr. A. Wilkie, M.P. (Shipwrights), Mr. Frank Smith (Cabinet Makers), and Mr. J. T. Brownlie (Engineers).

[3] Cole, *op. cit.*, pp. 189-190.

ADMINISTRATION OF THE TREASURY AGREEMENT

In order to carry into effect the terms of the agreement local munitions committees were set up in the chief centers of ship-building, especially on the northeast coast and on the Clyde. The committees were made up like the trade boards, of an equal number of representatives of employers and workmen with an additional number of impartial persons appointed by the government. The important difference between these committees and the trade boards, however, was the fact that they dealt not with wages " but with the management and control of industry." [1] Speaking enthusiastically of the committee formed on the northeast coast which had on it seven representatives of workers and seven of the employers, Mr. Cole has this to say of the possibilities of the new system:

The committee has, moreover, a far wider significance than any immediate advantage the workers can hope to gain from it. It will go down to history as the first definite and official recognition of the right of the workers to a say in the management of their own industries. Here, for the first time, the nominees of the workers meet those of the masters on equal terms, to discuss not merely wages, hours, or conditions of labor, but the actual business of production. Under stress of the emergency the workers are being recognized, however grudgingly, as partners in industry.[2]

This may be an extravagant statement, especially in view of the fact that shortly after the Munitions Act was passed these committees disappeared and their work passed into the hands of officials created under the authority of that act.[1] The real significance of the committees lies in the fact that in the new organization of industry being developed as a result of war needs, the trade unions were being given recognition as an essential part of the organization.

The Committee on Production appointed by the government in February continued its work during the spring of 1915, endeavoring to prevent stoppages of work on government contracts by adjusting wages, generally allowing increases in the form of

[1] *Labour Year Book*, 1916, p. 62.
[2] Cole, *op. cit.*, p. 198.

"war wages, recognized as due to and dependent on the existence of the abnormal conditions now prevailing in consequence of the war."[1]. The wage settlements seem to have been made in accordance with no general principle, such as the increase in cost of living. In some cases this seems to have been the controlling motive as, for example, on the Newcastle-upon-Tyne tramways when higher allowances were made "to employes who are householders" than to single men, and in other cases where bonuses were allowed only to men receiving below a certain stated sum per week. In other cases, however, other considerations dominated, as in the cement trade, where "the adverse effect that the war has exercised and is exercising upon the cement trade" was sufficient to influence the committee to allow no further increase of wages beyond the 5 per cent advance voluntarily offered by the employers.[2]

Meanwhile, trade disputes which, as we have seen, reached their minimum in intensity in December, 1914, began to increase at a rapid rate in the early part of 1915, as is shown by the following table:[3]

MONTH	No. of DISPUTES	No. of WORK PEOPLE AFFECTED	
		Directly	Directly and Indirectly
December, 1914.............	17	1,190	1,192
January, 1915	30	3,436	4,082
February, 1915.............	47	26,129	29,007
March, 1915	74	12,982	16,359
April, 1915.................	44	5,137	5,577
May, 1915.................	63	39,913	48,240
June, 1915	72	17,904	22,230

From the governmental standpoint the most serious phase of this increase was that the disputes were mainly in those industries, engineering, coal mining and transport, upon which the increasing output of munitions of war was mainly dependent. Most of the disputes were over the question of wages and in spite of the activity of the Committee on Production, it was evi-

[1] *Labour Gazette*, 1915, pp. 120-121, 162-164.
[2] *Ibid.*, pp. 203-205.
[3] *Ibid.*, pp. 66, 104, 141, 183, 222, 261.

dent that further steps needed to be taken if the output of war material was to be brought up to its maximum. Before these steps were taken, however, an event occurred which further tended to complicate matters.

THE DRINK PROBLEM

Mr. Lloyd George made a series of speeches in April, in one of which he laid great emphasis upon the influence of "the lure of drink " among the working classes as a factor responsible for the insufficient supply of munitions. The speech was widely circulated by the newspapers and was quickly seized upon by those who were advocating prohibition of the use of intoxicants during war time. The basis of the attack was, presumably, a report on lost time in war industries which was presented to the House of Commons by Mr. Lloyd George and was made public on Labor Day, May 1.

The report claimed that in the Clyde, Tyne and Barrow districts the situation in respect to shipbuilding, repairs and munitions of war work put briefly was

that now, while the country is at war, the men are doing less work than would be regarded as an ordinary week's work under normal peace conditions.[1]

Instances were cited where the time lost by riveters in the shipyards "equals about 35 per cent of the normal week's work; platers 25 per cent; and the caulkers and drillers about 22 per cent." Among fitters on submarine engine work " on the average each man did little more than three quarters of a day's work." "The problem," it was said, "is not how to get the workmen to increase their normal peace output, but how to get them to do an ordinary week's work of 51 or 53 hours as the case may be."[2]

[1] Report and statistics of bad time kept in shipbuilding, munitions and transport areas. p. 2.
[2] Ibid., pp. 2, 3, 5.

The reasons for the loss of time (continues the report) are no doubt various, but it is abundantly clear that the most potent is in the facilities which exist for men to obtain beer and spirits combined with the high rates of wages and abundance of employment. Opinion on this point is practically unanimous.

A great deal of statistical evidence was submitted by employers in the shipbuilding industry to show the extent to which lost time due, as they believed, to excessive drinking, interfered with the output. The report summarized this evidence in the following statement:

The evidence is really overwhelming that the main cause of this alarming loss of time is the lure of drink. The employers say so most emphatically; the Admiralty have received elaborate reports emphasizing the same conclusion in the case of shipbuilding, repairs, munitions of war and transport. The Home Office reports are to the same effect, and the detailed figures summarized above are, in themselves, strong evidence that drink is the cause. A section of each class of workmen keep perfectly good time throughout the week, and therefore the cause is not one which is common to all workmen, or due to any general industrial condition. The worst time is generally kept after wages are paid, and at the beginning of the following week. When absence from work occurs the workman is usually absent for several days together. Staleness and fatigue no doubt must arise from working during long hours over an extended period, but inasmuch as half the men are not in fact working for more than 45 hours a week, the cause must be found elsewhere. The testimony of observers in each district is that drink is by far the most important factor. . . . The contention that the cause of irregular hours is the excessive time worked is completely disposed of by observing that on average the time worked is unfortunately not so great as the standard in time of peace. The figures show, not that workmen who have been working long hours for days together occasionally take a day off, but that while some workmen are working steadily day by day for long hours, those who fail to work even ordinary hours are continually repeating this failure.[1]

While the evidence to the effect that much time was lost in the shipbuilding yards on account of drink seems overwhelming, it must be said that the impressions left by the report were more or less unfair to the majority of the men in the engineering and shipbuilding trades. This was pointed out in the report by one of the factory inspectors. He called attention to the fact that

irregular time is confined largely to certain specific trades: riveters, caulkers, platers, riggers, and to a very much less extent, engineers are the chief

[1] Report, etc., p. 15.

offenders; such tradesmen as pattern makers, molders, turners, and time workers generally keep relatively good time.[1]

Furthermore, he showed that drinking was not the only cause of lost time. Much of the lost time was due to the practice which we have already observed of riveters and platers working in squads. When, for any reason, one member of the squad failed to appear, four or five men would lose a morning's or even a day's work and the lost time of these men would figure in the employer's statistics.

The same inspector threw some light on the reasons for the absences of the riveters, which, if not an excuse, at least deserves a place in the explanation of their dereliction. He said:

Riveting is hard and exhausting work, and it is frequently and necessarily carried on in trying conditions—exposure in winter to bitter cold and damp. The temptation to take a morning or a day off during very cold or very hot weather is great, as the riveter knows he is indispensable at present, and will not lose his job if he does lie off. Moreover his pay is sufficient, even with a partial week's work, to keep him and his family in comfort. The machine men working under cover are in a comfortable shop and have not the same temptation to lie off. Again the pay is relatively much less, and being time workers they can not make up the lost time by a special spurt. Another important point frequently overlooked is that at present, owing to the extraordinary scarcity of skilled labor, men who in ordinary times would never be employed on account of their irregular habits, are at work in many yards, and materially affect the numbers of those losing time. Briefly, I am convinced that the " black squad " piece workers have not risen much above the social position of the man earning 30s. a week, yet their remuneration is equal to that of a professional man. They have not yet been educated to spend their wages wisely, and the money is largely wasted, for they have few interests and little to spend their wage on apart from alcohol.[2]

Mr. Lloyd George's speech and the allegations made in the report were warmly resented in labor circles and the Labor party in the House of Commons protested against the report, in which Mr. Arthur Henderson said " all the evidence against the workers is that of employers or officials," and demanded and secured the promise of the government to appoint a committee of inquiry on which labor should be represented.[3]

[1] Report, etc., p. 24.
[2] Ibid., p. 25.
[3] Cole, op. cit., pp. 200-207. Labour Year Book, 1916, pp. 62-63.

MINISTRY OF MUNITIONS

Dissatisfaction with the progress of the war caused a change in the government in May, 1915. The Liberal Ministry resigned and its place was taken by a Coalition Ministry in which Labor was represented. On the 9th of June a new government department was created known as the Ministry of Munitions, " for the purpose of supplying munitions for the present war," [1] and Mr. Lloyd George was appointed Minister of Munitions " to examine into and organize the sources of supply of any kind of munitions of war." [2]

At first it was believed, and apparently by Mr. Lloyd George himself, that the Defense of the Realm Acts conferred upon him sufficient power to control the labor situation. It was soon seen, however, that there were important gaps in that legislation. They gave the government power to take over any private works needed and to order the workers to work, so long as they remained there, exactly as the government directed, but it did not confer upon the government power to compel the workers to remain in its employ.[3] In other words the government had no authority to prevent strikes. There was much talk about this time of " conscription of labor."

Every one, it was urged, who was not a soldier or a worker in some absolutely essential trade, should be forced into the making of munitions, and martial law should be proclaimed in the workshops.[4]

In order to formulate a policy for the conduct of his work, the Minister of Munitions held a number of conferences with labor leaders to discuss proposals for meeting the emergency.[5] The National Labor Advisory Committee appointed by the government as a result of the Treasury Conference agreement in consultation with the minister drew up proposals which were put before " a full conference of trade union leaders representing

[1] 5 and 6 Geo. 5, c. 51. *Manual of Emergency Legislation, Supplement 4*, p. 14.
[2] Order in Council, June 16, 1915.
[3] *Labour Year Book*, 1916, p. 63.
[4] Cole, *op. cit.*, p. 208.
[5] *Ibid.*, p. 215.

the munition industries."[1] They were carried by a majority of the conference though a minority of the representatives were opposed to the provisions for compulsory arbitration.

Thus prepared, the Munitions Bill was introduced and with relatively little discussion was passed by Parliament on July 2. and became the Munitions of War Act, 1915.[2]

[1] Cole, *op. cit.*, p. 215. They did not include representatives of the miners or the cotton operatives.
[2] 5 and 6 Geo. 5. c. 54. *Manual of Emergency Legislation, Supplement* 4, pp. 17-26.

CHAPTER V

The Munitions of War Acts

The Munitions of War Act, 1915, together with its amendments (constituting practically a revision of the act) of January 27, 1916, and August 21, 1917, is the most important piece of labor legislation which has been enacted by Parliament during the war. Its foundation is the recommendations of the Committee on Production, made in February and March, 1915, modified and enlarged by agreements entered into between the government and leading trade unionists at conferences held in March and June, as already related. The act is entitled "An act to make provision for furthering the efficient manufacture, transport and supply of munitions for the present war; and for purposes incidental thereto," and it was made necessary by a realization of the fact that

an overwhelming supply of munitions of war for Great Britain and her allies was the essential element in the successful prosecution of the war, and, to attain this, the organization of an important section of the British industrial world upon a new basis became imperative.[1]

Although the act has been severely criticized by some of the labor writers and socialists in Great Britain, even to the extent of calling its acceptance by Parliament "scandalous,"[2] and of saying that its enactment came "like a thief in the night,"[3] yet it must be remembered that leading trade unionists and members of

[1] T. A. Fyfe: *Employers and Workmen under the Munitions of War Acts,* 2d ed., p. 1. For purposes of convenient reference I have in addition to referring to the sections of the Munitions Acts, 1915 and 1916, made references to the text of the codification of the acts as given by Mr. Fyfe. In my abstract of the principal provisions of the act I have also made free use of Mr. Fyfe's comments and interpretations, which is justified by the fact that Mr. Fyfe, in addition to being chairman of a munitions tribunal, is a judge of His Majesty's courts in Glasgow.
[2] Cole: *Labour in War Time.*
[3] Mary McArthur: *The Woman Worker,* January, 1916, p. 5.

the Labor party were consulted at every stage of its preparation and enactment and are, indeed, largely responsible for the form and substance of the acts. Whether or not, viewed from a labor standpoint, the Munitions Act be considered a wise or an unwise piece of legislation, it can not be truthfully said that it was enacted in defiance of labor or without giving their representatives an opportunity to consider it and to suggest amendments.

As a carefully drawn and consistently prepared piece of legislation, not much can be said for the original Munitions Act or for the government's clumsy method of amendment. As Mr. Fyfe says:

> It is to be regretted that the form the Amending Act (of 1916) took was not the total repeal of the original act, and the reenactment of its clauses along with the amendments in an entirely new act.[1]

In many respects the act seems to have been drafted backwards, since portions of Part III deal with matters necessary to an understanding of Parts I and II, and Part II contains sections and clauses which, logically, should come before Part I.

In the following abstract of the main provisions of the acts I have not attempted to follow the order in which the various sections appear in the parliamentary measure.

The acts are frankly stated to be emergency legislation; to " have effect only so long as the office of Minister of Munitions and the Ministry of Munitions exists,"[2] and the act creating the Ministry declared that it should cease to exist at a period not later than twelve months after the conclusion of war. It is also provided that the obligations contained in Schedule II, whereby the owners of establishments agree to restore prewar conditions among their employes, shall continue to be binding on such owners for twelve months after the end of the war.[2]

The act is divided into three parts. Part I deals with differences which may arise between employers and employes and the modes of settling them. Part II deals with what are known as

---

[1] Fyfe, *op. cit.*, 1st ed., p. 2.
[2] Sec. 20 (2), Fyfe, 2d ed., p. 83.

"controlled establishments," rates of wages and limitation of profits in such establishments, restrictions on the right to employ and be employed on munitions work, conditions under which workers may leave or be discharged from such service, and the conditions under which female labor may be employed on munitions work. Part III (made up largely of amendments) deals with the power of the Minister of Munitions to regulate or restrict the work of any factory or to remove machinery to any other factory or to control the supply of materials for the purpose of increasing the production of munitions. It also deals with matters of inspection, with information to be furnished by employers, with munitions tribunals, with penalties, and with the definition of terms used in the act.

The Munitions Acts may be considered as an extension of the Defense of the Realm Acts, especially of those portions which deal with the production of munitions.[1] They authorize the Admiralty or Army Council or Minister of Munitions to take possession of and use for the purpose of naval or military service any factory, workshop or plant and to regulate or restrict the carrying on of any work or the employment of any workmen therein, or to remove the equipment therefrom with a view to increasing the production of munitions, or to regulate and control the supply of materials that may be required for articles for use in war.[2]

In order that the Minister of Munitions may have at hand the information necessary to enable him to decide on the availability of any establishment for the production of munitions, the owner of any establishment in operation may be required to furnish to the Minister any information requested by the latter as to the persons employed and the nature of their work, the machinery used, the costs of production and other relevant matters, and to submit his premises and books to inspection by authorized inspectors in order that they may obtain such information or other-

[1] *Manuals of Emergency Legislation; Defense of the Realm Manual,* pp. 8-9.
[2] Defense of the Realm Act, sec. 1 (2) (a). *Defense of the Realm Manual,* p. 3 (note). Munitions of War Acts, Part III, sec. 10, Fyfe, *op. cit.,* pp. 73-74.

wise determine the availability of the establishment for munitions work.[1]

MEANING OF MUNITIONS WORK

The term " munitions work " has been given a very wide meaning by the revision of the act and by the interpretations placed upon it by the appeal tribunals. The amended act makes it include not only arms, ammunition and the like, but " any other articles or parts of articles intended or adapted for use in war " [2] and the appeal tribunals have interpreted this to mean anything " suitable for use in war." This does not mean, however, that anything which is " capable of use " in war is to be covered by the term.[3] Mr. Justice Atkin, in explaining the meaning of the phrase " intended or adapted for use in war," said:

"Adapted for use" means, I think, "suitable for use"; but it means in the context something more than merely capable of use. I think the word denotes fitness in some high degree to be determined on the facts in each particular case, taking into consideration, amongst other things, the extent to which articles of the particular class are in fact employed in war, the probability or otherwise of articles of the class in question being required by the military authorities, and the importance or unimportance of the articles in "furthering the efficient manufacture, transport and supply of munitions for the present war." I think it plain, however, that in considering this part of the definition the actual use, contemplated or intended, of the article is inconclusive and may be irrelevant; if its use in war is intended, the article will fall within the express words. "Adapted" must to my mind, when used disjunctively from "intended," convey some meaning independent of the intended use.[4]

It was accordingly held that the repair of railway wagons belonging to a colliery was " munitions work," since these wagons, though not at the time being used for war purposes, were " articles adapted for use in war." [5]

The act, as amended, provides that " munitions work " shall

[1] Munitions of War Act, 1915, sec. 11, Amend. Act, 1916, sec. 16 and 17. Fyfe, *op. cit.*, pp. 74-75.
[2] Amend. Act, 1916, sec. 9 (a). Fyfe, p. 82.
[3] In this respect Fyfe, p. 6, seems to have erred in his interpretation of Mr. Justice Atkin's decision.
[4] Shaw v. Lincoln Waggon and Engine Co., Ltd. (1916 A.M.T. 11), Chartres, Judicial Interpretation of the Munitions of War Acts, p. 2.
[5] Shaw v. Lincoln, etc. Chartres, p. 2. Fyfe, pp. 219-220.

also include the construction, alteration or repairs of building machinery and plant for naval or military purposes, including the erection of houses to accommodate munitions workers; the construction, repair and maintenance of docks, etc., where such work is certified by the Admiralty to be necessary for the successful prosecution of the war, and work necessary for the supply of light, heat, water or power, tramway facilities or fire protection where the Minister of Munitions certifies that such supply is of importance for carrying on munitions work.[1] The act does not specifically declare the production of raw materials or the mining of coal or ore as munitions work. No formal order of the Minister has, as yet, been issued to include such work and the appeal tribunals have declined to pass upon it in advance,[2] but it may be noted that formal orders have been issued specifying the manufacture of such articles as lead compounds, constructional steel, lime and all materials wholly or partially manufactured from wool as munitions work.[3] The Minister has also recommended employers to refrain from encouraging miners to transfer their services to munitions factories, and to assist men who had been engaged in coal mining to return to the mines if they desired to do so.[4]

Doubts having arisen as to the meaning of the words "workman" and "workmen" under the original act, the revised act declared that these expressions shall

include not only persons whose usual occupation consists in manual labor, but also foremen, clerks, typists, draughtsmen and other persons whose usual occupation consists wholly or mainly in work other than manual labor.[5]

CONTROLLED ESTABLISHMENTS

We have already observed that many trade unionists, especially those engaged in the engineering and shipbuilding trades, when urged by the government to abandon for the period of the war their rules restricting production and employment, met this pro-

---

[1] Munitions of War Amend. Act, 1916, sec. 9. Fyfe, *op. cit.*, p. 82.
[2] Chartres, *op. cit.*, p. 4, and note.
[3] Fyfe, pp. 181-182.
[4] Circular letter, 71, October 16, 1915, cited by Fyfe, p. 8.
[5] Munitions of War Amend. Act, 1916, sec. 12. Fyfe, p. 83.

posal with the counter demand that, in case this were done, employers surrender their right to excess profits resulting from government work. The supplemental agreement entered into with representatives of the Amalgamated Society of Engineers, following the Treasury Conference of March, 1915, shows that the government recognized the justice of this claim, and contains its promise to limit profits in important establishments engaged in the production of munitions. The principal method by which this promise was carried out was through the agency of what are known as "controlled establishments" dealt with primarily in Part II of the Munitions Acts.

Not all establishments engaged on "munitions work" are "controlled establishments," although the Minister of Munitions may, by order, declare any establishment where "munitions work" is carried on to be a "controlled establishment."[1] The effects of making an establishment a "controlled establishment" are fourfold:

(a) Four-fifths of the net profits of such an establishment, over and above the average profits for two years preceding the outbreak of the war, are to be paid into the Exchequer.[2] This means that if an employer had made on an average 5 per cent profits on his business during the two years prior to the outbreak of the war he is now entitled to retain only one-fifth of any excess above that amount. The remainder is to be paid to the Exchequer. Certain allowances are made, however, which probably in practice result in bringing the amount retained somewhat above the one-fifth excess contemplated.

(b) No changes in the rates of wages or salary of any employe in such establishment shall be made until the proposed change has been submitted to the Minister of Munitions, who may withhold his consent. Either the Minister or the owner of the establishment may

[1] Munitions of War Act, 1915, sec. 4. Amend. Act, 1916, sec. 1. Fyfe, *op. cit.*, pp. 62-63.
[2] Munitions of War Act, 1915, sec. 4 (1); sec. 5 (1), (2). Fyfe, pp. 63, 66.

then require that the matter be submitted to arbitration in the manner provided by the act.[1]

By an amendment made to the act in 1917 the undertaking which the owner of a controlled establishment was deemed to have entered into was made to include an undertaking not to change piece prices, time allowances or bonuses on output or the rates or prices payable under any other system of payment by results unless this change was made by agreement between the owner and his workmen or under certain conditions by direction of the Minister. This provision was not to apply, however, to changes in the rates of wages made by order of the Minister in the case of female workers employed on munition work or in the case of wages paid in shipbuilding yards where special rules were made applicable.[2]

(c) "Any rule, practice, or custom not having the force of law which tends to restrict production or employment shall be suspended in the establishment," but the owner is deemed to have entered into an undertaking to restore such rules, etc., at the close of the war, and to give preference in employment to former employes. In order that this undertaking may be carried out, this part of the act continues, as already mentioned, for twelve months after the close of the war. The Board of Trade is made the judge as to whether any rule, etc., tends to restrict production or employment.[3] The rules, practices and customs to which reference is here made are those dealt with in the Treasury agreement and relate to such matters as the restrictions imposed by the unions on the introduction of machines, the rules forbidding women or semi-skilled men from doing skilled work and the limitations on hours demanded by the unions, the use of nonunion labor, etc. Not all the rules which the

---

[1] Munitions of War Act, 1915, sec. 4 (2) ; 1916, sec. 2. Fyfe, p. 63.
[2] Munitions of War Act, 1917, sec. 8. *British Industrial Experience*, vol. 1, p. 263.
[3] Munitions of War Act, 1915, sec. 4 (3), (4) ; sec. 20. See also schedule 2, Fyfe, pp. 64, 83, 84-85.

act abrogated, however, were those laid down by trade unions. In one case dealt with by the High Court of Justice an employer who had maintained a nonunion shop was unwilling to employ members of a certain trade union, but the court held that a practice "which does tend to prevent workmen from entering employment who otherwise could reasonably be employed" was one of the practices which tended to hinder production and was therefore aimed at by the Munitions Act.

(d) Employers and employes in any such establishment become subject to any regulations made by the Minister of Munitions for that establishment, for the purpose of maintaining efficiency and discipline. They are also bound by his orders giving directions as to rates of wages, hours of labor or conditions of employment, so far as those relate to semi-skilled or unskilled workers doing work which before the war had usually been done by skilled labor.[1]

Thus it appears that the government has succeeded, as far as the language of the law is concerned, in tying together the limitation of profits in munitions establishments and the removal of the restrictive rules of the trade unions, while it seeks to bind the employer to a restoration of the prewar customs at the close of the war. Although the term "controlled establishments" is not specifically limited to the engineering and shipbuilding trades, it seems to have been in the minds of the framers of these sections of the original act to limit the operation of them to these trades and thus meet the issues raised at the Treasury Conference by the Amalgamated Society of Engineers. Later when the 1916 amendments to the act were being considered, it was apparently deemed best to give a broader meaning to the term "controlled establishments."

In February, 1917, the number of "controlled establishments" in the United Kingdom was 4,285 with approximately two million workers employed therein, twenty per cent of whom were

[1] Munitions of War Amend. Acts, 1916, sec. 7. Fyfe, *op. cit.*, p. 65.

women and girls. Since that date the proportion of female labor has increased considerably, but no figures are available which show the extent of the increase.

Although the undertaking given by employers to restore pre-war conditions in their establishments at the close of the war, as contained in schedule two, would seem to have been sufficiently broad to cover the exclusion of nonunionists where such exclusion had been the rule, unionists were apparently not satisfied with the statement and, in the amended act, succeeded in having this point specifically mentioned.[1]

Munitions Volunteers

Mention has already been made of the agitation for industrial conscription which was taking place in England during the spring of 1915. Mr. Lloyd George's earlier speeches indicated that he favored the idea, but he later expressed himself as not being in sympathy with this demand. He is quoted as having said at a conference with representatives of the unions on June 10:

They talk about the conscription of labor. I don't want conscription of labor at all. All I want to do is to be able to place men where they are most needed to increase the output of munitions.[2]

While the Munitions Act does not provide for "conscription of labor," it does impose such restrictions on the employment and mobility of laborers who volunteer to work in controlled establishments as to give this employment more or less the character of military service. Munitions volunteers, as they are called, enter into an agreement with the Minister to work at any controlled establishment to which they are assigned and to remain there for the period of the war, or for at least six months. If they fail to comply with the undertaking they become liable to penalties.[3] Subject to penalties for disobedience employers are forbidden to dissuade their employes from volunteering to do munitions work or to retain in their employment munitions volunteers who have received notice from the Minister of Munitions

[1] Munitions of War Amend. Act, 1916, sec. 15. Fyfe, *op. cit.*, pp. 64-65.
[2] Quoted by Cole: *Labour in War Time*, p. 213.
[3] Munitions of War Act, 1915, sec. 6 (1). Fyfe, p. 67.

that they are to work in some other establishment.[1] They are also forbidden to discharge from their employment munitions volunteers within a period of six weeks of the date of their agreement with the Minister unless " there was reasonable cause " for such dismissal.[2]

The usual mode of employing munitions volunteers is for the owner of a controlled establishment to make application to the manager of the central labor exchange for war munitions volunteers, stating the number desired, the occupations and special qualifications, the wages and hours of work and other conditions, and sign an agreement to employ the workers who may be assigned to him only on war munitions work and to pay them the district rate of wages for their work and to meet the other conditions applicable to munitions volunteers. His application must also contain the declaration that the employer has not already in his employ on private work men who are capable or who can be made capable for the work in question and that the local labor exchange has not succeeded in obtaining such men for him.[3]

The munitions volunteers are entitled to (a) the district rate of wages; (b) the sum necessary to make up the difference (if any) between the district rate and that received by the workman before his enrolment as a munitions volunteer; (c) traveling expenses, including railway fare at the commencement and completion of the work, and where necessary subsistence allowance at the rate of 2s. 6d. per day for seven days in the week.

It is clearly understood that the subsistence allowance is not intended to enable any workman to make a pecuniary profit.

When the workman's residence is within daily traveling distance of his place of work, he receives the cost of workman's tickets and, if the distance traveled exceeds one-half hour each way, he is paid one hour's traveling time per day at the rate of time and a half.[4]

The munitions volunteers plan was adopted by the government at the suggestion of the National Advisory Committee, made up

[1] Munitions of War Act, 1915, sec. 6 (2). Fyfe, *op. cit.*, p. 68.
[2] Munitions of War Act, 1916, sec. 3. Fyfe, p. 68.
[3] Form W.M.V. 19.
[4] *Ibid.*, p. 4.

of trade union leaders, as an alternative for conscription of labor. The plan was introduced even before the enactment of the Munitions Act, 1915, and 90,000 men had registered as munitions volunteers by July 10 of that year. There are no figures available which show registrations after that date. In November, 1916, the plan was extended by the trade card exemption system, under which whole unions enrolled as munitions volunteers.

The successful operation of the plan was hindered, however, by employers through patriotic motives and by other obstacles so that less use was made of the plan than had been expected. The plan has been revived and extended, however, since the abolition of leaving certificates in the fall of 1917.

THE DILUTION OF LABOR

Much has been said in the discussion of war labor legislation concerning the "dilution of labor." This apt expression has reference to the introduction of semi-skilled or female labor to do work which before the war was usually performed by skilled labor. Such substitution in the munitions trades had already been proceeding at a fairly rapid rate before the government directly interested itself in the question. The Board of Trade estimated that in February, 1915, the increase in the number of females in the engineering trades was 26.4 per cent over the 21,000 which the census of 1911 reported as employed in those trades. The number of men in these trades, on the other hand, showed a contraction of 9.1 per cent as compared to 1911.[1]

The unionists in the engineering trades offered strenuous opposition to the introduction of women and of unskilled labor into these well organized trades, especially where efforts were made to use this labor to accomplish what was regarded as skilled work. We have already noted that the government yielded to this opposition to the extent of making a separate agreement with the Amalgamated Society of Engineers in March, 1915, to the effect

that in the case of the introduction of new inventions which were not in existence in the prewar period the class of workmen to be employed on

[1] Edith Abbott: "The War and Women's Work in England," *Journal of Political Economy*, July, 1917, vol. 25, p. 662 .

this work after the war should be determined according to the practice prevailing before the war in the case of the class of work most nearly analogous.

Other clauses in the general agreement provided (1) that at the close of the war priority of employment should be given to workmen employed at the beginning of the war and to those serving with the colors; and (2) that the standard rates should be paid to semi-skilled and female laborers called upon to perform work which had been skilled labor. These safeguards were sufficient, it was believed, to cause the displacement in the skilled trades of female and unskilled laborers at the close of the war.

The Munitions Act of 1915 undertook to make definite these promises by Schedule 2 and by its scheme of controlled establishments. At the same time it gave the utmost encouragement to employers to make use of semi-skilled male labor and of female labor wherever it was possible to increase the output of munitions thereby. With the exception of the obligations imposed on owners of controlled establishments by Schedule 2, no special precautions in regard to the dilution of labor are found in the Munitions of War Act, 1915.

From the first, however, the dilution scheme caused uneasiness in the minds of unionists and in order to secure their cooperation, the government in September, 1915, appointed a joint committee representing the National Labor Advisory Committee (three of whose members were included) and the Ministry of Munitions, with additional members including Mr. W. H. Beveridge, Director of the Labor Exchanges, and Miss Mary Macarthur, Secretary of the National Federation of Women Workers,

to advise and assist the Ministry in regard to the transference of skilled labor and the introduction of semi-skilled and unskilled labor for munitions work, so as to secure the most productive use of all available labor supplies in the manufacture of munitions of war.[1]

In October, 1915, this committee, known as the Munitions Labor Supply Committee, drew up a series of recommendations in regard to the dilution of labor, and these " recommendations " were issued to employers in October as Circular L2 and Circular L3.

[1] *Labour Year Book*, 1916, p. 70.

EMPLOYMENT AND REMUNERATION OF WOMEN AND UNSKILLED LABOR

Circular L2 dealt with the "employment and remuneration of women on munitions work of a class which prior to the war was not recognized as women's work in districts where such work was customarily carried on." It dealt with rates of wages and allowances for overtime and holiday work, conditions under which women might be employed on piece work or the premium bonus system and contained a recognition of the principle "that on systems of payment by results equal payment shall be made to women as to the men for an equal amount of work done." After the amendment of the act in 1916, the government made the adoption of the provisions of Circular L2 mandatory.

Circular L3 related to the "employment and remuneration of semi-skilled and unskilled men on munition work of a class which prior to the war was customarily undertaken by skilled labor." Originally issued as mere "recommendations" of the Minister of Munitions, the provisions of this circular were, after the Munitions of War Amendment Act, 1916, had been passed, issued as government orders. The "general" clauses were as follows:

1. Operations on which skilled men are at present employed but which by reason of their character can be performed by semi-skilled or unskilled labor, may be done by such labor during the period of the war.

2. Where semi-skilled or unskilled male labor is employed on work identical with that customarily undertaken by skilled labor, the time rates and piece prices and premium bonus times shall be the same as customarily obtained for the operations when performed by skilled labor.

3. Where skilled men are at present employed they shall not be displaced by less skilled labor unless other skilled employment is offered to them there or elsewhere.

4. Piece work prices and premium bonus time allowances, after they have been established, shall not be altered unless the means or method of manufacture are changed.

5. Overtime, night shift, Sunday and holiday allowances shall be paid to such machine men on the same basis as to skilled men.

The circular also recommended time ratings for the manufacture of complete shell and fuses and cartridge cases, and these were likewise later converted into orders.[1]

When Parliament came to amend the Munitions Act in January, 1916, it gave the Minister of Munitions power

to give directions as to the rate of wages, hours of labor or conditions of employment of semi-skilled and unskilled men employed in any controlled establishment or munitions work, being work of a class which, prior to the war, was customarily undertaken by skilled labor, or as to the time rates for the manufacture of complete shells and fuses and cartridge cases in any controlled establishment in which such manufacture was not customary prior to the war.[2]

In the case of female workers " employed on or in connection with munitions work in any establishment " which had been brought under orders of the Minister of Munitions, the Minister was (subject to the provisions of the Factory and Workshops Acts, 1901 to 1911) empowered " to give directions as to the rate of wages or as to hours of labor or conditions of employment." [3]

It will be noted that the Minister's control extended much farther in the case of female workers than in the case of male workers, where it was limited to controlled establishments and to semi-skilled and unskilled laborers performing for the time being skilled work. The reasons for this greater control in the case of female labor are not entirely clear, but are probably due to the fact that the men were better organized in the skilled trades and felt able to control the situation in that class of work, and also to the fact that government control of the hours, conditions of employment and even the wages of women workers was something which had long since won recognition in Great Britain. It is probably also true that organized labor has less objection to the introduction of female labor into the skilled trades during the period of the war than it has to the introduction of semi-skilled male labor to do skilled work, believing that female labor will be much easier to displace " since the line of sex demar-

[1] See Fyfe, op. cit., Appendix 6, pp. 166-167.
[2] Munitions of War Amendment Act, 1916, sec. 7. Fyfe, p. 65.
[3] Munitions of War Amendment Act, 1916, sec. 6. Fyfe, p. 72.

cation is clearer than any line based upon classes of men." [1]

The government has undertaken to deal with the question of women's wages and work not only by making Circular L2 mandatory but by the appointment of a special tribunal with Lyndon Macassey as chairman and with two women among its six members, whose functions are to act as an arbitration tribunal to which the Minister may refer differences relating to the hours, wages and working conditions of women, and to advise the Minister in his dealings with these matters. The general tendency of the regulations has been to increase women's wages, but many difficulties have arisen in the effort to see that women were paid at the same rates for the same work as was performed by men when automatic machinery has been introduced.

The Amending Act of 1917 broadens greatly the power of the Minister of Munitions as to the regulation of wages. If he considers it necessary in order to maintain the output of munitions to give directions as to the remuneration of laborers employed in controlled establishments on time rates, he may, subject to any agreement which has been entered into between employers and the workmen with his consent, give such directions as he may consider necessary. A violation of these orders is punishable in like manner as violations of an award made in case of a settlement of differences between the parties. [2]

Another section of the 1917 Amending Act provides that where an award as to wages, hours or conditions of employment has been made under Part I of the act of 1915, or in pursuance of an agreement between work people engaged in the manufacture of munitions, and the Minister of Munitions is satisfied that the award is binding upon employers employing the majority of the employes in any branch of trade, he may direct that the award shall be binding on all or any employers and persons in the trade, either without modifications or with such modifications as shall insure that no employer shall be enabled to pay less wages than are required to be paid by parties subject to the original award. [3]

[1] Kirkaldy: *Labour, Finance and the War*, p. 136.
[2] Munitions of War Act, 1917, sec. 1. *British Industrial Experience*, vol. 1, p. 260.
[3] Munitions of War Act, 1917, sec. 5. *British Industrial Experience*, vol. 1, p. 262.

RESTRICTIONS ON THE MOBILITY OF LABOR

For several months prior to the enactment of the Munitions Act of 1915, the government had endeavored by means of an Order in Council dated April 29, 1915, to prevent the indiscriminate migration of labor needed in munition plants. The method of prevention was to forbid employers in factories engaged on munitions work to advertise for or otherwise seek to induce persons employed in other factories on government work to leave their employment in order to accept work in the establishment of this particular employer. Penalties were provided for enticing labor, and employers in munitions establishments desiring to secure additional laborers were forbidden to take any steps otherwise than to notify vacancies to one of the labor exchanges under the supervision of the Board of Trade.

This mode of restriction failed to accomplish its purpose since it did not apply to employers on other than munitions work; it did not prevent laborers in munitions plants from voluntarily leaving their places of employment to secure work elsewhere, and it did not furnish any method by which the offense of enticing laborers could be proved before the courts. Accordingly, under the Munitions of War Act of 1915, an effort was made to deal in a more direct way with restrictions on the mobility of labor. By section 7 of this act employers were forbidden to give employment to a workman who had been employed on, or in connection with munitions work within a period of six weeks preceding his application for work unless the laborer held a " leaving certificate " from the employer by whom he was last so employed or from a munitions tribunal to which an appeal might be taken in cases where his employer had refused to grant such a certificate. Munitions tribunals, set up under another provision of the act, were authorized to grant such " leaving certificates " whenever they had reason to believe that the refusal of the employer to grant such a certificate had been unreasonable.

More dissatisfaction arose from the operation of this section of the Munitions Act, 1915, than from any other section of the

act. Laborers complained that the restrictions on their right to
seek work in other munitions plants than those in which they
were for the time being employed were being taken advantage
of by employers to hinder their employment under conditions
best not only for themselves but for the country. New munitions
plants were being established all over the country and the services
of skilled workers were in great demand as foremen and managers and for giving instructions to unskilled laborers. Employers by their refusal to release workers to take such places were
preventing the skilled laborers of the country from being
employed in the most advantageous ways. Another ground of
complaint was that employers were using their power to refuse
" leaving certificates " as a means of discipline. Since laborers
could not be lawfully employed for a period of six weeks after
they left their employment unless they possessed " leaving certificates " they were forced either to remain in their present situations or to accept the penalty of idleness. It was also said that
employers in granting " leaving certificates " endorsed them with
comments on the conduct of their holders and thus made it more
difficult to secure employment.

With a view to remedying these difficulties, as well as to overcome certain difficulties in interpretation of such words and
phrases as " workmen," " munitions work," etc., the Amendment
Act of January, 1916, substituted for Section 7 of the original
act a new section (No. 5), which made more specific the obligations of munitions tribunals to grant " leaving certificates " where
they were unreasonably withheld by employers. They might also
require the employer who had refused such a certificate to pay
to the laborer a sum not exceeding £5, unless the laborer was
guilty of misconduct, for the purpose of securing his dismissal or
discharge. This penalty was also made applicable to the
employer of a workman

who applies for a certificate on the ground that he has for a period of more
than two days been given no opportunity of earning wages, or who leaves
his employment on account of conduct on the part of the employer, or any
agent of the employer, which would justify the immediate termination by the
workman of his contract of service in like manner as if he had been dismissed or discharged by his employer.

The workman was also under the provision of this section entitled to a week's notice of intention to dismiss him, or (in lieu of such a notice) to a week's wages, unless the employer reported such dismissal within twenty-four hours, under rules made by the Minister of Munitions, claiming that the work was of a temporary or discontinuous character or that the workman had been guilty of misconduct, and a munitions tribunal might be called upon to determine the legitimacy of this excuse and might require the employer to pay a sum, not exceeding £5, to the workman where the tribunal found that there was no reason or cause for dismissing him without a week's notice.

In spite of the improvements in the mode of administration of the section relating to "leaving certificates" made by the amendment of 1916, this section of the act continued to give great dissatisfaction to laborers employed in munitions plants. One of the reasons for this dissatisfaction is said to be the fact that although the act did not apply to workers engaged in civil establishments, employers in such establishments hesitated to employ workers who did not have "leaving certificates," in view of the penalties imposed upon employers hiring workers from munitions plants. "In other words," says Mr. Fyfe, "a 'leaving certificate' has come to be recognized in the industrial world as a passport to employment."

An effort was made to meet this difficulty by a rule promulgated by the Minister of Munitions to the effect that a worker might ask from a local munitions tribunal an exemption certificate which would state that in the opinion of that tribunal the workman had not been employed on munitions work within the past six weeks.

The munitions tribunals were authorized by the act to grant a "leaving certificate" to a workman who desired to leave his work in order to undertake work in which his skill or other personal qualifications could be employed to a greater advantage to the national interests, or where he had completed a term of apprenticeship and desired to obtain the full standard rate of wages, but these matters were left entirely to the judgment of the munitions tribunals and in all such cases the workman was supposed to remain in his employment until the question had been passed upon.

> It is possible, for example (said one of the appeal tribunals), that a man employed as a laborer might be indispensable in one establishment while his services, even in skilled work, might be of minor importance, from a national point of view, in another establishment. The question is, where can he render best service? [1]

Although the possibility of appealing their cases to the munitions tribunals enabled the workmen to secure their " leaving certificates " on reasonable grounds, the delays in such appeals and other causes for complaint led Parliament in the amendment of the Munitions Act, dated August 21, 1917, to give to the Minister of Munitions power to repeal the provision of the act relating to " leaving certificates " upon his being satisfied that this could be done consistently with the national interests. In the event such section was repealed certain "alternative provisions are to have effect, prohibiting the employment of the workmen concerned on work other than certain munitions work, except with the consent of the minister and, subject to certain exceptions, a contract of service between an employer, and a workman employed on or in connection with munitions work is not to be determinable by either party except by a week's notice or on payment of a sum equal to an average week's wages under the contract." [2]

Acting in accordance with this amendment, the government issued an order abolishing leaving certificates on and after October 15, 1917. Workmen may now leave their places of employment to engage on war work elsewhere on giving a week's notice or such other notice as is required by their contract.

A return to the war munitions volunteers scheme accompanies this abolition and the scheme has been extended to all men eligible to enroll, not as hitherto limited to those in certain trades and engaged on certain classes of work. The National Advisory

[1] Scottish Tube Company, Ltd. v. McGillivray, 1916, Scot. App. Rep., p. 19. Fyfe, op. cit., p. 19.
[2] Munitions of War Act, 1917, secs. 2, 3 and 4. British Industrial Experience, vol. 1, pp. 261-262.

Committee has voiced its approval of this plan by urging work-men not to change their employment " without definite and sub-stantial grounds and to show that the output of munitions will not suffer from the abolition of the leaving certificates." [1]

ARMY RESERVE MUNITIONS WORKERS

In addition to the munitions volunteers from civil life, the rules adopted by the Ministry of Munitions provide for the regulation of the employment of men from the army who have been temporarily released from the service in order that they may be employed in the production of munitions of war. We have already observed that it was not appreciated at the outbreak of the war that the success of military operations would be so dependent upon the increase of munitions that it would be unwise to allow men skilled in the production of munitions to enlist. Accordingly men from the engineering, mining and other essential war industries were allowed to enlist as freely as men from other trades until, after some months, the country came to a realization of the need of preventing further enlistments from these industries and steps began to be taken to secure release from the colors of men whose skill was required for munitions work. These released soldiers are known as army reserve munitions workers and, in general, the terms of their employment, as regards wages, traveling allowances, subsistence allowances, etc., are the same as for munitions [2] volunteers, but in addition to these regular allowances, there are supplemental allowances varying from 2s. 6d. to 5s. per week for soldiers having four or more children under fourteen (male) or sixteen (female) years of age. All these additions to the regular current wages of the district or for the job are paid by employers, but are recoverable by them from the Ministry of Munitions.

The soldier who has been released from military service to enter a munitions establishment enters into an agreement with the Minister of Munitions to remain in such employment during

[1] *Labour Gazette*, 1917, p. 356.
[2] Terms of Agreement, A.R.M.V. 1 and 2. Fyfe, *op. cit.*, pp. 193-195.

the war or " for so long as is required by the Minister," and the agreement includes the following clause:

> I understand that I am liable to return to military service at any time that I cease to be employed by any firm named by the Minister of Munitions, or if I am ordered to report myself for service with the colors by the competent military authority.[1]

Since November, 1916, the army reserve munition workers have included not only men released from the colors but men who have enlisted and who are unfit for military service. These men on being sent to the factories frequently make it possible to release for military service men employed therein. By February 23, 1917, over 12,000 men had started work under this plan and more than half of them were substitutes for men who had entered the service.

MUNITIONS TRIBUNALS

The munitions tribunals to which reference has several times been made are of two classes, which the act designates as first class and second class, but which are usually called " general " and " local " tribunals.[2]

The United Kingdom has been divided into 10 divisions—7 in England, 1 in Scotland and 2 in Ireland—in each of which a general tribunal has been set up. Each division has in turn been divided into districts, each of which has its local tribunal.

The general munitions tribunals deal with the more important offenses under the acts. These are, generally speaking, of two classes:

> (a) Offenses arising in connection with trade disputes—i.e., offenses under Part I of the act of 1915, and (b) all other offenses under the acts outside the scope of local munitions tribunals.

The offenses arising in connection with trade disputes are of three kinds:

[1] Terms of Agreement, A.R.M.V. 1 and 2. Fyfe, op cit., pp. 193-195.
[2] Munitions of War Act, 1915, sec. 15. Amendment Act, 1916, sec. 18. Fyfe, pp. 50-51, 77-78, Appendix 4, pp. 110-144.

(1) Failure to comply with an award, (2) the locking out by an employer of persons employed unless the difference has been reported to the Board of Trade and unless three weeks have elapsed since the report, without the Board of Trade referring the difference for settlement, (3) the taking part in a strike unless the conditions set out in the previous paragraph have been fulfilled.[1]

The other offenses dealt with by the general tribunals comprise (1) the employment of labor in violation of that provision of the act (now abolished) which declared that the laborer who had left his employment without a " leaving certificate " should not be employed within a period of six weeks after he had left his place of work; (2) failure to comply with any directions given by the Minister as to the rate of wages, hours of labor or conditions of employment of women workers or unskilled or semi-skilled men; and (3) wilful delay or obstruction of an inspector appointed by the Minister of Munitions in the exercise of his power or failure to give information or produce documents required by the inspector.[2]

The local munitions tribunals deal generally with (1) complaints that any person has acted in contravention of, or failed to comply with, regulations made applicable to controlled establishments in which he is either an employer or is employed; (2) breaches by war munitions volunteers of their undertaking to work in a controlled establishment; (3) complaints by a workman that he has been dismissed from his employment without reasonable cause; (4) breaches by an employer of his undertaking to employ a person temporarily released from naval or military service or a war munitions volunteer on a class of work designated by the Minister of Munitions; (5) complaints by workman that an employer had unreasonably refused or neglected to issue a certificate that the workman is free to accept other employment; (6) complaints by workman that he has been dismissed without a week's notice or without the wages to be given in lieu of notice; and (7) breaches by employers of the rules (now abrogated) relating to " leaving certificates." [3]

[1] Munitions of War Acts, 1915 and 1916, *Munitions Tribunals* (Pamphlet issued by Minister of Munitions, January, 1917), p. 1.
[2] *Ibid.*, p. 2.
[3] *Ibid.*, p. 3.

The general and the local tribunals are constituted in the same way. There is a chairman, appointed by the Minister of Munitions or by the Admiralty, and two or more assessors, one-half chosen by the Minister from a panel of employers or their representatives and the other half chosen by the Minister from a panel of workmen or their representatives.[1] Chairmen of general tribunals are usually barristers or solicitors and of local tribunals are usually chairmen of courts of referees under the National Insurance Act.

The amended act (1916) gives a right of appeal from a decision of either a general or a local munitions tribunal to a judge of the highest law courts in cases which involve "a question of law or a question of mixed law and fact" or on any other ground sanctioned by rules of procedure.

The amended act (1916) also provides that in the munitions tribunal the chairman, before giving his decision, shall consult with the assessors and in all cases where they are agreed he shall in his decision give effect to their opinion, except in questions which appear to him to be questions of law. It is further provided that, in cases affecting female labor, at least one of the assessors representing the workers shall be a woman.[2]

The penalties provided by the act for failure on the part of workmen to comply with the orders of the Minister, and which the munitions tribunals alone were empowered to impose, no longer include imprisonment.[3] Moderate fines may be imposed and in case they are not paid the munitions tribunal has the power to order the employer of the penalized workman to deduct the fine in instalments from the wages of the workman and to give an accounting for such deductions.[4] Imprisonment may be the penalty imposed by the criminal courts, however, for tamper-

[1] Munitions of War Act, 1915, sec. 15. Fyfe, *op. cit.*, pp. 51, 77-78.
[2] Munitions of War Amendment Act, 1916, sec. 18 (3). Fyfe, *op. cit.*, p. 79.
[3] Imprisonment was inflicted for nonpayment of a fine by a general tribunal in Scotland early in 1915, but the decision created great ill feeling among laborers. The imprisoned man was released by order of the Minister before completing his term and when the act was amended the power to imprison was taken away from the tribunal.
[4] Munitions of War Act, 1915, sec. 15 (4). Fyfe, p. 80.

ing with certificates, or disclosing information obtained for the use of the Minister of Munitions.[1]

The number of things which employers are forbidden to do and which if done by them render them liable to fine are more numerous than those specified as violations by workmen.[2] Like workmen, employers and others are liable to prosecution in the criminal courts for granting false certificates, tampering with leaving certificates, giving false information to the government, etc.[3]

PROHIBITION OF STRIKES

The Munitions Act, we have observed, was enacted at a time when there had been a recrudescence of strikes following a short interval of industrial peace, and it was intended, among other things, to put an end to stoppages of work in the munitions industry. The act accordingly forbids strikes and lock-outs in establishments engaged on munitions work until the industrial difference has been referred to the Board of Trade[4] and twenty-one days have elapsed without the Board of Trade having taken steps to secure a settlement in ways provided by the act.[5]

There are several methods (the choice between them being optional with the Board of Trade) for settling industrial differences when they have been referred to the Board of Trade for purpose of securing a settlement.

(1) The Board of Trade may itself " take any steps which seem to them expedient to promote a settlement of the difference." [6]

(2) The Board of Trade may, " if in their opinion suitable means for settlement already exist in pursuance of any agreement between employers and persons employed,"

---

[1] Munitions of War Amendment Act, 1916, sec. 17 (2), sec. 14. Fyfe, *op. cit.*, pp. 75-76.
[2] *Ibid.*, pp. 43-48.
[3] Munitions of War Act, 1915, sec. 15 (4). Fyfe, p. 80.
[4] Since the establishment of the Ministry of Labor it performs the functions ascribed to the Board of Trade in this chapter.
[5] Munitions of War Act, 1915, sec. 2. Fyfe, p. 61.
[6] Munitions of War Act, 1915, sec. 1 (2). Fyfe, pp. 59-60.

refer the difference " for settlement in accordance with those means," and if the settlement is unduly delayed, it may annul the reference and substitute any of the other means.[1]

(3) The Board of Trade may refer the difference to the Committee on Production, this being the same committee which was appointed by the government on February 4, 1915.

(4) The Board of Trade may refer the difference to a single arbitrator selected by the parties to the difference, or if they fail to agree, by the Board of Trade.

(5) The Board of Trade may refer the difference to " a court of arbitration consisting of an equal number of persons representing employers and persons representing workmen with a chairman appointed by the Board of Trade." [2]

(6) The Minister of Munitions may constitute a special class of arbitration tribunals to deal with differences relating to the wages and working conditions of female workers employed on munitions work or those involving semi-skilled and unskilled workers employed on munitions work in controlled establishments and the Board of Trade may refer any such differences for settlement to these tribunals. The Minister may also ask these tribunals for advice " as to what directions are to be given by him " in regard to these classes of workers. Whenever the differences relate to female workers the tribunals must include in their membership one or more women.[3]

The arbitration awards are not subject to appeal, are binding on all parties and may be retrospective.[4] A failure to comply with an award makes the guilty party liable to a fine not exceeding £5 for each day during which the noncompliance continues, and (if the guilty party is an employer) for each employe in respect of whom the failure to comply takes place.[5] The same

[1] Munitions of War Act, 1915, sec. 1 (2), (3). Fyfe, op. cit., pp. 59-60.
[2] Munitions of War Act, 1915, sec. 1 (2), schedule 1. Fyfe, pp. 60-84.
[3] Munitions of War Amendment Act, 1916, secs. 8, 6 and 7. Fyfe, pp. 35, 60-61, 65, 72.
[4] Munitions of War Act, 1915, sec. 1 (4). Fyfe, p. 60.
[5] Munitions of War Act, 1915, sec. 14 (a). Fyfe, p. 76.

penalties apply to violations in the shape of strikes or lockouts.[1]

The Arbitration Act of 1889 does not apply to disputes covered by the Munitions Act,[2] but all "differences as to rates of wages, hours of work, or otherwise as to terms or conditions of or affecting employment on or in connection with munitions work" are subject to the arbitration provisions of the Munitions Act whether or not such differences have resulted in strikes or lockouts.[3]

The arbitration provisions of the Munitions Act are applicable not only to munitions work, but may be made applicable "in connection with any work of any description" if they are made applicable by the government on the ground that the existence or continuance of the difference is likely to be prejudicial to a supply of munitions.[4] It was under the authority of this section that the government acted when it attempted to apply the arbitration provisions of the Munitions Act to the strike of the Welsh coal miners.

To say that all differences in regard to wages, hours, etc., of workers employed on munitions work are subject to arbitration is, however, not tantamount to saying that, when such differences arise, they are immediately referred to the Board of Trade to be by them referred to one of the agencies for effecting a settlement. For when a difference arises in a contrölled establishment or as regards the employment of female workers, the first question to be asked is as to whether any proposed change in wages or hours has been submitted to the Minister of Munitions for his approval. It is only when the Minister has withheld his consent that arbitration of the matter is called for. The Minister may, however, as we have already observed, refer the matter to a special arbitration tribunal for advice before he either gives or withholds his consent.[5]

Complaint having arisen that differences under section 1 of the act of 1915 were not always reported promptly to the Board of

[1] Munitions of War Act, 1915, sec. 14 (b), (c). Fyfe, op. cit., pp. 76-77.
[2] Munitions of War Amendment Act, 1916, sec. 23.
[3] Munitions of War Act, 1915, sec. 3; Amendment Act, 1916, sec. 9. Fyfe, pp. 61-62.
[4] Munitions of War Act, 1915, sec. 3. Fyfe, pp. 61-62.
[5] Munitions of War Act, 1915, sec. 4 (2); Amendment Act, 1916, sec. 8 (2). Fyfe, pp. 36, 62, 60.

Trade (Minister of Labor), the amending act of 1917 provided that the Minister of Labor might make regulations with respect to the reporting of differences with a view to preventing undue delay in negotiating for the settlement of such differences.[1]

The act of 1917 also provides that no workman employed on or in connection with munition work may be discharged on the ground that he has joined or is a member of a trade union or that he has taken part in any trade dispute.[2]

[1] Munitions of War Act, 1917, sec. 6. *British Industrial Experience*, vol. 1, p. 262.
[2] Munitions of War Act, 1917, sec. 9. *Loc. cit.*, pp. 263-264.

CHAPTER VI

The Supply and Distribution of Labor

The chief purposes of the Munitions Acts were to secure continuity and regularity of effort on the part of employes engaged on munitions work and to stimulate the maximum production of war supplies by both government and private establishments. To accomplish these ends the securing of an adequate labor supply was the most important and most difficult task.

SHORTAGE OF LABOR EARLY IN THE WAR

The shortage of male labor, which developed in many industries as early as December, 1914, made itself felt especially in the engineering trades, upon which the government was most directly dependent for its supplies of munitions. Recruiting had been allowed to proceed unchecked in these trades, as well as in others, with the result that ere long skilled workers had to be withdrawn from the army to supply the most urgent need created by the shortage of labor in engineering establishments. The rapid change in conditions affecting the labor supply during the first half of 1915 is well reflected in the short reviews of the labor market which are given each month in the Board of Trade *Labour Gazette*.

In January, 1915, says the *Gazette*, many trades were still depressed. Only those " concerned with the equipment of the Allied forces " were unusually busy and " in some of these trades there was a shortage of skilled labor partly owing to pressure of work and partly to enlistments." [1] In March " there was a shortage of male labor in many industries, especially in engineering and

[1] *Labour Gazette*, 1915, p. 37.

shipbuilding, coal mining and agriculture, and of female labor in some branches of the clothing trade." [1]

In June " a scarcity of male labor was reported by nearly all trades owing to the previously existing surplus in some having been absorbed by others or drawn off by enlistments. This shortage is now extending to female and boy labor in many occupations." [2]

To supply this deficiency of male labor the thoughts of employers and government officials turned first to the possibility of securing labor, especially skilled labor, from other industries and from other districts. No figures are available which show the full extent of this transference of labor, most of which doubtless took place during the first year of the war on the mere initiative of the workers, who, finding their services in greater demand away from their homes or in other industries than those in which they were customarily employed, migrated thither in search of employment and better wages.

TRANSFERS OF LABOR THROUGH THE EMPLOYMENT EXCHANGES

Every effort was made by the government to assist in this movement through the labor exchanges in so far as it related to a transference from other industries to the munitions trades. From the records of the exchanges we can gain some idea as to the extent of the movement from one exchange district to another. There are in the United Kingdom about 400 public labor exchanges or employment offices in each of which registrations are received and each one of which endeavors to fill vacancies in its own district or immediate locality or, failing in this, in an outside district by cooperation with the exchange in that district.

In 1913, a year of great prosperity, the total number of vacancies filled by all exchanges was 921,853. Of these placements 110,992 or 12.4 per cent were in exchange districts outside those in which the applicants were registered. In 1914 the

[1] *Labour Gazette,* 1915, p. 115.
[2] *Ibid.,* p. 195.

total number of vacancies filled was 1,116,909 and of this number 177,312 or 15.8 per cent were placements outside the exchange district in which registration took place. Furthermore the statement is made that " the increase is mainly accounted for by the transference during the last six months of the year," *i.e.*, during the war period.[1] Only 24,201 of these transferences in 1914 were from one of the eight divisions into which the kingdom is divided to another.

In 1915, although there was a decline in the total number of registrations as compared to 1914, amounting to 7.4 per cent, yet the number of vacancies filled amounted to 1,308,137, an increase of 17.1 per cent compared to the preceding year. Although the increases in the registrations and vacancies filled in 1915 were almost entirely among women and girls, yet " the number of persons for whom work was found in a labor·exchange area other than that in which they were registered was 283,644. (Men 196,057, women 53,096, boys 19,976, girls 14,515.) This means that 21.6 per cent of the placements for the year were outside the districts in which registration took place. The proportion of men transferred was, of course, much larger. Furthermore the average distance traveled was much greater since 67,557 of the transfers were from one labor division of the kingdom to another.[2]

Not all the transfers were caused by the war, but most of them seem to have been made in response to the demands of the war industries. Thus 89,638 of the men transferred were employed in the building of huts and military camps and in the construction of munitions factories and of public works. Of those transferred, 50,564 of the men, 11,238 of the women, 9,868 of the boys and 443 of the girls were employed directly in the munitions trades.[3]

GOVERNMENTAL EFFORTS TO PREVENT ENLISTMENTS FROM ESSENTIAL INDUSTRIES

Governmental efforts to control the supply and distribution of labor were next turned to the problem of preventing or restrict-

[1] *Labour Gazette*, 1915, pp. 44-45.   [2] *Ibid.*, 1916, p. 50.

ing enlistments from the industries and occupations of primary importance to the conduct of the war. As already mentioned the recruiting campaign had proceeded without reference to the industrial training of the recruits and with but little consideration of the need for skilled workers in those trades upon which the output of war supplies depended.

The necessity of maintaining the transportation system in a state of high efficiency was realized at the very beginning and as early as September, 1914, recruiting officers and agencies were instructed by the war office to allow no railway man to enlist " unless he presents a written statement from the railway company who employs him to the effect that he has approached the head of his department and has obtained the necessary permission to enlist." [1]

In spite of these restrictions the railways were under steady pressure from the military authorities and from the employes themselves to allow enlistments and they complied with these requests, whenever possible, by employing as substitutes for men of military age men who were ineligible for military service and women. By the middle of October, 1914, 56,000 railway men had joined the colors and this meant nearly ten per cent of the entire railway staff of the country. By June, 1916, the ten larger railway systems had released 94,411 men for military service and this constituted from 15.1 to 22.2 per cent of their total staffs. By November of that year evidence presented to the man power distribution board showed that nearly 140,000 men, or about 25 per cent of the total staff at the outbreak of the war and over 50 per cent of the men of military age had been released for the army.[2]

Among coal miners, enlistments were especially numerous during the early months of the war. A wave of enthusiasm spread throughout the coal mining districts following the invasion of Belgium and this stimulus to recruiting was contributed to by the small industrial demand for coal which was a feature of the early weeks of the war. By February, 1915, it was officially estimated

[1] Leland Olds: *Railroad Transportation*, Part 4 of *British Industrial Experience during the War* (Senate Document No. 114, 65th Cong., 1st Sess.), vol. 2, p. 1119.   [2] *Ibid.*, pp. 1120-1123.

that approximately 167,500 miners or 17.2 per cent of the total number had joined the colors. The output of coal had begun to fall off and because of the curtailed production inconvenience was being experienced in some of the manufacturing districts.[1]

Among the manufacturing industries the enlistments from the engineering, shipbuilding, chemical and leather trades were especially serious in their effects on output because of the direct dependence of the war upon these industries and the degree of skill required of the operatives.

A Board of Trade report made in December, 1914, gives the following estimates as to the number of enlistments from various trades and the percentage which the enlistments made of the total number in the trade according to the census of 1911:[2]

NUMBER EMPLOYED IN EACH TRADE OR INDUSTRY ACCORDING TO INDUSTRIAL POPULATION CENSUS OF 1911, AND PER CENT IN EACH TRADE KNOWN TO HAVE JOINED THE COLORS

Trade and Industry	Approximate Industrial Population Census, 1911	Per cent Known to Have Joined the Forces
Shipbuilding	164,000	13.6
Leather and leather goods	67,000	14.2
Chemicals (including explosives)	122,000	15.4
Engineering	665,000	14.6
Woolen and worsted	129,000	7.2
Boot and shoe	199,000	9.9
Hosiery	18,000	7.5
Iron and steel	311,000	13.9
Food	315,000	13.4
Sawmilling	44,000	14.2
Coal and other mines	1,164,000	13.7
Clothing	235,000	12.5
Paper and printing	240,000	12.5
Linen, jute and hemp	42,000	15.0
Cotton	259,000	9.6
Cycle, motor carriage and wagon building	202,000	14.3
China, pottery and glass	83,000	13.3
Building	1,023,000	12.2
Furniture and upholstery	141,000	13.5
Brick, cement, etc.	78,000	13.5
Tin plate	23,000	8.3

[1] W. J. Lauck: *Coal Mining*, Part 5 of *British Industrial Experience during the War*, vol. 2, p. 1170.
[2] W. J. Lauck: *Manufacturing Industries*, Part 3 of *British Industrial Experience during the War*, vol. 2, p. 947.

The fight at Neuve Chapelle aroused Great Britain to a realization of the fact that the success of the war was as much dependent upon a plentiful supply of munitions as upon a supply of fighting men and it then became evident that a mistake had been made in permitting enlistments of skilled workers from certain trades. As already mentioned, this mistake was remedied to a certain extent by the actual withdrawal from the army of skilled workers in the engineering trades.[1] No figures are available which show the extent to which men were withdrawn from the army for work in munitions plants, but such withdrawals were difficult to make, largely because of the opposition of the military authorities to the withdrawal of men whose superior abilities had made them especially valuable soldiers. No proper register of the occupations of men who enlisted had been made at the time of their enlistment. It was therefore necessary to create an elaborate system of inspection of regiments both to guard against the fraud of men who wished to escape from military service, by claiming to have the skill needed for munitions work, and to prevent really skilled men from being retained in the army because of the insistence of their commanding officers when such men might be more useful in the manufacture of munitions. After these inspections had been completed, arrangements were made to facilitate the release of skilled workmen for whom applications had been received from the firms which had previously employed them and which were engaged in the manufacture of munitions. These men withdrawn from the colors remained liable to be returned to military service, but while employed in munitions establishments they were subject to the same law as civilian workmen and were subject to military discipline only in regard to such matters as their behavior on streets, etc. They received the same wages as civilian workmen, performing similar duties, but the proviso was made that these wages were to be not less than the rate of army pay they were receiving at the time of their release.

[1] British Association for the Advancement of Science, sec. F. *Draft Interim Report of the Conference to Investigate into Outlets for Labor after the War*, p. 6.

Further efforts were made by the government to prevent the enlistment of skilled workers in November, 1915, when it was announced that an interdepartmental advisory committee was " engaged in preparing lists of reserved occupations, *i.e.*, occupations from which enlistments should be restricted in view of the necessity of maintaining the trade of the country as far as possible," and employers in these trades were invited to make recommendations to the secretary of the committee " with reference to indispensable and irreplaceable classes of labor." [1] This schedule of indispensable occupations superseded the system of badges to munitions volunteers in May, 1916.

Overtime Work as a Cure for Labor Shortage

The way in which many employers sought to solve their labor difficulties during the first year of the war, in particular, was by working their existing forces overtime. There were several circumstances which favored this. The employes filled with the spirit of patriotism and anxious to help the men in the trenches win the war entered little objection during these early months to working long hours. Higher rates of pay for overtime naturally contributed to their willingness to work, and it was not long until the higher earnings secured in this way were actually made necessary by the increased cost of living. Employers, on the other hand, were not reluctant to pay the higher rates for overtime because the terms of their contracts with the government easily made this possible. Furthermore, as far as skilled labor was concerned there was no immediately available supply on which to draw and even the existing supply was being steadily depleted by enlistments. Overtime, therefore, became the rule, at first in those trades working directly on government orders, but later in other trades as well.

Under section 150 of the Factories Act of 1901 the Secretary of State is authorized in case of any public emergency to exempt from the act, by order made by him, any factory or workshop in respect to work which is undertaken on behalf of the Crown.

[1] *Labour Gazette*, 1915, p. 391.

The question now arose as to how much latitude should be given to employers to work the protected classes long hours under the provisions of this exemption. It was generally held that overtime work was necessary, especially in the munitions trades, and those who deplored the necessity comforted themselves with the thought that the war would be a short one. During the year 1915 the authority to suspend the Factories Act was extended by clause 6A of the Defense of the Realm Regulations to "any factory or workshop in which the Secretary of State is satisfied that by reason of the loss of men through enlistment or transference in government service, or of other circumstances arising out of the present war, exemption is necessary to secure the carrying on of work required in the national interests." [1]

Applications to work overtime began to pour in on the Factories Department from all over the kingdom as soon as government orders began to be placed and such applications have continued to be made throughout the war, although, perhaps, lately with less frequency. The earliest trades to be affected were those directly concerned with the manufacture of munitions. Next came the demand from the woolen trades, from hosiery factories and from the clothing trades, especially those engaged in the manufacture of army clothing and of boots and shoes. Other applications were received from those trades manufacturing surgical dressings, metal accessories, such as buckles, spurs, bits and horseshoes, and from a large number of miscellaneous trades.

The department's method of handling the problem was to make temporary orders permitting overtime, not to exceed two hours a day, on not more than five days a week. Additional hours were permitted in the munitions trades. In these trades the hours of labor oftentimes extended to fourteen or fifteen per day and Sunday labor and night work were usual. Between August 4, 1914, and February 19, 1915, not less than 3,141 orders were granted permitting overtime work for women and young persons to whom alone the Factories Act applies. Of this number 748 were in the woolen manufacture, 231 in the hosiery manufacture, 514 in the manufacture of uniforms, 245 in the manufacture

[1] Annual Report of Chief Inspector of Factories and Workshops, 1915, p. 5.

of boots and shoes, 151 in the manufacture of munitions of war and 137 in the manufacture of canvas equipment.

Not all manufacturers awaited the pleasure of the factory inspectors in the matter of working overtime. Although the inspectors endeavored to make it clear to all that permission to work overtime was for only a limited number of hours, the impression prevailed in many quarters that the government had suspended the Factories Acts for the period of the war. There were, accordingly, many cases where long hours were worked without legal permission having been given.

For men workers the Factories Acts of course do not apply and therefore no permission was necessary to employ male adults beyond the usual number of hours. During the first year of the war it seems to have been the aim of most manufacturers to work as much overtime as the workers themselves were willing to allow. At the time the Health of Munitions Workers Committee conducted its investigation on the subject of "Hours of Work," in 1915, it found that men were being worked sometimes as many as 108 hours a week. Boys under 18 frequently worked as many as 90 or 100 hours, and some women and girls were regularly employed for 77 hours a week.

Requests for permission to work overtime continued unabated throughout 1915, but the Chief Inspector of Factories notes the fact that there was "a marked reduction in the amount of latitude sought and allowed; for instance, fresh demands for permission to work on Sundays are now rarely received and are confined to cases where sudden and unexpected emergencies arise or the processes are continuous. Requests for Saturday afternoon work have also become less common and there seems to be a more general recognition of the advantages of a week-end rest."[1]

The Factories Department also became more strict in its allowances of overtime. The Chief Inspector reported that there was no set scheme throughout the kingdom for the general arrange-

[1] Annual Report of the Chief Inspector of Factories and Workshops, 1915, p. 5.

ment of hours when overtime was worked.   Different systems were adopted in different localities and employers seem to have been governed chiefly by the custom of the district.   In some instances there was overtime on each day of the week, while in other places overtime was worked on only two or three days.. The desire of the workers not to work late in the evening had led in some instances to a long spell of work in the afternoon without any interval for the evening meal, but experience seemed to indicate that long spells of work without interruption did not lead to high output.   Accordingly, the department established the rule that for the protected classes of labor not more than five continuous hours should be worked in textile factories, nor more than five and one-half hours in nontextile works, and that even these hours might not be worked unless tea or other hot refreshments were available in the rooms for the workers during the spell.   A break of a quarter of an hour in the afternoon, instead of a half hour, was permitted provided (a) that the working spell did not exceed six hours; (b) that a whole hour was allowed for dinner; and (c) that the inspectors were satisfied that adequate arrangements had been made for serving tea to workers as soon as they stopped work.[1]

In munitions establishments the demand for overtime work was more urgent than elsewhere and permission to work overtime was granted with less reluctance.   We have already noted the wider latitude given employers in these trades.   After six months' experience with such work the department issued a general order applicable only to munitions establishments and which provided for overtime work in accordance with any one of three schemes.

1. Overtime with a limit of five hours per week for women, boys between 14 and 16 and girls between 16 and 18 years of age, and of 7½ hours for boys over 16 years and also (in a few cases of special urgency) for women.

2. Day and night shifts for women and boys over 16 years, and in certain cases for boys 14 years of age.

3. Eight hour shifts for women, girls over 16 and boys over 14 years of age.

[1] Annual Report of the Chief Inspector of Factories and Workshops, 1915, p. 8.

For the large munitions establishments it was found necessary in some cases to issue special orders which permitted overtime somewhat in advance of that covered by the general order. Even as early as 1915, however, it had been noted that there was a distinct tendency towards a reduction of hours in munitions plants as well as elsewhere. Sunday labor had been found to be especially objectionable. Not only had the Health of Munitions Workers Committee recommended the abandonment of Sunday work but the Ministry of Munitions had also recommended to employers that they abstain wherever possible from Sunday work, especially where overtime was worked during the week.[1]

During the year 1916 the Chief Inspector reported that " there has been a notable decrease in the requests for the long hours that were common in the early months of the war. The general tendency has been to restrict the weekly hours of work to an amount very little, if at all, in excess of those allowed under the Factories Act, and to arrange for more elasticity in the daily limits.

While in many of the munitions factories and in the machine tool and similar works full use had been made of the overtime allowed, in other cases overtime work was intermittent. It was noted that in those cases where special orders had been granted to meet sudden emergencies, advantage had not been taken of the permission granted in every case. One employer expressed what seemed to be a general opinion when he said that the special orders were " like a drop of brandy, a useful thing to keep in the house, but you don't want to be always taking it." [2]

Even in the case of adult male labor it began to be realized that excessive hours of labor and Sunday labor were inadvisable. Although the Minister of Munitions had no statutory power to restrict the hours for men workers, recommendations were made by him that moderation be shown in the matter of overtime and by the end of the second year of the war Sunday labor had been generally discontinued in controlled establishments and the Min-

[1] Annual Report of the Chief Inspector of Factories and Workshops, 1915, p. 6.
[2] *Ibid.*, 1916, p. 3.

istry was endeavoring to get it discontinued throughout the country on the ground that it hindered, rather than facilitated, maximum production.

APPEALS FOR VOLUNTARY REGISTRANTS FOR MUNITIONS WORK

Reluctance to use the compulsory powers of the government to mobilize the industrial forces of the nation even in war times is a characteristic of Anglo-Saxon countries, and English experience in this matter is in sharp contrast with that of the continental countries, in which compulsion for civilian as well as military purposes was adopted with little hesitation in the early months of the war.   Although there was during the early months of the year 1915 much talk in England of " conscription of labor," apparently intended to serve as a parallel to, and an excuse for, conscription for military purposes, there was so much objection to the plan among the working classes that the government found it desirable to disavow any such intention [1] in making its appeal for the passage of the Munitions of War Act, 1915.

Instead of conscripting men and women for industrial purposes, the government has sought by every means possible to discover the extent and character of the labor supply of the United Kingdom, and by a policy of classifying the trades and restricting the entrance of labor into the non-essential ones has left it little alternative but to enter those trades and industries which have been deemed essential for the successful prosecution of the war.

The first step in this direction was taken in March, 1915, when the President of the Board of Trade issued an appeal to the women " who are prepared, if needed to take paid employment of any kind—industrial, agricultural, clerical, etc.—to enter themselves upon the register of women for war service which is being prepared by the Board of Trade labor exchanges."   The object of registration it was said " is to find out what reserve force of women's labor, trained or untrained, can be made avail-

[1] See *ante*, p. 94.

able, if required." Women were urged to register by this appeal to their patriotism: "any woman who by working helps to release a man or to equip a man for fighting does national war service."[1]

Measured solely by the number who availed themselves of this opportunity to register for war service, this appeal to the patriotism of the women was fairly productive; 110,700 women were said to have enrolled by the middle of September. Judged by the immediate availability of this potential supply of labor, however, but little was accomplished by the registration, for an examination of the returns showed that only 5,500 women were able to undertake the skilled jobs open to them.[2]

Not discouraged with the results attained by this registration the government next proceeded to invite registration of men from those trades whose relation to the conduct of the war was most intimate. In June, 1915, the Ministry of Munitions acting in cooperation with the National Advisory Committee of the Trade Unions invited "all skilled workers in the engineering, shipbuilding and allied trades, not already engaged on war contracts," to register themselves at munitions work bureaus open for this purpose at some 400 places throughout the United Kingdom. Registration rendered a man liable to transfer to government work in any part of the country on the following conditions:

1. The rate of wages paid will be the rate of the district to which he is transferred unless the rate of the district which he leaves is higher, in which case he will be paid at the higher rate.

2. Certain traveling and subsistence allowances will be paid in reasonable cases.

3. The first period of enrolment to be for six months, but workmen may volunteer for a further period when this has expired.

4. Any workman transferred from employment shall, if found suitable, be guaranteed employment during the war for a period not exceeding six months.

5. The workman agrees that any breach of his undertaking shall be dealt with by a Munitions Court, consisting of a chairman appointed by the Minister of Munitions, with assessors, equally representing employers and workmen, which may, if it thinks fit, impose a fine not exceeding £3.[3]

[1] *British Industrial Experience during the War.* vol. 3, p. 709.
[2] British Association. *Credit, Industry and the War,* p. 72.
[3] *Labour Gazette,* July, 1915.

This plan of voluntary registration had been adopted by the government at the urgent request of the trade unions in the engineering and shipbuilding trades while the Munitions Bill was under consideration in the House of Commons. They hoped to show that voluntary enlistment was sufficient without any degree of compulsion, and hoped that the success of the scheme would be such that the government would abandon, or at least materially modify, the Munitions Bill.[1]

At first the plan seemed likely to succeed. Registration began on the evening of June 24 and 46,000 men enrolled the first week. By July 10 about 90,000 volunteers were registered. When the lists were carefully inspected, however, it was seen that four-fifths of the volunteers were already engaged on government work and that dilution of labor must be resorted to. The government found the plan sufficiently useful, however, to continue it and made a place for it in the Munitions of War Act, 1915.[2] Those who register under this plan are technically known as " war munitions volunteers," to distinguish them from the army reserve munitions workers who are released from military service to work in munitions plants. In order to protect these volunteers from insistent appeals from recruiting officers, the act provided a scheme of war service badges to be worn by such workers and rules were drawn up by the Ministry of Munitions to govern the use of these badges and to prevent their fraudulent transfer to other workers.[3] There was no guarantee that wearers of these badges would be exempt from military service and in May, 1917, it became necessary to withdraw the privileges conferred by these badges and to make their wearers subject to the military service acts.

COMPULSORY REGISTRATION FOR INDUSTRIAL PURPOSES

The government next undertook to secure registration on a much larger scale. On July 15, 1915, the National Registration

[1] H. L. Gray: *War Time Control of Industry*, p. 32.
[2] Sec. 8. Fyfe: *Employers and Workmen under the Munitions of War Acts*, p. 72.
[3] Fyfe, pp. 171, 174.

Act was passed, which provided for the registration " of all persons, male and female, between the ages of 15 and 65 " who were not in the naval or military service, together with a record of their ages, nationalities, marital conditions, number of dependents, professions or occupations. The record was also to indicate:

(1) Whether the work on which he (the registrant) is employed is work for or under any government department.

(2) Whether he is skilled in and able to perform any work other than the work (if any) at which he is at the time employed, and, if so, the nature thereof.

The Registrar General, acting under the directions of the Local Government Board, was made the central registration authority and the common councils of the various metropolitan and municipal boroughs and of urban and rural districts were made responsible for the registration in their respective areas.

The instructions issued by the Local Government Board to the local authorities in charge of this registration emphasized the importance of stating occupations with the utmost care, " especially by persons having technical knowledge or skill, such as workers in engineering, shipbuilding and other metal trades, and by persons engaged in agriculture."

The nation seems to have entered upon this registration with much enthusiasm and the press declared that it " marked the decision of the people that the whole man and woman power of the kingdom should be applied to the task of beating Germany," [1] but although penalties were provided for persons refusing or neglecting to register and to furnish the information required by the act, it does not appear that the registration was at all complete or that the information secured was of much value to the government in its efforts to mobilize the industrial forces of the nation, although it was made much use of by recruiting officers.

INDUSTRIAL EXEMPTIONS UNDER THE MILITARY SERVICE ACTS

The Military Service Act of January 27, 1916, called into the military service " with the colors or in the reserve for the period

[1] *British Industrial Experience during the War*, vol. 1, p. 42.

of the war" every unmarried man between the ages of 18 and 40, inclusive, and the Amendment Act of May 25, 1916, made conscription applicable to "every male British subject" within the ages mentioned. Both acts, however, provided that exemptions might be granted to any man on grounds of ill health, infirmity, conscientious objection to military service, exceptional financial or business obligations or domestic position, or "on the ground that it is expedient in the national interests that he should, instead of being employed in military service, be engaged in other work in which he is habitually engaged or, if he is being educated or trained for any work, that he should continue to be so educated or trained." Exemptions might also be granted by any government department, after consultation with the army council, to "men who are employed or engaged or qualified for employment or engagement in any work which is certified by the department to be work of national importance and whose exemption comes within the sphere of the department."

Provision was made for the representation of labor, whether organized or unorganized, on the military service tribunals which were created to pass on the question of exemptions. The circular of instructions issued by the Local Government Board to local bodies charged with the selection of the military service tribunals urged these tribunals to "be most careful to avoid the slightest tendency to what might appear to be industrial compulsion."[1]

Armed with the powers of military conscription, the government has been in a measure free to dispose of the services of its male population of military age in whatever way it has seen fit, whether in the army, the navy or in industry. During the year 1916, the need of men for the war industries appears to have been felt fully as keenly as the need for fighting men and a liberal policy of exemptions was followed. Taking advantage of that provision of the Military Service Act which allowed a government department to grant exemption, after consultation with the Army Council, to men engaged in work of national importance

[1] *British Industrial Experience during the War*, vol. 1, p. 719.

and whose exemption comes within the sphere of the department, the Board of Trade on June 9, 1916, granted exemption from military service to dock and wharf laborers and other persons, " excluding clerks," employed on the maintenance of ports, docks, wharves and waterways."[1] In November, 1916, the government entered into arrangements with certain unions, notably the Amalgamated Society of Engineers, whereby no recruiting officer could call up for service with the colors any workman who held a " trade card " evidencing his membership in any one of certain specified trade unions of skilled craftsmen. In May, 1917, this arrangement had to be withdrawn owing to the growing need of men for military service. Both the limited character of the agreement and its withdrawal caused great irritation throughout the working districts and led to a strike of large proportions in the engineering trades in the spring of 1917.

Although the government may fairly be charged with lack of consistency in its policy of exempting workers for industrial reasons, it may be said that the military situation was such that the pursuit of any consistent policy was well nigh impossible. By the beginning of the last quarter of 1916, the need of men for military service had become so urgent that it was deemed necessary to release for military service certain men who had previously been granted exemption badges on the ground that the work on which they had been engaged was of national importance. In October and December of that year unskilled and semi-skilled men of military age who were engaged on munition work and for whom substitutes could be found were to be released for military service, if found medically fit. Their substitutes were to come mainly from the following sources:

(a) Men in the army unfit for general service and surplus to military requirements;

(b) Men granted exemption by tribunals on condition of taking up work of national importance;

(c) Men called up by recruiting officers and not required for the army because of their medical category.[2]

[1] *British Industrial Experience during the War*, vol. 1, p. 720.
[2] *Labour Gazette*, 1917, p. 56.

Employers in the munitions trades were to furnish to the Ministry of Munitions lists of men to whom badges had been issued and such men after a medical examination had disclosed their fitness for military service were to be released for such service as soon as the employment (labor) exchanges in collaboration with other government departments and the Army Council had arranged for their substitutes, as above mentioned.

These substitutes who were suitable for munitions work and who were willing to undertake it were enrolled by the officials of the employment exchanges at first as army reserve munitions workers. Men who were not found suitable for munitions work were nevertheless registered (though not as army reserve workers) as possible substitutes in other industries.[1]

By the first of December, 1916, the need of men in the army had become so urgent that the government had to announce that tribunals could no longer grant exemption " on grounds of business or employment," except for highly exceptional reasons, to any man under 26 years of age, since any such man " who is fit for general service is of more value to the country with the forces than he would be in civil employment,"[2] and by January 20, 1917, the same rule was laid down for men under 31 years of age.[3]

NATIONAL SERVICE SCHEME

In December, 1916, Lloyd George announced that the universal national service policy which had been determined upon by the late government would be put into effect with Neville Chamberlin, Lord Mayor of Birmingham, as director. In accordance with this plan, industries and occupations would be scheduled according to their essential utility in war time and laborers would be invited to enroll for war work. If they did not respond in sufficient numbers the government would use its powers to direct them where they were most needed.[4]

[1] *Labour Gazette*, 1917, p. 56.
[2] *British Industrial Experience*, etc., vol. 1, pp. 723-724.
[3] *Ibid.*, pp. 724-725.
[4] Gray, *op. cit.*, pp. 45-46.

It was in accordance with this plan that the Minister of Munitions found it necessary to issue an order under the authority of the Defense of the Realm Regulation 8A, whereby men of military age (18 to 60 inclusive) were not allowed to enter any one of a long list of occupations contained in a schedule accompanying the order, except "with the consent of the Director General of National Service, given on the ground that the employment is expedient for the purpose of executing a government contract, or on the ground that the work on which the men are to be employed is of national importance." These occupations included the manufacture of a large number of commodities, either luxuries or generally believed to be not essential in war times, and also included the distribution and sale of such commodities. The effect of this order was not to cause an immediate cessation of these industries, but to prevent their expansion unless such expansion could be secured by the employment of women, boys or old men.

The Director General of National Service issued at about the same time as the issuance of the order of the Ministry of Munitions containing the list of restricted occupations, a list of " trades and occupations of primary importance " [1] into which new labor was urged to go in the national interest. This list included not only the munition trades but many other industries deemed essential for the health and efficiency of the people and for the successful conduct of the war.

The Ministry of National Service was created by act of Parliament, March 28, 1917, " for the purpose of making the best use of all persons, whether men or women, able to work in any industry, occupation or service." [2] The Minister was given the title of Director General of National Service. By him an appeal was made for volunteers to be known as national service volunteers who were to go into any work to which they might be sent. It was for the purpose of guiding the employment exchanges in allocating these volunteers to their work that the Director Gen-

---

[1] *British Industrial Experience*, etc., vol. 1, pp. 725-729.
[2] *Ibid.*, pp. 733-734.

eral of National Service issued this list of " trades and occupations of primary importance " just referred to.

The Ministry of National Service was organized on a large scale. Much labor and money was spent on organization and advertising and several hundred thousand men were enrolled within a few weeks as national service volunteers. The plan at first seemed to be a failure. Three months after it had begun it was said that the number of men shifted from one occupation to another deemed to be more essential " was actually smaller than that of the staff employed at St. Ermin's Hotel in shifting them."

Several reasons are given for the failure of the plan as originally constituted :

1. The plan duplicated in large measure the work of the employment exchanges instead of supplementing it.

2. Men were enrolled for service without any attempt having been made to ascertain where there was any demand for their services. " Seven-eighths of the volunteers are men who can not possibly be spared from their present posts, and no one knows how to extract the other eighth or what to do with it when it is extracted." [1]

According to the original plan the enrolment of volunteers was done by the national service department and the men were to be placed by the employment exchanges.

3. Organized labor seems to have regarded the scheme as a thinly veiled substitute for industrial conscription which was unpopular with the trade unions and with laborers generally. Men who were willing enough to be drawn into the service of the state at an arbitrary wage and for dangerous duties were not willing to have even a mild form of compulsion applied to service for a capitalist employer working for profit.

An effort was made to amend the scheme during the spring of 1917, by placing the responsibility for selecting the persons to be shifted from the less essential to the more essential industries upon joint committees of employers and workers in each organized trade and upon local national service committees selected to deal with the unorganized trades in every urban area. Those who volunteered under this scheme were to be called " substitution " volunteers. They were to be allocated to their work by the

[1] *The New Statesman,* April 7, 1917, p. 5.

substitution officers of the national service department and not through the employment exchanges. The terms of their transfer were made more attractive than they had previously been, as will be seen from the following statement:

A "substitution" volunteer will not be asked to leave his employment except to take up a definite job on work of national importance on terms which will be clearly notified to him. If the terms are clearly acceptable to him, he will be free to refuse the offer without going before any appeal court. He will either take the place of a man of military age and fitness who has been called up to join the colors or he will reinforce the labor supply in industries of special national importance for war purposes. In either case he will have the satisfaction of feeling that he is engaged in direct war work as truly as the men who are actually with the colors. The terms of employment as regards wages are such that the volunteer is not now asked to make any pecuniary sacrifice by transferring his services from private to national work.[1]

In spite of these modifications in the national service scheme it does not appear to have been immediately practicable. The select committee on national expenditure appointed by order of the House of Commons to examine into current expenditures and see what if any economies might be effected, through a subcommittee reported on the work and expenditures of the Ministry of National Service from its beginning (end of December, 1916, to August 8, 1917). The expenditures up to that time had been £223,720; the total staff was 762 on March 31 and 491 on August 9. The result of this expenditure had been that 351,383 men and 41,984 women were enrolled. Employment for 19,951 men had been found as national service volunteers. Of these 8,747 were placed by employment exchanges; 9,187 part time workers (men) had also been found work, or a total of 29,768. In the Women's Section, 14,256 had been found employment, or a total of 44,024 men and women.

The committee concludes its report on this subject with this statement:

We are of opinion that the results obtained were not commensurate with the preparations made and the heavy preliminary outlay of money.[2]

[1] *Labour Gazette*, 1917, p. 161.
[2] Special Report and Reports from the Select Committee on National Expenditure together with the Proceedings of the Committee, April 12.

The New Statesman in July declared that national service was dead, although the government kept up the pretense that it was alive. This was, to say the least, an exaggeration. The plan had up to that time proved ineffective, but it was not dead and later in the year was enlarged and wide powers given to its director. In the meantime the way for a more successful distribution of the man power of the country had been paved by the decision of the war cabinet to call into military or naval service men who had been employed on munitions work and who had been protected from calls for enlistment by their trade cards or war service badges.

THE PROTECTED OCCUPATIONS LIST

A list of protected occupations was issued by the Ministry of Munitions which went into effect May 1, 1917. Employers were required to send a list of all their male employes who were over the age of 16, together with the total of women and boys employed, to the munitions area dilution officer of the area in which the establishment was situated. They were to mark the names of these men for whom they claimed protection under the schedule. The actual selection of the men who were to be released was made by the district representatives of the Admiralty or director of army contracts. Only men who were found "indispensable for the fulfilment of the varying programs of ship construction, munitions and other essential government work were protected from recruiting" and even these men were protected only provisionally. The army's need might again be urgent or experience might show that operations performed by the protected men could be undertaken by men released from the army or by women.

All exemptions previously granted by trade cards or war service badges or certificates were canceled and those workmen who were protected (temporarily) from recruiting were given red cards (army form W. 3476A), while those who were engaged on Admiralty, War Office or munitions work but were not protected by the schedule were given cards printed in black (army form W. 3476B).

Men who were employed on Admiralty, War Office or munitions work and who did not hold red or black cards, but claimed exemption, might present their claims to an enlistment claims committee set up in every munitions area recruiting office and which consisted of one labor representative and one government representative.   A central committee for each of the eight divisional areas passed upon claims on which the local committees were unable to agree.

Where men were called up and their employer considered that substitutes were needed, the government promised that efforts would be made to supply them.   Employers were warned, however, that " the need of the army for men is too urgent to admit of the release of men being delayed in every case until substitutes have been provided and that the supply of male substitutes is likely to prove unequal to the demand." [1]   Employers were urged to employ women wherever possible, even if they had to be trained for the work, and to effect a transfer or rearrangement of labor within their works.

NATIONAL SERVICE AND THE EMPLOYMENT EXCHANGES

It was in connection with the work of providing substitutes that the National Service Department was connected up with this scheme, and by means of which it apparently gained a new lease of life.   In every munitions area recruiting office an area employment officer representing the Ministry of Labor and an area substitution officer representing the National Service Department were located, and on them fell the responsibility of providing substitutes where required.   The first 33 per cent of the total quota of men from each district required for military service were to be furnished without reference to the provision of substitutes.   Thereafter the release of men was made dependent upon the finding of substitutes and the munitions area dilution officer was to notify the munitions area recruiting office of the men made available for military service by the provision of substitutes.

[1] Letters issued by Ministry of Munitions (April 21, 1917), *British Industrial Experience*, vol. 1, p. 736.

The line of division of work and authority between the employment exchanges and the National Service Department in the efforts to supply substitutes, was at first not clearly defined. Circular R133 issued June 8, 1917, attempted a division along the following lines :

(a) The employment exchanges were to deal with war munition volunteers and with army reserve munition workers in addition to their ordinary work of placing men in employment. They were also to deal with persons of the professional or business classes, whether enrolled as national service volunteers or not.

(b) The national service department was to place the national service volunteers and the substitution volunteers.

The National Service Department drew up a list of certified occupations, which was issued as Circular R136 on June 23, 1917, and which took the place of previous lists of protected occupations. Inclusion of an occupation within this list was evidence that the government departments and the Army Council had agreed that the work was of national importance, and that men employed or engaged in these occupations were entitled to exemption from the military service acts when individual certificates of exemption had been issued to them by the appropriate tribunal. Mere employment at an occupation included in this list did not automatically exempt the individual workman. It was distinctly stated that " men who have a bad record for absenting themselves from work " should not be granted exemption and exemption having been granted should not continue in such cases.

NEW NATIONAL SERVICE PLAN

The division and distribution of powers among the several authorities concerned with recruiting and the provision of substitutes for men called up apparently did not work smoothly for in October, 1917, it was decided to transfer to the Director General of National Service " the powers and duties of the Army Council . . . which relate to recruiting, the calling up of the reserve forces, exempting from service or otherwise to the provision of men to the army."[1]

Under a new director (Sir Austin Geddes) the National Service Department issued an outline of a new scheme for enrolling volunteers for work of national importance. Some of the defects made evident by the early experience of the department were remedied.

(1) Arrangements were made to determine the demand for labor in undertakings of national importance accurately and regularly. The lists of all vacancies to be filled were to be compiled and published from day to day in each locality.

(2) Men required to fill these places were to be secured from less essential industries. Men of the type required and of the number actually wanted were to be invited to enroll as war work volunteers.

War work volunteers were asked to sign an enrolment form on which they agreed to undertake work of national importance either for the duration of a particular job or for a year. The enrolment of national service volunteers ceased and those already enrolled who had not been transferred to work of national importance were released from their obligations, but the hope was expressed that when definite vacancies occurred for which they possessed the necessary qualifications, they would then enroll as war worker volunteers.

Those national service volunteers who had been transferred to work of national importance were classed and described as war worker volunteers (special), but were to continue under the terms and conditions under which they were transferred until the expiration of their jobs, when they were invited to enroll under the new terms when vacancies occurred for which they possessed the necessary qualifications.

(3) The war worker volunteers were to be divided into three categories:
    a. War worker volunteers (trade): This class of workers was to be obtained by trade committees of employers and workers and were to be placed by the committees in vacancies selected by them from lists supplied to them. The committees were to utilize the employment exchanges for transferring the men, as for example in securing railway transportation.
    b. War worker volunteers (general): Those who volunteer for a year.
    c. War worker volunteers (special): Those who volunteer for a specific job.

Classes (b) and (c) were to be obtained and dealt with by the employment exchanges. All war work volunteers were to receive

---

[1] Ministry of National Service Orders, October 23 and 30. *British Industrial Experience*, vol. 1, p. 815.

on transfer the rate of wages they were receiving before they were transferred or the time rate of the district to which they were transferred, whichever was the higher. If sent away from their homes, they were to receive railway fares and, under certain conditions, the usual subsistence allowances, and those enrolling for a year's service might receive out of work pay or a guaranty of employment for six months.[1]

In the fact that volunteers are enrolled only after a demand for their services has been demonstrated and in the closer coopera- tion with the employment exchanges, the new scheme for national service is undoubtedly vastly superior to the old one of register- ing a miscellaneous lot of volunteers whose qualifications are not easily ascertainable and for whom there may be no demand. The scheme has also profited by the larger authority given to the director in the control of recruiting.

INDUSTRIAL CONSCRIPTION A REALITY

A conclusion to which one arrives from a study of the develop- ment of the government's policy of exercising control over the supply and distribution of labor during the war is that, despite the objection raised to conscription of labor and despite the caution imposed upon the local administrators to avoid anything in the nature of compulsion in their dealings with labor, the policy which has been evolved is little short of compulsion for men of military age.

It is true that men are not called up and arbitrarily assigned to a given task as they are under the military service acts, but the fact that men of military age are not allowed to enter many oc- cupations except with the consent of the National Service Direc- tor means that they are limited for new employment to the war industries or to those of national importance. Having entered such occupations nominally as volunteers they are subject to the terms of their contract with the government for the period stipu- lated. If they do not fulfil their contract or if they are charge- able with bad time keeping they are liable to be withdrawn from

---

[1] *British Industrial Experience*, etc., vol. 1, p. 817.

industry for the army, at any time. As long as they are engaged in one of the certified occupations they are in a measure protected from the recruiting officer, but even this protection does not avail when the need of men for military service grows urgent or the dilution officer finds satisfactory substitutes from the lists of those not available for military service. The demand for more men in the army has become more urgent with every passing month and the industries of the country have been " combed " time and again. The success of the policy of withdrawals has been dependent upon the success of the dilution policy to be described in the following chapter.

Doubtless such control of labor as is being exercised under the national service scheme is necessary as a complement to the military service acts and because of the imperative need of men by the war industries, but when one considers the length to which the government has gone in its restrictions on the employment and movement of labor, he is led to wonder whether organized labor has in reality accomplished much by its apparently successful resistance to the industrial conscription of labor.

CHAPTER VII

The Dilution of Labor

By the middle of the year 1915 it had been generally recognized that neither the transference of workers nor overtime work would be sufficient to secure the increased production required by war needs. Employers as well as the government recognized that some reorganization of industries must be effected which would permit the employment of a larger proportion of unskilled workers. This policy of introducing a larger proportion of semi-skilled and unskilled workers into trades which had hitherto been regarded as suitable only for highly skilled workers, is aptly expressed by the phrase " dilution of labor."

As early as March, 1915, the government had taken steps in the direction of diluting labor. The Chancellor of the Exchequer, Mr. Lloyd George, in opening the conference of government officials and trade union representatives which led to the Treasury agreement, called attention to the great need of an increased supply of munitions and the difficulty of bringing it about owing to the scarcity of skilled labor. In asking the trade unionists to suspend their rules restricting output for the period of the war, he said that there is the question " of the number of machines which one man is permitted to attend to; there is the question of the employment of semi-skilled labor, where under normal conditions you could not assent to it; and there is the question of the employment of female labor. In France there is a vast amount of work being done by women and by girls in the ammunitions factories. In that country they have suspended all these rules and regulations for the time being, because they realize that the security of their country depends upon it." [1]

[1] Forty-seventh Annual Report of the Trade Unions Congress, 1915, p. 220 ff.

Trade Union Opposition to Dilution

Although the Treasury agreement provided for dilution of labor, in accordance with the proposals of the Chancellor, and although the Munitions of War Act, 1915, was intended to make possible the adoption of this policy, little progress in the way of such dilution had apparently been made during the year 1915. In spite of the fact that their leaders had signed the agreement to permit the substitution of unskilled male labor and female labor for skilled workers in munitions plants, the rank and file of trade unionists were greatly dissatisfied with the policy, the reasons for and the necessity of which they did not fully understand. In order to make clear this necessity, Mr. Lloyd George, then Minister of Munitions, attended the Trade Unions Congress at Bristol, in September, 1915, and in an address to the congress set forth the reasons which had led to the adoption of the policy and explained more fully the methods by which this dilution was to be brought about.

" The war," he said, " has resolved itself into a conflict between the mechanics of Germany and Austria on the one hand, and the mechanics of Great Britain and France on the other. . . . This is a war of material. Inadequate material means defeat, sufficient material means victory." [1]

Having called attention to the increased number of casualties which occurred as a result of the shortage of munitions and having emphasized the necessity of having the factories manufacturing munitions operating continuously, by night as well as by day, Mr. Lloyd George went on to say:

The first fact I want to get into the minds of trade unionists is this—that if you employ every skilled workman in the kingdom you would [sic] not have enough labor for the task we have on hand. Therefore, when it is a question of our diluting skilled labor with unskilled, it is not a question of turning out the skilled workman in order to put a cheaper workman in his place. We have plenty of work for the skilled workman, we have not enough skilled workmen to go around.

The second point I want to put is this—there is a good deal of the work which is being done by skilled workmen now, highly skilled workmen who

[1] Report of Trade Unions Congress, 1915, p. 353.

have years of training, which can just as easily be done by those who have
only had a few weeks' or a few days' training. We want to turn the unskilled on to work which unskilled men and women can do just as well as
the highly skilled so as to reserve the highly skilled for work that nobody
can do except those that have great experience, training and skill.

Another thing we want to do is this—you can not leave the unskilled to do
the work alone without having a skilled person to look after them. For
instance, take shell making, instead of putting skilled people to do that work,
what we should like to do would be to put on, say ten or eleven, unskilled
men or women to one skilled man to look after them. . . 'This is work
which is done in France and Germany by women. It is done in parts of
this country by women also. It does not require very long training. A
few weeks and they are trained. In a few days intelligent men and women
are able to do it. It is a waste of material, of which we have got far too
little, to turn highly skilled men on to do work of this kind and, therefore,
we have got to make arrangements with the trade unionists by which they
permit us to mix the skilled and the unskilled so as to let the skilled go as
far as it possibly will, and unless that is done we have not got enough labor
to go around.

Speaking of the results of the Treasury agreement, Mr. Lloyd
George said that although the state had kept its part of the bar-
gain by the passage of the Munitions Acts, which provided for a
restoration of prewar conditions and for limitation of profits,
the unionists in many cases were not keeping their part of the
contract. The parliamentary committee decided to investigate
these charges.

Government Assists in Dilution

During September, 1915, the Central Munitions Labor Supply
Committee, upon which the trade unions were represented, was
appointed to advise and assist the Minister of Munitions in carrying out its dilution policy. A circular (No. 129) was dispatched
to owners of controlled establishments explaining what was
meant by dilution of labor and instructing them to introduce it
as extensively as possible and without delay. Dilution of labor,
as explained in this circular, implies that:

(1) The employment of skilled men should be confined to work which
could not be efficiently performed by less skilled labor or by women.

(2) Women should be employed as far as practicable on all classes of
work for which they are suitable.

(3) Semi-skilled and unskilled men should be employed on any work

which does not necessitate the employment of skilled men and for which women are unsuitable.

In order to assist employers in carrying out the policy of dilution the government sent special representatives, among others the factory inspectors, to the most important districts in which munitions plants were located, to explain the methods by which dilution could be brought about. As the result of conferences with employers, substitution for skilled workers proceeded rapidly throughout the year 1916. Agreements were entered into by employers and employes not only in the munitions industries but in cotton, hosiery, woolen and worsted, silk, felt hat, printing, bleaching and dyeing, woodworking and furniture, boot, wholesale clothing, earthenware and china manufactures, which provided for the substitution of men not available for military service and women for men of military age, together with the agreement that at the close of the war, the workers dismissed for military service were to be reinstated under conditions which prevailed in the prewar period.

SCARCITY OF MALE SUBSTITUTES

The number of men available for substitution was not large. The unskilled male labor which might have been substituted for skilled labor was as much in demand for military purposes as were the skilled laborers. Something was done in the way of substitution by the introduction of men over military age and by the earlier promotion of boys serving their apprenticeship to undertake men's work—the place of these boys being taken in many instances by women or girls. However, the result in most instances where an attempt was made to make substitutions was that the employers had to fall back upon female labor for their supply of substitutes.

There are no figures which show the total numbers of skilled and of unskilled men in all industries in the United Kingdom. Indeed such figures would be hard to collect since the line of demarcation between skilled and unskilled, in most trades, is very uncertain. Some indication of the extent of this mode of substitution is afforded by the figures furnished by the labor exchanges for the insured trades which include, it will be remembered, among others engineering, shipbuilding and works of construction.

In 1914 the number of " skilled vacancies " filled by men in the insured trades registered in the labor exchanges was 228,800. In 1915 it had fallen to 223,800, in spite of the war demands, and in 1916 there was a further decline to 194,237. The number of " unskilled vacancies " in these trades filled by men registered in the labor exchanges was, in 1914, 182,824. By 1915, this number had risen to 209,057 and by 1916 to 210,680.[1]

A slightly better showing is made if the engineering trades alone are considered, but it is at once obvious that the enormous war demand for labor in these industries was to be met in only a very small degree by the use of unskilled male labor to take the place of skilled workers.

FEMALE LABOR AVAILABLE EARLY IN THE WAR

Owing to the scarcity of male labor of all sorts, in the efforts to find substitutes for skilled labor, emphasis was of necessity placed upon the utilization of women and girls. The extent of the changes which took place during the first year of the war in the way of substituting female labor for male labor is not easy to trace, on account of the absence of official statistics and the lack of government participation in the movement to effect this substitution. While the great majority of these women laborers were hired by private employers, independent of efforts made by the labor exchanges, the reports of these exchanges nevertheless indicate, probably with a fair degree of accuracy, the tendency to exhaust the supply of male labor by military service and the extent to which women workers have supplied the lack of men.

The number of men and women remaining on the registers of the exchanges at the end of each month is the number of persons

[1] The figures for 1917 are not comparable, for they include additional " insured trades."

who have registered for employment and for whom places have not as yet been found. In normal years the numbers remaining on the register fluctuate with the seasonal changes in industry, being highest in winter and lowest in midsummer.

During the first half of 1914 the figures reflected this general movement, the number of men on the registers declining from 115,767 on February 13 to 85,185 on July 17, while the number of women on the registers, which had been 17,650 in February, was only 17,115 in the middle of July.[1]

The disorganization of industry which followed the outbreak of the war caused a rapid increase in these figures so that on September 11, when unemployment had reached its maximum for both men and women, the numbers remaining on the registers were 148,391 men and 37,599 women. Thereafter, the figures at six months' intervals show not only the seasonal fluctuations but the extent to which the decline in the number of men available is made good by the increase in the number of women seeking employment.

NUMBERS OF MEN AND WOMEN REMAINING ON THE REGISTERS OF THE LABOR EXCHANGES AT SELECTED PERIODS, 1914-1917

Period Ending	Men	Women
July 17, 1914	85,185	17,115
January 15, 1915	67,215	30,864
July 16, 1915	40,539	46,623
January 14, 1916	39,522	71,429
July 14, 1916	33,315	78,641
January 12, 1917	53,590	64,779
July 13, 1917	32,364	64,152
January 11, 1918	18,541	32,565
July 12, 1918	30,661	53,949

A few words of explanation seem necessary to interpret these fluctuations. After the brief period of unemployment in the late summer of 1914, the decline in the number of men remaining on the registers is to be explained not only by the number of enlistments, but also by " the heavy demand for labor for munitions work, hut building, etc." [2] The increase in the number of women,

[1] *Labour Gazette*, 1915, p. 43.
[2] *Ibid.*, 1916, p. 48.

however, does not admit of so simple an explanation. For the latter part of 1914 and for some months in 1915 the number of women remaining on the registers represents a demand for employment which met with no adequate response on the part of employers. In September, 1914, nearly a quarter of a million of women in strictly industrial occupations, were unemployed compared with the numbers in industry at the beginning of the war.[1]

From September onwards women unskilled and industrially ill equipped, as the great majority of them were, poured into those trades, leather, tailoring, metal trades, chemicals and explosives, food trades, hosiery and the woolen and worsted industries, which had been suddenly revived by the placing of large orders by our own and the Allied governments. Between September and December over 130,000 women were drawn into the ranks of industry proper, but still 80,000 unemployed women remained in spite of the net shortage of men which amounted to about a quarter of a million.[2]

The contraction of women's employment had not disappeared in February, 1915, when the number of employed women in industries was still 1.5 per cent less than in the preceding July.[3] The recovery seems to have been most marked in those branches of the clothing and food trades on which the government was dependent, for its supplies, such as military clothing, boots and shoes, canned and preserved foods. Unemployment was most marked in other branches of the clothing trades and was partly due to economies being practised and partly to the fact that many men were going into khaki. Women were, in increasing numbers, finding their way into the metal trades, but for this work many of the unemployed were untrained and while, in some cases, employers undertook to furnish the training necessary, " in most cases time was too short, the experiment too risky and the pressure of business too great, for employers to become enthusiastic over such schemes."[4] Most men seem to have believed that the war would be of short duration and were therefore reluctant to undertake important readjustment plans.

[1] British Association for the Advancement of Science, *Draft Interim Report of the Conference to investigate into outlets for labor at the end of the war*, p. 4.
[2] *Ibid.*, etc., p. 5.
[3] Kirkaldy, *Labour, Finance and the War*, p. 63.
[4] British Association, Draft Interim Report, p. 5.

During the year 1915 and the first half of 1916 the number of men available for industry steadily declined, while the number of women offering themselves for employment steadily increased. At the labor exchanges the number of registrations for the four years was as follows:

	Men	Women
1914	2.316,042	707,071
1915	1,512,335	1,232,891
1916	1,229,171	1,921.826
1917	1,167,864	1,893,706 [1]

WOMEN IN CLERICAL AND COMMERCIAL OCCUPATIONS

Governmental efforts to substitute women for men seem to have been made at first in certain occupations in which women had already been employed and had demonstrated their abilities. A Clerical and Commercial Employment Committee was appointed early in 1915 and made its report in the autumn of that year.[2] The committee said that its work was forced upon it by a realization of the fact that "a very large number of men of military age are at present engaged in clerical and commercial occupations and the certainty that most of these men will offer themselves for service with His Majesty's forces." This raised the question of finding "an adequate supply of competent substitutes." The committee said that there were about 300,000 male clerks of military age in England and Wales and of these about one-half would be available for military service. The classes from which their substitutes could be drawn were as follows:

(1) Men above military age and women already trained in clerical work and unemployed.

(2) Lads under military age.

(3) Sailors and soldiers previously employed in these occupations who are invalided out of the service.

(4) Women without clerical experience and not at present employed.

At the time the committee made its report, it was believed that the first class had been so heavily drawn upon that "the number now remaining is very small." The supply of lads in many dis-

[1] *Labour Gazette*, 1918, p. 48.
[2] Cd. 8110, 1915.

tricts was small and their utilization had the disadvantage from the standpoint of employers that the lads were rapidly attaining military age and might be lost to employers at just the time when they were beginning to be useful. Soldiers and sailors released from the service were, so far, few, but the committee urged that the authorities take steps " to release from service all invalided men as soon as it is seen that there is no reasonable prospect that they will be able to serve again in the fighting ranks."

" The bulk of the substitutes," said the report, " must be drawn from the ranks of women not at present employed." Some of the work to be done was of a routine and mechanical character, but much of it would require for its satisfactory performance education and capacity for responsibility and the committee believed that many women who had been educated in the secondary schools and universities, or who had had other educational advantages, were well fitted for clerical duties and would be glad to have the opportunity to render service in the national interest. The large business organizations, banks, insurance offices, etc., were already recruiting their staffs from this class of workers. Employers were urged to give a preference to the wives and families of men on their staff who had enlisted.

In spite of the fact that many women already enjoyed educational advantages for such work, the committee believed—and it was the opinion of employers—that some training was desirable and, in the case of the smaller business establishments where the work was of a less routine character, it was essential.

A short whole time training lasting from one to two months would go some way towards familiarizing women with business routine, and enable them to adapt themselves more readily to their work and surroundings on actually entering employment.

To give this training and to study local needs the committee proposed that in all commercial centers

a local body representative of higher education and of the commerce of the district should be formed to organize the supply and training of women clerks.

Steps had already been taken to accomplish this end in London, Manchester and other places, and the committee had sent a letter to the secondary education authorities throughout England

and Wales to urge that such bodies be established as soon as possible and that they undertake the following tasks:

(1) To ascertain the present and prospective requirements of employers in the locality, both as to number of substitutes and kind of training.

(2) To organize emergency classes to give a general groundwork in commercial knowledge and office routine, bearing in mind the special requirements of any important class of business peculiar to the locality.

(3) To take steps to attract women of sufficient education to this class of work.

(4) To compile a register of those who pass through the emergency classes with a view of getting them placed in employment.

The committee reported that it had also addressed a circular to a number of commercial and professional associations asking them to call the attention of their members to the urgency of reviewing at once their position, in order that their businesses might not unduly suffer when men were called under the new recruiting scheme. Strong representation had been made to the committee, however, by important business and professional concerns as to the importance of retaining

a sufficient nucleus of trained men to carry on the businesses which are essential to the maintenance of national commerce and finance.

The committee stated that it must be made clear that the employment of women under this scheme was intended to be only temporary and men replaced should be assured that their positions will be kept open for them. The committee also suggested that the scale of wages payable to women should, " in so far as conditions permit," be based upon the rate of wages paid to men for similar work.[1]

To what extent the increase in the number of women employed in clerical and commercial occupations was due to the efforts of the government and to what extent it is to be explained by the natural preference of the women for this work it is difficult to say. Certain it is that employers themselves, faced with the necessity of substituting women for men, preferred to begin the substitution at this point.

The conditions which explain this are set forth by the report

[1] Report of committee as reviewed in *Labour Gazette*, 1915, p. 395.

of the Conference Committee of the British Association for the Advancement of Science as follows:

Clerical work is obviously suitable for women, and employers have had far less hesitation in introducing a greater portion of female labor in this side of their business than in the industrial side proper. The conditions of the clerical labor market, including, as it does, a great majority of clerical workers who belong to no trade organization, have made it easier to introduce female labor without encountering serious opposition from the trade unions concerned, than in those trades where the group of workers is smaller and the workers are more highly organized. Enlistment was exceptionally heavy, in some cases over 30 per cent, among men such as clerks whose occupation is sedentary, and, in spite of the restriction of business, the net shortage of men was soon apparent, and women, mostly young girls from school, or middle aged women from professions which have been hit by the war, were rapidly drawn in to make up the shortage. Into government departments, local authorities, banks, insurance and other offices, as well as ordinary business houses, women are being drawn in increasing numbers to do work previously done by men.[1]

In clerical and commercial occupations, although women were oftentimes not directly substituted for men, the resemblance between the work done by the two sexes was closer than it was in most industrial occupations. The failure to make direct substitutions seems to have been due less to any inferiority in ability than it was to lack of training, although to a certain extent women's lack of physical strength was responsible for the change in organization. Women were employed more largely, during the first two years of the war at least, on the more mechanical side of the clerical work: typing, shorthand writing, copying and filing. It is even said that the women preferred the routine occupations.

Employers who were interrogated as to the success of the women workers placed a lower estimate on the value of women as clerks than on that of men, due primarily to women's lower physical strength and inability to stand overtime. There was a general opinion that on routine work the women were better workers than men and that they were more conscientious and painstaking, although probably less accurate on the whole.

In the case of ticket collecting on the railroads, where at first

[1] Draft Interim Report of the Conference to investigate into outlets for labor after the war, 1915, p. 9.

sight men and women appeared to be doing the same work, it was found on inquiry that the women were working shorter hours and were employed on three shifts, whereas the men were employed on two. Furthermore, the shifts of the women were arranged when the traffic was relatively light. In many of the large stores it is said that three women were required to do the work formerly done by two men.[1]

INCREASED EMPLOYMENT OF WOMEN IN INDUSTRIES ALREADY EMPLOYING WOMEN

In industrial occupations the increased employment of women took place, first of all, in those lines in which women had been employed in large numbers before the war. The report of the Chief Inspector of Factories, for 1914, says that—

The large trades concerning women in most of which there has been an incessant increasing demand for their labor are: woolen and worsted textiles (khaki, flannel, blankets); hosiery; clothing (military tailoring and fur coat making, cap making, shirt making); boots and shoes and other leather articles; ordnance and ammunition; rations and jam; haversacks, kitbags, holdalls, bandoliers; surgical dressings and bandages; tin canisters and box making. This demand has been limited only by difficulties in (a) absorbing undue proportions of unskilled workers at a time when available skill was more needed for production than usual; (b) shortage of machines and of machine parts, *e.g.*, hosiery needles; (c) shortage of raw material, *e.g.*, dyes and yarn, wool at times in woolen weaving mills, khaki cloth in military tailoring.[2]

The increased employment of women in these trades did not result in the replacement of men to such an extent as the figures would seem to indicate. This was largely because the increased need of war supplies was felt not only in the trades in which women had hitherto been largely employed, but in the very branches of those trades in which women were normally employed under peace conditions. Thus in the tailoring trade, which in peace times normally employed about 130,000 women, there was a decline in the demand for high grade tailoring work in which men were largely employed, whereas the increased demand for military clothing took place in the medium branches of the trade in which female labor normally predominates.

[1] Draft Interim Report, p. 9.
[2] Annual Report of the Chief Inspector of Factories and Workshops, 1914, p. 34.

This part of the trade has drawn women and girls from its other branches and from its fringe of casual labor, as well as from other trades in which there was a surplus of female labor.

It thus shows a great increase of female labor since the war which has been drawn in, not to undertake work previously done by men but merely to cope with a huge increase of orders in that branch of the trade in which a larger proportion of women than men is normally employed. Again, the cloth from which the uniform is made is not the very finest suiting and the huge demands upon the wool and worsted trade for it have resulted, as in the tailoring trade, in a larger demand for female labor compared with the demand for male labor than the trade as a whole would normally employ. The great increase of women's employment since the war in the leather trade has to a certain extent been in the lighter accoutrement branches on processes normally done by women, while in the boot and shoe branch there has actually been a replacement of women by men, owing to the heavier nature of the work required in the military than in the civilian boot.[1]

WOMEN IN THE MUNITIONS TRADES

The second stage in the employment of women was reached when they began to be employed directly in the manufacture of munitions. In some establishments this was reached even during the first year of the war, but the great increase in the employment of women came after the middle of 1915 and was directly due to government efforts following the agreement with the trade unions already referred to.

The report of the Chief Factory Inspector for 1914 says that in ordnance and munitions works large numbers of girls and women have been employed who had previously never worked in a factory or workshop[2] and the committee of the British Association, in its first report made in August, 1915, says that many thousands of women had been pouring into the armament branches of the metal and engineering trades since February of that year. Up to February the metal trades as a whole had shown a contraction in the employment of women amounting to over 1,200. By July of that year, according to Mr. Lloyd George, 50,000 women were engaged in munitions branches of the metal trades and this number was between one-tenth and one-fifth the number employed in France.

[1] British Association Draft Interim Report, p. 8.
[2] Annual Report of the Chief Inspector, 1914, p. 33.

The number of women employed in munitions work increased rapidly after the creation of the Ministry of Munitions and the establishment of new government factories. Women were for the most part engaged during " the early stages of their employment on repetition work and automatic machinery involving little or no departure from the work to which they are ordinarily accustomed—their work is mainly in the filling, capping and cleaning of shells, boring and drilling bombs, fuses of all kinds, English and French, and cartridge cases." [1] In the shell factories, however, even as early as August, 1915, women were in some cases executing the entire process of shell making from start to finish, involving twenty-one operations in the case of eighteen-inch highly explosive shells and Russian three-inch shrapnel.

Although most of the women were employed on repetition work, the possibility of their undertaking work of a higher order had already been demonstrated. A quotation from *The Engineer* of August 20, 1915, shows that women had thus early undertaken work requiring a high degree of excellence. This must be regarded, however, as an exception, for all reports seem to agree that women were mainly employed at the simpler tasks, especially during the first eighteen months of the war. Where a shortage of men required substitution it was found that boys who had already received some training were best adapted to undertake the men's work and women and girls were then employed to do work which had been done by the boys. Experience brought out the fact that where a very high degree of accuracy was demanded girls could at times be employed to do such work as limit gauging and would perform the work better than the men or boys. This, it was said, was " for no other reason than that it is purely a mechanical operation and requires no judgment, whereas men will frequently use judgment in testing a piece of work which is inaccurate to some trifling degree."

The inability of women to take up the work of skilled men during the first year of the war seems to have been mainly due,

[1] Draft Interim Report, p. 47.

not to unwillingness on their part to undertake such work, but
to lack of training and experience. At this time there was no
lack of semi-skilled and unskilled labor, either male or female,
but the absence of skilled workers created what seemed to be " an
almost insuperable obstacle " to the employment of the willing
but unskilled female labor. The British Association Report,
made in 1915, expressed the opinion that the problem was not
likely to be solved during the time of war. It was said that
women were in many industries working on processes which
had previously been done only by men, but that " the extent to
which this has occurred is inconsiderable." [1]

INDUSTRIAL TRAINING FOR WOMEN

Up to this time about the only experiments in training of
women for industry had been those made by the Central Committee on Women's Employment. Little work of a practical
nature had been accomplished, for the suggestions made by the
committee had to do with the making of toys, artificial flowers,
baskets, hair nets, surgical bandages and work of a decorative or
ornamental character. There was no opportunity in these trades
to displace men by women and the suggestion seems to have been
due to a belief that in order to relieve unemployment among
women it was necessary to discover new occupations for them.

The British Association report for the year 1915 embodied a
scheme for training women, as well as boys, in trades in which
men had hitherto been employed. It called for an increase in
the number of technical and trade schools which should work
in close cooperation with the trades concerned and advocated
a development of " part time " continuation schools, in place of
evening instruction at the end of a day's work, and advocated
workshop training, systematized and reduced to the shortest
period compatible with efficiency. The opinion was expressed
that, especially in the metal working trades, women could be
successfully trained to undertake skilled work. Experiments
made in some engineering shops had shown that women, within

[1] Draft Interim Report, p. 7.

a few days, were able to turn out accurate work and that they possessed initiative as well as manipulative dexterity.

Doubtless the government was more or less influenced by these suggestions when in July, 1915, steps were taken in conjunction with the Board of Education to organize training classes for men and women who were willing to become munition workers. Close cooperation between the factories and the schools was secured so that students might, so far as possible, be taught in the schools to use precisely similar machines to those which were in operation in the factories. Over 25,000 persons were trained in these schools during the years 1915 and 1916 and a large proportion of the students were women.

It was not intended to give a complete technical training; in fact the Ministry of Munitions stipulated that the course should provide not less than thirty nor more than one hundred hours instruction. It was suggested that, so far as possible, learners should be men or women who had secondary education or who had been skilled in other trades. Preference was to be given to those who were willing to leave the town where they lived and go where there was demand for their labor. No fee was charged for the course, but each learner was required to give a written undertaking that he would work whole time in a munitions factory on the completion of his course and, if he failed to do this, the cost of his training was to be recoverable from the worker. No male student was to be accepted who was of military age.

It is at once obvious that such a brief training would suffice only for the semi-skilled work in the munitions factories. It was on such work, we have observed, that women were chiefly employed during the first two years of the war and their employment was facilitated by the introduction of machinery which could be used in the turning out of standardized products. Standardization itself was made practicable by the enormous output of the munitions factories.[1]

[1] How far the great use of woman's labor has been dependent on standardization and specialization is illustrated by the following statement from the *Dilution of Labour Bulletin* of March, 1918, p. 85:

" In order to render the bulk of the women's work productive rapidly, it

WOMEN EMPLOYED ON SKILLED WORK

The third stage in the employment of women was reached when they began to replace men in the performance of skilled work. In some munitions establishments this took place as early as 1915 when the British Association report showed that women "are slowly undertaking processes in many trades which were previously thought just above the line of their strength and skill." Examples of such employment were chiefly in the leather, engineering and the wool and worsted trades, as well as in certain trades which had been depressed since the beginning of the war, as the cotton, pottery and printing trades.[1]

While the use of women to perform skilled work was the exception this early in the war, experience in those few establishments in which employers had been willing to make experiments in the use of women had shown that it was not lack of ability but lack of training and opportunity which was holding women back from the skilled branches of these trades. Trade union opposition and the prejudice of employers were also responsible for the failure of women to do other than mechanical and routine work.

As early as August, 1915, it was said that in a factory engaged in the manufacture of projectiles in sizes up to those required for 4.5 inch guns, women, working under the direction and supervision of a few expert men, were able to do "good work turned out accurately to gauge, much of the work demanding intelli-

---

was no good attempting to teach a woman a trade but only that part of it which she was going to be employed on—in fact to specialize.
  "This specialization was made possible in the branches of employment new to women by the war itself.
  "It is probable that since this war began more fuses and shells have been turned out of the engineering workshop, all practically to one pattern, than of any other complex appliances since engineering workshops began to exist. Their numbers, indeed, are comparable with those of typical repetition parts such as bolts, nuts, split pins, screws, etc. For the bulk of the available unskilled labor, therefore, every sort of stop, jig and appliance must be introduced—the job had, in short to be made fool proof. If there was a right and a wrong way of using these appliances as first made, that had to be altered until there was only one way of using them, and that the right one."
  [1] Draft Interim Report, 1915, p. 9.

gence of a high degree and involving intricate operations." [1]
The British Association report indicated at this time that it was
only the prejudice of employers and the selfishness of the trade
unions which were standing in the way of serious attempts to
substitute women for men on skilled work.[2] Women were said
to be particularly suitable to perform the delicate work necessary
for time fuses, and even the more arduous work of forging and
of handling machine tools had been successfully performed by
them.[3]

The longer the war continued the less serious became the
opposition to the introduction of women on skilled work. The
prejudice of employers was broken down when one task after
another was taken over by women and successfully performed by
them. Only two things, it was seen, stood in the way of the
substitution of women to do men's work in the manufacture of
munitions. One was the lack of training necessary to enable
any one to perform the most skilled operations and this was
being gradually overcome by experience and by using the skilled
male laborers as instructors. The other obstacle was women's
lack of physical strength to perform the heavier tasks and, in
part, this situation was remedied by a more careful classification
of work so as to subdivide the processes and grade the labor
accordingly. Mechanical devices for lifting, etc., were also
introduced wherever practicable.[4]

The women who have performed this skilled work have been
secured, for the most part, from the ranks of those who have
passed through the training schools. The more promising ones
in these schools have been given further training and have thus
been fitted for the more skilled tasks. An especial effort has been
made, however, to train for this work disabled soldiers who have
had some previous mechanical experience.

The training given to the women in the technical schools and
by the firms which employ them is intended to meet the needs of
the situation in the smallest possible time. The short period of

---

[1] *The Engineer* quoted in Draft Interim Report, p. 12.
[2] Draft Interim Report, p. 12.
[3] *Ibid.*, p. 46.
[4] *Ibid.*, p. 10.

training intended to fit a woman for shell making does not, of course, suffice when she is intended for general engineering work. But the purpose of even the longer training is not to turn out all around skill. On the contrary, women are trained to one type of machine, which they are taught to set up accurately as well as work. Generally about six weeks instruction is necessary for this kind of work.

Women with a good general education are mostly in demand and profit most by this system of education. Several of the schools allow from 15s. to 25s. per week to each woman who takes the training course. The Ministry of Munitions, in order to help firms who desire to improve the efficiency of their women workers, lends the services of demonstrator-operatives, women who are experienced in such work as machine operating, turning, drilling, tool setting, bench fitting, oxyacetylene welding, etc. These women are sent to a factory to demonstrate to the women what can be done. The Ministry is also ready to supply a nucleus of women workers to any firm which has difficulty in starting women in a new shop or new type of work. This nucleus of trained workers remains permanently in the employment of the firm.[1]

The experiments made during the year 1915 to utilize women to do work which hitherto had been done by men did little more than show the possibilities of such substitution. The continued withdrawal of men for military service and the need of larger and larger quantities of munitions soon left no other alternative than to make the fullest possible use of women in the manufacturing establishments.

Government Urges Further Dilution

Following the appeal made by the Minister of Munitions to the trade unionists to permit dilution, the Home Secretary and the President of the Board of Trade early in 1916 called the attention of employers in the manufacturing industries to the situation created by the continual withdrawal of male labor for

[1] Kirkaldy, *Industry and Finance*, pp. 68-72.

military purposes and to the need of concerted action in order to maintain " in the fullest vigor the manufacturing industries which are necessary to the provision of government supplies, the support of the population and our export trade." The appeal went on to say:

> There is one source, and one only, from which the shortage can be made good—that is, the great body of women who are at present unoccupied or engaged only in work not of an essential character. Many of these women have worked in factories and have already had an industrial training—they form an asset of immense importance to the country at the present time, and every effort must be made to induce those who are able to come to the assistance of the country in this crisis. Previous training, however, is not essential; since the outbreak of war women have given ample proof of their ability to fill up the gaps in the ranks of industry and to undertake work hitherto regarded as men's.
>
> We appeal, therefore, on behalf of the government to every employer who is finding his business threatened with diminished productivity through the loss of men, not to accept such diminution as an inevitable consequence of the war, but to make every possible effort to maintain his production by using women, whether in direct substitution for the men who have been withdrawn or by some subdivision or rearrangement of his work.[1]

The government promised to give every assistance possible in bringing about this dilution, but emphasized the importance of the employer taking the initiative in reviewing the organization of his works in order " to ascertain how it is possible by re-arrangement of work and other measures profitably to employ, as temporary substitutes, as large a number of women workers as possible." It was admitted that the employer would have some difficulties in arranging for conditions of work suitable to women or complying with the requirements of the Factory Acts, but it was asserted that in many industries these difficulties had been overcome as a result of discussion between employers and the factory inspectors. Employers were urged to make their wants for women labor known through the local labor exchanges and to give the fullest possible details as to the classes of work and the qualifications required.

Governmental assistance in bringing about dilution came from several sources:

[1] *Labour Gazette*, 1916. p. 83.

(1) The factory inspectors, as already mentioned, held conferences with employers in nonmunitions as well as in munitions industries to further the introduction of women to perform work formerly reserved for men.[1]

(2) After the creation of the Ministry of Munitions in June, 1915, a labor supply department was created whose functions were to supply labor of the character and amount required wherever needed and to carry out the policy of dilution. For the purpose of organizing the manufacture of munitions nearly the whole of Great Britain had been divided into forty-three districts and in August, 1915, the Minister of Munitions appointed three commissioners in each district to promote dilution. It was the business of these officials to proceed from establishment to establishment within their respective districts to discover the employer's need for labor and to work out with him a plan whereby unskilled labor and especially women could be utilized in place of or to supplement skilled men.

(3) To assist employers in determining where women could be used to advantage, the Ministry of Munitions issued in the early part of 1916 a book entitled *Notes on the Employment of Women on Munitions of War, with an Appendix on the Training of Munition Workers.* This book was filled with a description of processes on which women had been employed together with pictures of women performing these processes. Employers were urged to make inquiries from time to time of the labor officers in their districts as to new processes on which it had been found that women could be successfully employed.

NUMBERS AND PROPORTION OF WOMEN EMPLOYED IN MUNITIONS WORK

By these means and others dilution proceeded so successfully that in February, 1917, in the various government establishments

[1] Report of Chief Inspector of Factories and Workshops, 1915, p. 13; 1916, p. 3.

the following were the number and proportion of females employed in the manufacture of munitions.

Group	Total Number of Employes	Percentage of Female Employes
National shell factories	18,500	62
National projectile factories	52,000	46
National filling factories	77,000	79
National factories (high explosives and propellants)	23,000	48
Other government factories (miscellaneous munitions)	2,500	40

In addition to these government owned establishments there were on January 30, 1917, 4,285 " controlled establishments," 3,934 of which reported in February that they were employing 1,752,381 persons, of whom 21 per cent were females and over 11 per cent were boys under 18 years of age.[1]

The proportion of women employed in these various munitions establishments has greatly increased within the last year although no later figures are available which are comparable with those just given. The *Labour Gazette* in reviewing the extension of employment of women during the first three years of the war reported that while " the number of women engaged in making munitions can not be stated exactly, it is believed that about 670,000 are employed on munition work, whilst 632,000 are engaged in other government work such as the manufacture of clothing and food for the troops."[2]

The number of women employed in the metal and chemical trades grew from 210,000 in July, 1914, to 616,000 in July, 1917, and while not all of these women were engaged in the manufacture of munitions, the majority were so employed. Furthermore, these figures did not include government owned establishments, where 204,000 women were employed in July, 1917, as compared to 2,000 three years before.[3]

[1] Memorandum (manuscript) on the organization and work of the Ministry of Munitions of War, April 19, 1917.
[2] *Labour Gazette*, 1917, p. 395. By October, 1917, these figures had been raised to 700,000 and 650,000 respectively (*Labour Gazette*, 1918, p. 49).
[3] *Ibid.*

Mr. H. W. Garrod of the Special Mission from the British Ministry of Munitions to the United States in November, 1917, reported that 80 per cent of the munitions work was at that time being carried on by women.[1] Since March 31, 1917, all contracts for shells have been let on the condition that 80 per cent of the employes must be women when work on shells from two and three-quarters to four and one-half inches is being performed, and on larger shells the instructions of the Labor Supply Department as to the proportion of women and semi-skilled male labor must be followed.[2] In April, 1918, Mr. Winston Churchill said that 750,000 women were employed in the British munitions factories and that 90 per cent of the work was performed by them.

Employment of Women in Nonmunitions Work

During the first two years of the war, government efforts to dilute labor were mainly limited to the munition industries, although by March, 1916, as we have observed, an appeal was issued to manufacturers by the Home Secretary and the President of the Board of Trade to take concerted action in the way of hiring " women unoccupied or engaged only in work not of an essential character " to make good " the loss of labor caused by withdrawal of men for the forces." [3]

The Treasury agreement with the trade unions made in March, 1915, provided for dilution of labor in connection with production for war purposes only, and the sections of the Munitions Acts of 1915 and 1916 which deal with dilution likewise relate only to the manufacture of munitions, though, as we have seen, the term munitions was given a very broad interpretation by the appeal tribunals. Such increase in the employment of women as took place in other than the munitions industries during the first two years of the war was made with govern-

[1] Andrews and Hobbs: *Economic Effects of the War upon Women and Children in Great Britain*, p. 38. (Preliminary Economic Studies of the War issued by Carnegie Endowment for International Peace, 1918.)
[2] *Ibid.*, p. 54.
[3] *Labour Gazette*, 1916, p. 83.

ment encouragement, but without such direct government intervention as took place in the industries directly engaged on war work. In those industries in which the laborers were well organized, dilution took place usually as a result of agreements made by employers with the unions. These conferences were frequently called at the request of the Army Council which urged that as many men as possible be released for the army. The initiative was usually taken by the Home Office, whose factory inspectors participated in the conference. During the year 1915 agreements to allow women to undertake work hitherto carried on by men were made in the cotton, hosiery, leather, woolen and worsted, silk and felt hat, printing, bleaching and dyeing, woodworking, biscuit, pastry baking, wholesale clothing, boot making, earthenware and china trades. During 1916 further agreements were made in some of these trades and there was an extension of the trades conferences to the lace, hosiery, finishing, silver plate and cutlery and brush making industries.[1]

Much opposition to dilution in these industries was shown by the trade unionists and agreements were only reached after promises had been made that women should be employed on " men's work " during the war period only and that the men who had left these industries to undertake military service should have their places kept open for them on their return. Women were to be employed only on work which " they were physically fit to perform " and were to be paid the same rates of wages as had been paid to men when performing similar work. An important item in the agreement reached with the union in the leather industry was that the local trade union officials were to be consulted whenever it was thought advisable to substitute women for men.[2]

Many of the nonmunition industries were those in which women were most largely employed prior to the outbreak of the war and it was therefore natural that as soon as they had recovered from the first shock of the war and had entered upon

[1] Annual Report of the Chief Inspector of Factories and Workshops, 1916, p. 3.
[2] British Association Report, *Credit, Industry and the War*, p. 151.

a period of great activity they should have added to the number of women employes. Between December, 1914, and July, 1915, it is estimated that there was an increase of "nearly 150,000" in the number of women employed in the nonmunitions industries as compared to an increase in the munitions trades of only 39,000.[1] After July, 1915, the preference of women for the munitions industries became very marked. There was only a slight increase in the number of women in the nonmunitions trades during the year ending July, 1916, and during the next half year there was an actual decrease in the number of women employed in industries other than the metal and chemical trades. The decrease was greatest in the textile trades (32,000) and the clothing trades (11,000),[2] precisely those industries in which women have normally been most largely employed.

It was thought at the time that the decline in the number of women employed in the above industries meant not only a decline in the demand for women's labor but an actual shortage of female labor, but since January, 1917, increased employment in the clothing trades throws some doubt on the assertion that there is any real shortage of female labor.[3]

Less effort on the part of the government seems to have been needed in securing increased employment for women in other than the manufacturing industries. Women's fitness for clerical work and to serve as shop assistants (retail clerks in stores) was so obvious that employers needed little persuasion to attempt the substitution of women for men in these occupations. The report of the Committee on Clerical and Commercial Employments has already been considered. A Shops Committee, appointed at about the same time, which undertook to find out how many men could be released from the wholesale and retail stores for the army, reported in the autumn of 1915 that, except in the heavier branches of the wholesale trade, very few men needed to be retained and under the inspiration of this committee's report, many trade conferences were held in London and throughout the

---

[1] *Labour Gazette*, 1917, p. 395.
[2] *Ibid.*, p. 125.
[3] *Ibid.*, p. 275.

country at which those present agreed to do everything possible " to substitute women for men." [1]

In the railway service there has been a very great extension in the employment of women as clerks in the offices, as ticket collectors, carriage and engine cleaners, porters and as laborers in the shops. On the tramways of the large cities women have for some time been employed as cleaners, conductors and even as drivers. They are also largely employed in other branches of the municipal service, as in power stations, gas works, in parks and in road cleaning. In the government postal service the employment of women as mail carriers and in other capacities has become one of the familiar incidents of the war.

Considerable substitution of women for men has taken place in grain milling, sugar refining, brewing and in sawmilling. Even in building, mining and quarrying it is said that women have replaced men, although " only in comparatively small numbers." [2] The very novelty of women's appearance in these trades, some of which seem entirely unsuited to their character and capacity, has doubtless caused an exaggerated idea as to the extent to which women have replaced men in industry.

The year 1917 has seen further extensions of the employment of women in new industries although it has also shown, according to the report of the Chief Inspector of Factories, " a quiet dropping off from processes not found practically adaptable for women." The mainly new industries into which women have found their way during the year include ship and marine engineering yards, blast furnace and forge work, copper works, spelter construction work for factories, airdromes, large electrical stations, maintenance work in gas works and in certain occupations in breweries. The extent to which the women are being substituted for men is further illustrated by this same report, which mentions a cement works run almost entirely with women's labor, " the only men remaining being foremen, engineers and rotary kilnmen," and " a large tobacco factory in

[1] Andrews and Hobbs, op. cit., pp. 62-63.
[2] Labour Gazette, October, 1916, p. 357.

which a staff of women mechanics do the running, repairs, oiling and setting all the machines."

The inspectors report that the relatively few failures of women's work seem to be due to " (a) insufficient care in selection of appropriate women for the kind of work needed; (b) insufficient care in instruction and training so as to make the women really efficient, or in gradually accustoming them to new and heavy work; (c) insufficient care or understanding in adapting and organizing to women's needs the conditions and methods of work; (d) opposition on the part of men workers, leading in a very few cases to positive obstruction of the women in doing or learning their work." The first two are said to be the main hindrances and the last mentioned the least.

The Chief Inspector's report calls attention to the fact that the possibility of rapid extension of the substitution of women for men depends in large degree on the extent of use of modern plant, machinery and labor saving appliances. Factories with up to date construction and equipment have found relatively little difficulty in releasing men for military service. The possibility of substitution has also depended in no small degree on the willingness of employers to introduce welfare work, which the inspectors report is rapidly finding its way into not only new establishments but into those in which women have long been employed.[1]

WOMEN IN AGRICULTURE

Many efforts have been made to increase the employment of women in agriculture, but these have had only a partial success, if we are to judge by the official estimates. As late as December, 1916, it was admitted that " the progress has been slow and is in no way commensurate with that achieved in industrial and commercial occupations." The obstacles were said to be prejudice on the part of the farmers, reluctance on the part of the women, insufficiency of housing accommodations and low wages.[2]

[1] Special report appended to annual report of Chief Inspector of Factories for 1917. *Labour Gazette*, 1918, pp. 305-306.
[2] *Labour Gazette*, 1916, p. 447.

To overcome these obstacles a campaign of propaganda was instituted in the spring of 1915 by the Board of Trade and the Board of Agriculture. Women's county war agricultural committees were formed to carry on the propaganda, to register women willing to undertake farm work and to arrange to place them on the land. Sixty-three such committees had been formed by the end of the year 1916 and these committees in turn worked through village registrars, 4,000 in number. Meetings were held to arouse enthusiasm and to explain to women the need for their services. The meetings were followed by a house to house canvass and the names of those women willing to work whole or part time were entered on the village register. The registrar then cooperated with the nearest employment exchange in endeavoring to place these women on the land. About 140,000 women registered for agricultural service, but not all could be placed for the reasons given above.

A list of the occupations in which women were engaged in agricultural work in various parts of the country includes 20 classes of work with eight subclasses under general farm work and five under gardening. The report on their activities claims that while the experience gained during the war shows that some women " can do anything and everything on the land and do it well," the average woman is useful chiefly in the following occupations: general farm work, milking, stock tending and rearing, butter making, cheese making, poultry rearing, hay making, fruit picking, hop picking and gardening. They were said to be especially successful in milking and in tending and rearing stock.[1] In a few cases women had been given short courses of training in milking, general farm work and gardening and one of the notable successes reported was the plan of having " organized gangs of women, working under a leader, who visited farms in rotation, undertaking jobs at piece work rates." [1]

The efforts made during the year 1916 to substitute women for men on the farms were generally held to be successful in England, especially in the eastern and southeastern counties,

[1] *Labour Gazette*, 1916, p. 448.

where a considerable increase in the number of women engaged in farm work at the beginning of the war was shown. In Scotland and Wales, however, the efforts were not sufficient to prevent an absolute decline in the number of women engaged in agriculture, owing to the migration of women to munition establishments and other places of work where higher wages were offered.[1]

Further efforts to increase the number of women engaged in agricultural occupations took place during 1917, but they do not appear to have been generally successful, if we are to judge by the figures given, which show that there was an increase during the year ending July, 1917, of only 3,000 women employed as permanent laborers, while among women employed as casual laborers there was an actual decrease. The need of women for munition plants and in industry and commerce, generally, had become so urgent and the inducements offered were so much greater than those offered on the farms that relatively few women were attracted to the latter.

Statistics of Extension of Employment of Women

The following table shows the effect of the first three and one half years of the war in extending the employment of women in the various occupational groups in Great Britain, as far as this can be shown by official estimates. No estimates were prepared for the year ending July, 1915, and comparison must therefore be limited to the rate of growth between July, 1916, and July, 1917, as compared to the two year period ending in July, 1916.

[1] *Labour Gazette*, 1916, p. 448.

EXTENSION OF EMPLOYMENT OF WOMEN IN GREAT BRITAIN DURING THE WAR

Occupations	Estimated number of females employed July, 1914.	Estimated number of females employed July, 1916.	Percent increase over 1914.	Estimated number of females employed July, 1917.	Percent increase over 1914.	Estimated number of females employed January, 1918.	Direct replacement of men by women.
1. Industries	2,184,000	2,545,000	16.5	2,702,000	23.7	2,708,500	503,000
2. Government establishments (arsenals, dockyards, munition factories, etc.)	2,000	81,000	3950.0	204,000	9596.7	209,500	197,000
3. Transport (other than local tramways)	17,000	54,000	217.6	89,000	422.0	93,000	78,000
4. Commercial occupations	496,000	736,000	48.3	820,000	65.4	839,000	342,000
5. Finance and banking	9,500	41,500	336.8	63,500	570.5	70,500	57,000
6. Professions	67,500	81,500	20.7	87,500	30.2	100,500	22,000
7. Hotels, public houses, theaters, picture shows, etc.	176,000	196,000	11.3	198,000	12.5	207,000	45,000
8. Civil service (including post office)	65,000	124,000	90.7	163,000	150.7	189,500	123,000
9. Local government (including public utilities and public school teachers)	198,000	228,000	15.1	247,000	24.7	249,500	44,000
10. Agriculture (permanent labor)	80,000	100,000	25.0	103,000	28.7	74,000	31,000
Total	3,295,000	4,183,000	26.9	4,677,000	41.9	4,741,000	1,442,000
11. Agriculture (casual labor)	50,000	96,000	92.0	89,000	77.0	89,000	38,000

The highest rate of increase throughout the first three years, it will be at once observed, took place in government establishments where very few women had been employed prior to the war. Women in these establishments are of course almost exclusively employed on war work.

The table does not reveal the fact that in the manufacturing industries under private ownership the increase in the numbers of women employed has also been mainly in the munitions establishments. Figures have already been given which show the number of women employed in the "controlled establishments" early in 1917 and also the increase in the number of women employed in the metal and chemical trades, most of whom are employed in making munitions. If we exclude these latter from our calculations we find that the number of women in industries increased during the three years by only 112,000—from 1,974,000 in 1914 to 2,086,000 in 1917. Nearly all this increase took place during the first six months of 1915. During the last year for which the figures are given the number of women employed in the nonmunitions group has barely maintained itself.[1]

The table shows that in commercial occupations, in the professions and in the local government service the rate of increase in the employment of women has been fairly steady during the first three years of the war. There had been an accelerated rate of increase during the last of these years in transportation, in finance and banking and in the civil service while the rate of increase had slackened considerably in hotels and amusement places and in agriculture, casual labor in agriculture showing an actual decline. To some extent, this slower rate of increase, or even decline, in numbers indicates a lessened demand for the products of women's labor, a decline in the demand for luxuries, for instance, but in the main it probably means that the demand

[1] *Labour Gazette*, 1917, p. 395; 1918, p. 216. Figures have not been published for a period later than January, 1918. By October, 1917, there had been an actual decrease in the number of women in the nonmunition industries. The decrease was entirely in the cotton trades as a result of a shortage of raw materials, but in all the principal trades the rate of increase between July and October, 1917, was less than during the period April-July, 1917.

for women's labor in the " essential " industries, those minister-
ing directly to war needs, is slowly but steadily absorbing the
supply of female labor. The latest figures available, those for
January, 1918, furnish corroboration of this statement, for
it shows that while there had been an increase of 4,000 in the
number of women employes in all occupations during the
quarter October to January, the increases were confined to private
industrial establishments, to finance and banking, to commercial
occupations, to the civil service and to industries under local
government authorities. All other groups showed a decline or
at best a stationary condition of affairs.[1]

SOURCES OF SUPPLY FOR WOMEN WORKERS

No phase of the labor situation in Great Britain has excited
so much popular attention and comment as the increased employment of women in industry and many inquiries have been made
as to the source of supply of these women workers. To the
popular imagination there have been pictured the figures of
duchesses and other ladies of fine breeding running the lathes
in the munition factories or pouring the deadly TNT into the
endless rows of shells.

Individual instances of the industrial employment of patriotic women of the higher classes undoubtedly may be found in
Great Britain, but they have not constituted an important source
of the war labor supply.[2] Women accustomed to manual work
and dependent, wholly or partially, on such work for their
maintenance have furnished the great bulk of the female labor
which has been drawn into industry as a result of the war. Many
women, who had retired from industrial service after marriage,
have felt obliged to reenter industry since their husbands,
fathers or other male support have entered the military or naval

[1] *Labour Gazette*, 1918, p. 261.
[2] The employment of the "higher class" women seems to have largely
taken the form of "the week end munition relief workers" who worked
Sunday to relieve the regular staff. There were not many of these workers,
and their number was not increasing. Andrews and Hobbs, *op. cit.*, pp. 70-71.

service. Others have been attracted to industry by the high wages paid, by the increase in the cost of living and, in some cases, for patriotic reasons.

In a report made by the Standing Joint Committee of Industrial Women's Organizations to the Joint Committee on Labor Problems After the War, the increase in the number of women employed in July, 1918, over the estimated number employed in July, 1914, is put at 866,000, of whom 462,000 were absorbed by industry, transport and government work alone.[1] The report offers the following succinct statement as to the sources from which this increased number of employed women has been drawn:

(1) A large number are women who have transferred their services from the ranks of domestic servants. This number is probably much larger than the estimate of 100,000 given by the Board of Trade.

(2) Many transferences have been made from the ranks of outworkers, small employers on their own account, etc.

(3) The wastage at the later years has been less; women remaining in industry to a later age, after marriage, etc., while girls from school have come quickly into employment.

(4) Married women, widows, etc., have returned to employment in large numbers, both for economic and patriotic reasons.

(5) A certain number of middle class women have entered industry, commerce, etc., for patriotic or economic reasons, who would under normal circumstances not have become wage earners.

No reliable estimate can be made as to the number of women employed that has come from each of the above classes, but a statistical analysis has been made of the prewar occupations of 444,137 female workers (380,470 women and 63,667 girls) to whom unemployment books had been issued up to January, 1917, under the National Insurance (Part II) Munition Workers Act of 1916, and who had stated their occupations definitely enough to make a tabulation possible. This analysis shows clearly enough the extent to which munition workers have come from other industries and the extent to which they are made up of women and girls not previously employed in gainful occupations.

[1] These are the Board of Trade estimates.

OCCUPATIONS IN JANUARY, 1917

Prewar Occupations	Metal Trades (excluding engineering)	Chemical Trades Including	Clothing Trades	Other Trades	All Insured Trades
Same trade	53,249	14,634	38,256	30,399	136,538
Household duties and not previously occupied	18,927	52,407	9,334	17,843	98,511
Textile trades	3,408	6,226	1,000	4,374	15,008
Clothing trades	4,635	17,911	8,430	8,787	39,793
Other industries	12,458	20,879	5,745	10,065	49,147
Domestic service	12,502	44,438	4,970	12,062	73,992
Other non-industrial occupations ..	5,449	17,079	3,643	4,977	31,148
Total insured	110,628	173,604	71,378	88,527	444,137

The *Labour Gazette*,[1] which publishes the above figures, offers the following comment upon their character and significance:

Subtracting the number of persons who have remained in the same trade it will be seen that the table accounts for nearly 308,000 persons who have changed their occupations. In July, 1917 (the latest date for which figures are available), the number of women drawn into industrial work, using the term to include government establishments, was 720,000, or rather more than double the number drawn into the trades here considered. The proportion of the total increase covered by these figures is therefore sufficiently large for them to be taken as fairly typical. Assuming that the whole of the increase of 720,000 could be accounted for in the same manner as the increase analyzed above, it would mean that it was made up of 231,000 women and girls who were previously unoccupied, 173,000 who were domestic servants, 243,000 who came from other industries, including 93,000 from the clothing trades, and 73,000 from non-industrial occupations other than domestic service. These figures can, of course, only be taken as a rough indication of the change that has taken place, but they must be sufficiently near the truth to be of considerable interest.

The fact that so many persons have left a trade can not be taken to indicate that the numbers employed have decreased by an equal amount, as these trades in their turn have drawn in workers from the outside. Thus in January, 1917, at the date to which these figures refer, taking the clothing trades as a whole, the numbers of women and girls employed had decreased by 32,000, whereas it appears from the above table that the newly insured alone had drawn in nearly 40,000 females from the clothing trades, which must therefore have found at least 8,000 workers from outside. In the textile trades, the loss shown in the table is 15,000, although at that time the textile trades had increased the number of female employes by 25,000.

[1] 1917, p. 438.

A discussion of the sources of female labor capable of substituting directly or indirectly for male labor withdrawn for military service inevitably raises the query as to the extent of this supply. How many women are still available for employment in the essential industries?

No exact answer to this question can, of course, be given. The Board of Trade estimated in July, 1916, when 866,000 women had already been added to industry, that there were still over a million and a half women who had had industrial or commercial experience and who might be used to take the place of men. Up to October, 1917, 560,000 more women had found employment, which would indicate that there were then probably less than a million of women who have had industrial or commercial experience, but who were at the time not in any wage earning occupations. But this, as has been pointed out, is not equivalent to saying that these women are to any large extent now available for industrial purposes. Most of them are over 35 years of age and probably most of them are married.

> It must be realized that, although these women may not be working for wages, they are usually working, and working very hard, too, in keeping their homes and looking after their children. To take such women into industry will not be a national advantage. If the homes are to be kept so that the rest of the workers and the children may be properly cared for it is necessary that somebody give their energy and time to the task. Already many women have had to find substitutes to do the work of their homes, and many are also acting as the unpaid substitutes for domestic servants.[1]

Some evidence of a shortage of female labor was revealed in the latter part of 1916 and the first part of 1917, when the number of women remaining on the registers of the employment exchanges at the end of the month showed a tendency to decline and when employers in the textile, clothing and other trades making large use of female labor reported a shortage. This was at first thought to be due to a transference from these industries to " munition work or other better paid occupations," [2] but the

[1] Report of the Standing Joint Committee of Industrial Women's Organizations presented to the Joint Committee on Labor Problems After the War.
[2] *Labour Gazette*, 1916, pp. 8, 126.

experience of the latter half of 1917 threw doubt on this interpretation and seemed to indicate that the decrease in the number of women employed in these trades was due to a check in the demand for labor in these trades.[1]

The quarterly reports for October, 1917, and for January, 1918, again raised the query as to whether the supplies of female labor were not approaching exhaustion. In October the report for the quarter showed that the increase in the number of women employed was only 48,000 as compared to 140,000 the preceding quarter. The number of women in agriculture showed an actual decline, but this might possibly be explained by seasonal variations. In industrial occupations, the increase had been only 21,000 as against 63,000 the preceding quarter.[2]

The report for January, 1918, is even more striking. The total gain in the number of female employes in all occupations was only 4,000 and, as we have shown, the slight increases in a few of the groups were nearly met by decreases in other groups. The most notable decreases were in agriculture (13,000) and in government establishments (3,500). "The falling off in the number of males employed," says the *Gazette*, "has been conspicuously small, probably owing largely to the reinstatement of men returning from the forces."[3]

From such evidence as is available, however, it would seem as if the continued demand for labor in the munition industries would have to be secured in the main by a shifting of labor from the less essential trades and by an increased use of men released from the army because of their disabilities.

MOBILITY OF WOMEN'S LABOR

The shifting of women from one industry to another has frequently, though not always, meant a transference of residence from one part of the kingdom to another. Such a transfer before the war was hard to bring about, as female labor was thought to

[1] *Labour Gazette*, 1917, p. 274.
[2] *Ibid.*, 1918, p. 48.
[3] *Ibid.*, p. 216.

be especially immobile. Domestic ties, of course, made it difficult for many women to move, but even in the case of women without strong domestic ties there were two obstacles which stood in the way whenever the labor exchanges undertook to make such transfers. These obstacles were:

(1) The low wages which made it difficult for women to support themselves while away from home, and

(2) The "lack of a compelling motive strong enough to counteract the working woman's natural distrust of new conditions of employment amongst strange surroundings." [1]

These difficulties largely disappeared during the war. High wages on government contract work and economic pressure combined with a patriotic desire to serve the country by engaging directly in the manufacture of munitions broke down, at least for the time being, the reluctance of many women to leave their homes to engage in work.

Probably most of the transfers of women made by the employment exchanges from one district to another and which rose from 32,988 in 1914 to 160,003 in 1916 [2] do not indicate any great mobility. They oftentimes mean simply that women have gone from one village to another at no great distance or from one district in London to another. In many instances, however, the transfers were for considerable distances. In the earlier days of the war women went from the pottery districts to silk mills in the neighboring towns; cotton operatives and carpet weavers were transferred to the Yorkshire woolen mills; tailoresses from Cambridge, Cardiff, Belfast and elsewhere went to work in the clothing factories of Leeds.

In the West Midlands district alone, where before the war the migration of industrial women was practically unknown, over 4,000 women were during 1915 placed by the employment exchanges in employment away from their own districts, the greater number on munitions work, and others as artificial silk workers, rubber workers, chocolate makers, farm hands and as substitutes for men in various kinds of work.

In the great majority of cases the occupations were entirely new to the

[1] *Labour Gazette*, 1918, pp. 92-93.
[2] Later figures not available.

workers, who were drawn from such diverse occupations as carpet weaving, chain making, domestic service, dressmaking, fustian cutting, lock making, millinery, shopwork, tailoring, web making and pottery decorating.

Similarly, much useful work was accomplished during this early period by the exchanges in transferring inland to other employment women from seasonal resorts on the east coast, and fisher girls and other women engaged in subsidiary industries in fishing towns.[1]

During the year 1916 women were transferred through the exchanges to act as substitutes for men in clerical and commercial occupations, in staple industries, in munition plants and in agriculture.

The policy of the Ministry of Labor was to avoid as far as possible disturbing the labor employed on other important work in munition centers and this policy led the exchanges to conduct their recruiting campaign for munition plants in non-industrial areas remote from the centers where labor was required. Appeals were made to women in the eastern and southern coast towns and in Tyneside towns where there is little industrial activity to take up work in munition plants. During one month (February, 1917) 5,118 women from some 200 different exchange districts were brought into eight large munition centers.

To one factory, for example, in the South of Scotland 1,641 women were brought during this period (February, 1917) from 63 different districts, including 228 from two Tyneside towns alone, 40 from Berwick, 55 from Inverness and 9 from one small Fifeshire village. To another in the West Midlands 772 women were imported from centers as far apart as Aberdeen and Penzance.[1]

The transfer of these women has necessitated unusual precautions on the part of the employment exchanges to see that proper arrangements have been made for their transportation, for their reception, board, lodging and general welfare. " Women submitted for work in national factories have to pass a medical test before they leave home and in all cases before proceeding on their journey, women are fully informed as to the conditions of employment, the details of the journey, the address of the

[1] *Labour Gazette*, 1917, p. 93.

exchange at the other end, and the nature and approximate cost of the lodging accommodation available." [1]

REPLACEMENT OF MEN BY WOMEN

The extent to which the extension of women's employment during the war has meant a replacement of men naturally varies in the different industries and occupational groups. In the munitions trades, speaking generally, the increase in the number of women has meant oftentimes an actual increase in the number of persons employed, although there has been, of course, much replacement. "In the metal and chemical trades, in which the volume of work has developed enormously, the increase in the number of women employed," says the *Labour Gazette*,[2] "is much in excess of the numbers replacing men. The reverse is true for all other industries; that is to say, the number of women employed on what was previously regarded as women's work has declined, and the increase in numbers is due entirely to replacement."

The extent to which women have replaced men in the various industries and occupations depends largely upon the interpretation given to the word "replacement." During the first two years of the war, in manufacturing industries there appears to have been very little direct replacement, *i.e.*, few women were employed to do precisely the same work which had been done by men. The reasons are, of course, not hard to discover—lack of training in the skilled trades and lack of physical strength in the unskilled ones. Some sort of reorganization of the industry was usually necessary to allow of the employment of women. In the munitions trades this was not hard to bring about, for the enormous increase in output permitted a splitting up of the processes, the introduction of machinery and therefore the conversion of work which had required the services of the highly skilled machinist into repetition work requiring little judgment. In shell making, for example, it was said that

[1] *Labour Gazette*, 1917, p. 93.
[2] *Ibid.*, p. 395.

The worker must be able to adjust the shell in its right position in the lathe, to manipulate the different levers and to apply the gauges. But since the "stops" are all arranged for her it requires little intelligence to know when to stop applying a given tool. It is unnecessary for the girls to lift the shells by hand, since there is a simple form of crane for this purpose adjacent to every lathe.[1]

Conditions were somewhat different in other than the engineering industries, but the general character of substitution was much the same wherever large numbers of women were employed.

In some industries replacement was made easier by a shifting in the demand. In the tailoring trade, for example, there was a lessening in the demand for high grade clothes requiring skilled male labor for their manufacture. Many men went into khaki and others undertook to practise economy. The result was an increased demand for military clothing and lower priced garments in whose manufacture cheap female labor could be utilized.[2]

There were, of course, certain instances in which women directly replaced men, in the sense that they did the same work which men did before the war. Most instances of this kind, at least during the first two years of the war, were to be found in other than the manufacturing industries. Even in these cases, although the work done by the women was substantially the same as that done by men, changes in working conditions and rules had sometimes to be made. On the tramways, for example, the old rule that conductors after six months' service must serve as drivers, which service required 12 days' training, was abandoned when women were employed as conductors.[3]

In the munitions trades, in which the agreement with the trade unions provided for dilution, the reorganization made necessary by the employment of women was readily secured by the government's demand that dilution be adopted as a condition to receiving government contracts. In other industries employers hesitated to undertake the necessary reorganization for a number of

[1] Kirkaldy, *Labour, Finance and the War*, pp. 146-147.
[2] *Ibid.*, p. 193.
[3] *Ibid.*, pp. 197-198.

reasons: uncertainty as to how long the war would last, uncertainty as to whether women would want to continue in industry after the war, unwillingness to furnish the training necessary, reluctance to incur the expense for new equipment, and the fear of opposition from trade unions.

Trade Unions Continue to Oppose Dilution

As the continuation of the war has called for the release of more men for military service the government has felt obliged to bring pressure upon employers in the nonmunition trades to attempt dilution and with this end in view it prepared early in 1917 to amend the Munitions of War Acts so as to give the government power to require dilution upon private work. The trade union opposition to this proposed amendment was so strong, however, that the government abandoned the attempt, but has sought to accomplish the same result by other means. By its plan of forbidding the employment of male labor of military age to fill vacancies in "the restricted trades," as described in the last chapter, and by its steady withdrawal of men for military service from these trades it has forced the employers to lessen their output or to attempt dilution.

In spite of the Treasury agreement which the government made with the representatives of the leading trade unions in March, 1915, and in spite of the authority conferred upon the Ministry of Munitions by the Munitions of War Act, trade union opposition to the policy of dilution did not cease, but continued to embarrass the government in the execution of its policy. Complaint was chiefly to the effect that employers were not consulting with workers already employed in their shops when they desired to introduce unskilled or female labor, in accordance with the terms of Schedule 2 of the Munitions of War Act, 1915, which provides among other things that:

Due notice shall be given to the workmen concerned wherever practicable of any changes of working conditions which it is desired to introduce as a result of the establishment becoming a controlled establishment, and opportunity for local consultation with workmen or their representatives shall be given, if desired.

Many local trade unionists seem to have considered that this practically amounted to a promise to obtain consent of the men in the shop before dilution was attempted. In order to clear up this point the Ministry issued in October-November, 1915, a circular (L6), which set forth the procedure recommended when an employer planned to change working conditions in his establishment. It was suggested that the employer consult with a committee appointed by the men in his shop and with the local trade union representative and obtain their consent, if possible, but the circular went on to say:

It is not intended that the introduction of the change should be delayed until concurrence of the work people is obtained. The change should be introduced after a reasonable time, and if the work people or their representatives desire to bring forward any question relating thereto they should follow the procedure laid down in Part I of the (Munitions) act.

In order to lessen the opposition to dilution on the part of the trade unionists the government enlarged the National Advisory Committee by adding other labor leaders and made it the Central Labor Supply Committee, whose function it was " to advise and assist " the Ministry of Munitions regarding the " most productive use of all available labor supplies." Local labor advisory boards were also established (Circular L57) "in such districts as the National Advisory Committee shall determine" to see that the provisions of Schedule 2 were being carried out by employers, etc., and to " aid dilution by pressing the abandonment of trade union restrictions in accordance with the Treasury agreement."

Keeping Records of Departures from Prewar Practices

Complaint has constantly been made by the workmen that paragraph 6 of Schedule 2 of the Munitions of War Act, which provides that

a record of the nature of the departure from the conditions prevailing when the establishment became a controlled establishment shall be kept and shall be open for inspection by the authorized representative of the government,

has not been observed by the employers. The difficulty here lies largely with the interpretation of the word " departure." Many changes made by the employer which he considers are not departures from the prewar practices have been made and no record kept because they have been due to changes in machinery or methods of production which call for the employment of a different grade of labor. Under the circumstances the employer calls this *new* work, while the laborers, having in mind the performance of similar work before the war, insists that this is a " departure " or " change," which requires a " record." Problems of this sort have been particularly perplexing in connection with dilution and the Ministry of Munitions has endeavored to lay down the principles to be followed although admitting that many cases arise in which there is a large element of doubt.

Thus in a memorandum (95) issued in September, 1916, by the Ministry of Munitions, it is stated that

> The introduction of new machinery or the alteration or improvement of existing machinery is not in itself a departure which requires to be recorded, but if such introduction, etc., is accompanied by, *e.g.*, a change in the class of labor employed on the job or the machine or which would have been employed on the machine in ordinary circumstances, a record of the facts should be made.[1]

The following rules are laid down for controlled establishments in the matter of dilution:

> 5. When the workshop or department, etc., has been started since the war or the job is new to the establishment and the work is carried on under different conditions, *e.g.*, with different classes of labor, from those which would customarily have obtained before the war, a change in working conditions for the purpose of records under the Munitions of War Acts, must be deemed to have taken place and a record should be made. The record should clearly state the existing conditions, *e.g.*, the class of labor employed, and state that the job or department, etc., is a new one, and that the establishment therefore had no previous practice. . . .
> 6. The following are examples of cases in which records are required in regard to a change in the class of labor employed: ·

[1] Memorandum M. M. 95 (embodying Circulars L65 and M. M. 56). Paragraph 7, *British Industrial Experience*, vol. 1, p. 376.

a. The employment of women on work formerly done by men or boys, whether skilled, semi-skilled or unskilled.
b. The employment of unskilled men on work formerly done by semi-skilled men.
c. The employment of unskilled men on work formerly done by skilled men.
d. The employment of semi-skilled men on work formerly done by skilled men.
e. The employment of men in one trade on work formerly done by another trade.
f. The employment of one class of tradesmen in a trade on the work of another class in the same trade, such as (1) riveters doing platers' or calkers' work, and (2) light platers doing sheet iron workers' work.
g. The mode of doing work as by splitting a skilled man's job into two parts, one of which continues to be done by a skilled man and the other is thereafter done by an unskilled man or woman.

It must be remembered that the making of this record is not an admission by the employer that such a change has been made in his mode of operations as requires the restoration at the close of the war of the prewar conditions, including the displacement of the laborers taken on during the war. This may or may not be the case. The principle is that during the war all such questions are in abeyance. The record is to be kept in order that reliable and accurate data may be available for the purpose of deciding questions as to the restoration of prewar conditions when once the war is over.

It is this very uncertainty as to how far restoration of prewar conditions can go which has been in part responsible for the restlessness and discontent of the rank and file of trade unionists. Week by week changes are taking place in the factory and workshop which apparently are fundamental and which the workmen believe can not be undone, no matter how solemn the pledge of Ministers and the House of Commons that the old conditions will be restored.

The discontent caused by dilution reached its head in April and May, 1917, when the apparent determination of the government to amend the Munitions Act so as to extend dilution to private work was one of the prominent reasons for an extensive series of strikes in the engineering establishments.

Very reluctantly the government abandoned the plan to require dilution of labor on private work. Repeated conferences were held between the government and the leading trade unionists in the engineering trades and changes in the mode of safeguarding skilled labor in these trades were suggested with the idea of making the dose more palatable. Progress seemed to be made and for a time at least the leaders seemed reconciled to the plan.[1] Opposition continued, however, on the part of the rank and file of the trade unionists and the " silent strike " of May, 1917, showed the futility of attempting to coerce them. When Mr. Churchill became Minister of Munitions, it was decided to abandon that part of the Munitions (Amendment) Bill of 1917 which provided for dilution on other than munitions work.

Dilution has nevertheless taken place on a large scale in private plants and, as we have seen, employers have been aided in bringing it about by the factory inspectors and other officials. It has been greatly facilitated, of course, by the government program forbidding the entrance of men of military age into the restricted occupations and by the rapid withdrawal from the nonessential trades of able bodied men for military service. In such cases probably the word " substitution " is more appropriate than " dilution."

[1] *British Industrial Experience*, vol. 1, p. 383.

CHAPTER VIII

Wages, Cost of Living, Hours of Labor, Welfare Work and Unemployment

We have already described the changes which took place in the rates of wages during the first year of the war and have observed that the advances made after January, 1915, generally took the form of bonuses "limited to the duration of the war."

EXTENT OF WAGE INCREASES

The official statistical report of wage changes for the year 1914, considered as a whole, may be said to have yielded only negative results. Of the 834,240 work people whose rates of wages were reported to have changed during the year, 407,230 had received a net increase amounting to £40,210 per week, while 404,960 sustained a net loss of £35,148 per week. The remaining 22,050 had had upward and downward changes which left their wages at the same level held at the beginning of the year.

The increases which took place were most marked in the building, engineering and shipbuilding and transport trades, while the decreases appeared in the mining, pig iron and iron and steel industries, where wages fluctuate with the selling prices of the products.[1]

The first trades to be affected by the upward changes in wages following the outbreak of the war were those more directly concerned with the output of munitions and the transport of troops and supplies, but the movement soon spread to all industries, as the number of enlistments rose, the shortage of labor became evident and rising prices not only justified demands for

[1] *Labour Gazette*, 1915, p. 30.

increased remuneration of labor but made such increases possible.

In October, 1915, the Board of Trade presented a table which showed that in various groups of trades, so far as reported to the department, 2,846,000 work people had received, since the beginning of the war, increases in wages estimated at £493,800 per week. These figures relate only to manual workers and are exclusive of shop assistants, clerks, salaried officials and domestic servants. The same authority estimated that 1,600,000 railway servants, seamen, agricultural laborers, police and governmental employes received in the aggregate increases in wages amounting to £270,000 per week.

While the wage increases affected all the principal trades, they were most marked in coal mining, engineering and shipbuilding, with large advances to general laborers in all districts throughout the country, and the advances were less noticeable in the building, printing and furnishing trades, in linen manufacture and in certain luxury trades.

Apart from these advances in the rates of pay, many workers had received substantial additions to their weekly earnings, owing to overtime work, speeding up and greater regularity of employment.[1]

Taking the year 1915 as a whole, the total number of people who were reported to the Board of Trade as having received war bonuses or increased rates of wages was 3,165,000. The total increases were £603,000 per week or an average per person of 3s. 10d. The increases were greatest in the trades mentioned in the October report.

There were three periods of rising wages and two of falling wages in the nineteen years preceding 1915, said the *Labour Gazette*, the periods of rising wages being the five years 1896-1900, the two years 1906-1907, and the five years, 1910-1914, but the increase for the single year 1915 was greater than the increase for any of these periods. Compared to the £603,100 weekly increase in 1915, the greatest increase recorded in any single year prior to 1915 was £208,588 in 1900.[2]

---

[1] *Labour Gazette*, 1915, pp. 354-355.
[2] *Ibid.*, 1916, p. 4.

All these figures relate only to changes in rates of wages. They do not take account of increased earnings resulting from overtime, greater regularity of employment, or the transference of work people from lower paid to higher paid employments. On the other hand they do not take into account the extensive substitution of women and young persons for men, which has tended to lower wages per head of those employed.[1]

The upward movement in rates of wages continued throughout the year 1916, affecting approximately the same number of persons, so far as these were reported. The number of persons reported to have received an increased rate of pay was 3,400,000 and the net weekly increase amounted to £595,000 over the preceding year, an average of about 3s. 6d. per person.

It should be remembered, said the *Labour Gazette*, that these figures " include increases granted not only to men but to boys and women and girls. The amount of the advances granted to men has usually been greater than that given to females and boys, and accordingly, if the average increases per head in the various trades be calculated, it will be affected by the proportion of male and female labor employed, and the average increase for men alone would be greater." [2]

As in the preceding year the advances in wages were greatest in coal mining, engineering, shipbuilding and the textile trades.

No complete account can be given (says the *Labour Gazette*) at this time, of all the changes in rates of wages which have been made since the beginning of the war, as among unorganized work people many changes escape attention, but so far as reported it appears that up to the end of December, 1916, nearly six million work people had received some advance. The amount varied, but, on average, the weekly increase to these work people was about 6s. per head, and in some of the industries directly concerned with the supply of war requirements ranged from 10s. to 12s. per week. [3]

The records for all previous years were dwarfed by that of the year 1917, when the number of work people reported to have received increases of wages was 4,690,000 and the total amount of the weekly increases was £2,183,000. The increases came

[1] *Labour Gazette*, 1916, pp. 4-5.
[2] *Ibid.*, 1917, p. 4.
[3] *Ibid.*, p. 3.

about in some trades by the operation of the sliding scales based
on the selling price of the products.   This was true in the
pig iron and the iron and steel industries.   In the engineering
and shipbuilding industries the awards of the Committee on
Production explain a large part of the increases and statutory
orders by the Ministry of Munitions, and arbitrators' awards or
trade agreements were responsible for others.   War grants and
bonuses were largely responsible for the advances in the textile,
the boot and shoe and other trades.   Of agricultural laborers it
is said that the rates of wages "continued to rise, partly as a
result of the rise in retail prices and the shortage of labor, and
partly, in some districts, in consequence of the enactment for
Great Britain of a minimum wage for adult able bodied men, at
the rate of 25s. per week, inclusive of the value of allowances in
kind." [1]

During the first six months of 1918, changes in wages have all
been in an upward direction.   A net increase in their weekly
wages of £1,174,700 had been received by 2,506,000 workers.
The increases were largely in the shape of war bonuses or war
grants by the Committee on Production.[2]

WAGE REGULATION

The government seems to have made no efforts to regulate
wages or to interfere in any way with the wage contract until
the passage of the Munitions of War Act of July 2, 1915.   Even
then, such regulations or interferences were limited to controlled
establishments, except that, under the compulsory arbitration
provisions of Part I of the act, differences in regard to the rates
of wages were among the differences which might be settled by
the methods there laid down, if such differences arose in munition establishments, or in other establishments, provided Part I
of the act had been applied to them by the King's proclamation.

The Act of 1915 applied to wages in controlled establishments
in that it provided that any proposal for any change in the rate
of wages, salary, etc., of any class of persons employed in such

[1] *Labour Gazette*, 1918, pp. 4-5.
[2] *Ibid.*, pp. 234, 279.

establishments must be submitted to the Minister of Munitions, who had power to withhold his consent within fourteen days of the date of the submission or to require that the matter be submitted to the arbitration tribunal.   Schedule 2 of the act also provided that " the relaxation of existing demarcation restriction or admission of semi-skilled or female labor shall not affect adversely the rates customarily paid for the job.   In cases where men who ordinarily do the work are adversely affected thereby, the necessary readjustments shall be made so that they can maintain their previous earnings."

This provision was inserted at the request of the unions and was intended to protect the wage rates which they had built up through a long process of collective bargaining.   It had the unexpected result that under the stimulus of piece rate production and with the aid of machinery and a high degree of division of labor these irreducible piece rates were made to yield to the semi-skilled workers earnings much in excess of those formerly received by the skilled laborers whose places had been filled and, what was more trying, in excess of the earnings of skilled workers who remained at work on a time wage basis.

Nevertheless, the men were at first not concerned with this problem of inequality of earnings, but feared to put forth their full exertions through fear of a reduction of the piece rates.   In November, 1915, therefore, the Minister of Munitions issued a notice (Circular 53) to the effect that workmen in controlled establishments need not fear that any considerable increase in output would lead to a reduction of the piece rates then being paid, in view of the fact that no change in wages or piece rates could be made without his consent.   He stated that he was prepared to exercise his powers, if necessary, in order to prevent a reduction of piece rates as a consequence of the increase of output due to suspension of restrictions.[1]

The amendments to the Munitions Acts made in January, 1916, made considerable extensions in the authority conferred upon the Minister of Munitions to regulate the wages of female labor engaged in munitions work and of semi-skilled and un-

[1] *British Industrial Experience during the War*, vol. 1, p. 288.

skilled male laborers employed in controlled establishments.
The substance of these amendments has already been given in
the chapter dealing with the Munitions of War Acts.[1] We there
noted that the powers of control extended much further in the
case of female laborers than in the case of male labor.

REGULATION OF WOMEN'S WAGES

The regulations issued by the Ministry of Munitions relating
to the wages of female laborers were numerous, but can be dealt
with here only in condensed form.[2]

Circular L2 which had been issued in October, 1915, to controlled establishments had fixed £1 a week as the time rate for
women and prescribed the same piece rates as for men. Lacking
the power to enforce these rates the Minister could only recommend them to employers. After the amendment to the act in
January, 1916, the prescribed rates of this circular were issued
as Order 181 (February 24, 1916)[3] to establishments in engineering and allied industries and were made binding on employers in those establishments. The £1 a week was made the minimum rate for piece workers as well as time workers and the
order stated that "the principle upon which the directions
proceed is that—on systems of payment by results—equal
payment shall be made to women as to the men for an equal
amount of work done." This order applied only to women doing
men's work and still left open the question as to the wages of
women doing work not recognized as men's work.

The Minister in March, 1916, acting under authority conferred
by the amended Munitions Act appointed a special arbitration
tribunal to deal with women's wages. To this tribunal were
promptly referred cases dealing with the wages of women munition workers for work not recognized as men's work.[4] The

[1] See pages 90-94, 98-100.
[2] This whole subject is fully covered in the study in this series by Andrews and Hobbs entitled *Economic Effects of the War upon the Women and
Children.* See chap. 10.
[3] *British Industrial Experience*, vol. 1, pp. 397-399.
[4] *Ibid.*, pp. 1029-1030.

tribunal issued awards which allowed a minimum wage of 4½d. per hour to women time workers and somewhat more to piece workers. Later these awards were gathered up into a general order issued by the Minister of Munitions applicable to women engaged on " munitions work of a class which prior to the war was not recognized as men's work."[1] Another order (No. 456)[2] issued the same day fixed rates of pay for girls under 18 when engaged on work which prior to the war was customarily done by male labor of 18 years of age and over. The time rates prescribed varied from 14s. a week for girls under 16 to 18s. a week for girls 17 years old and the piece rates allowed were from 30 to 10 per cent under those paid to men.

The terms of Order 447 called forth a vigorous protest from the women's trade unions. They claimed that making the rate of £1 a week a prescribed rate instead of a minimum rate was contradictory to the promises made by Mr. Lloyd George.[3] The reply was that the Minister's promise was only in regard to the wages of women on men's work. There were also complaints that no allowances had been made for overtime and Sunday work and that piece rate workers were not allowed to earn more than the time rates. A supplementary order (No. 618) was therefore issued on September 13, 1916, which regulated the rates for overtime, Sunday and holiday work and which provided that the piece rates should be so arranged that a woman or a girl of ordinary ability could earn at least one third more than her time rate for the same class of work.[4]

When first issued Order 447 had not been made applicable to all controlled establishments, but only to about 1,400 establishments engaged in the manufacture of armaments and ammunition ordnance and explosives, shipbuilding and the various branches of mechanical engineering. In January, 1917, upon recommendation of the arbitration tribunal, the Ministry of Munitions issued Orders Nos. 9 and 10 (the latter applicable to establish-

---

[1] Order No. 447 (July 6, 1916). *British Industrial Experience*, vol. 1, pp. 401-402.
[2] *Ibid.*, pp. 403-404.
[3] Andrews and Hobbs, *op. cit.*, p. 94.
[4] *British Industrial Experience*, vol. 1, pp. 407-408.

ments in rural districts)[1] which applied the main provisions of Order 447 to a number of additional trades.

One of the leading causes of complaint in connection with the operation of Order 447 was that women were not adequately paid when they were doing only a part of the work of skilled men. The women in most cases had to have the machines set up by skilled men. The trade unions held that this should not preclude their receiving the skilled men's rate. The employers held that this was unreasonable. There was no provision made in Circular L2 and the subsequent orders based thereon for any rate for women between the £1 a week and the fully skilled tradesmen's rate to women on time work, nor was there any allowance for work of a specially laborious nature or where there were exceptional local conditions.

To settle this controversy the Minister asked the advice of the Central Munitions Labor Supply Committee, which had drawn up the original Circular L2. That committee made recommendations which were referred to the special arbitration tribunal for its consideration. The recommendations of the two bodies were embodied in Order 888 issued on January 1, 1917,[2] which fixed £1 as the lowest rate for a week's work of 48 hours or less and an additional 6d. per hour for every hour up to 54 hours per week. Provision was made for the payment of higher rates for work of a specially laborious or responsible nature or performed under special circumstances. The specific rates of wages were not fixed for this work, but it was to be paid for "according to the nature of the work and the ability of the women."

The question of the pay for women employed on "work customarily done by fully skilled tradesmen" was not finally dealt with, but it was said that a further order on this subject would be issued. This was done on January 24 on the basis of arrangements which had been made by the dilution commissioner on the Clyde and on the Tyne in cases where women were employed on fully skilled men's work.[3] Order 49[4] declared that "a

---

[1] *British Industrial Experience*, vol. 1, pp. 417-422.
[2] *Ibid.*, p. 415.
[3] *Ibid.*, vol. 2, p. 1033.
[4] *Ibid.*, vol. 1, pp. 423-427.

woman shall be considered as not employed on the work customarily done by fully skilled tradesmen, but a part or portion only thereof if she does not do the customary setting up, or where there is no setting up, if she requires skilled supervision to a degree beyond that customarily required by fully skilled tradesmen undertaking the work in question." The women who did only a part of the work customarily performed by skilled men were to serve a probationary period for three months and were not entitled to the full pay until the end of such period. Thereafter, they were to be paid at the district rate of the tradesmen whose work they were performing, but, where it was necessary to incur extra cost for setting up or skilled supervision, the employer was allowed to deduct from the wages not more than 10 per cent to cover this extra cost.[1]

By April, 1917, the wages of women in controlled establishments had been regulated in approximately 3,585 establishments where women and girls were employed on men's work, in about 3,875 establishments where women and girls were employed on work not recognized as men's work, and in 90 establishments in which women and girls were employed on wood work for aircraft. In this last named group, although the wages fixed in September, 1916, approximated those fixed for men's work, there was no recognition of the principle, equal pay for equal work. The aircraft industry had expanded enormously since the war began and " it was felt that to legislate for women's wages on the customs existing prior to the war might unduly hamper its development." [2]

On April 4, 1917, the Minister of Munitions decided after consultation with the special arbitration tribunal, " in view of the increasing cost of living and of the general increase in the wages of men in the engineering and shipbuilding industries," to allow certain increases in the wages of women workers to take effect from April 1, 1917. The increases amounted to 4s. a week for women time workers employed on men's work and

---

[1] *British Industrial Experience*, vol. 1, p. 425. A consolidated and amended order relating to women's wages was issued May 8, 1918. Reprinted in *Labour Gazette*, 1918, pp. 255-257.
[2] *British Industrial Experience*, vol. 2, p. 1032. See also Andrews and Hobbs, *loc. cit.*, pp. 98-99.

1d. per hour for those employed on work not recognized as men's work, with corresponding adjustments in the wages for girls and for piece workers.[1]

Another advance in the wages of women and girls employed on munitions work was made on August 16, 1917.[2] The increase amounted to 2s. 6d. a week for women 18 years of age and over and 1s. 3d. per week for girls under 18. They applied to both time and piece workers and were payable to all women and girls over their weekly earnings. The advances were intended to meet the increased cost of living and were made as a result of representations made by several trade unions. It was understood at this time that, as in the case of the men munition workers in the engineering trades, women munition workers would have the right to have their wages reviewed by the Committee on Production or other tribunal every four months and have them adjusted to the change in the cost of living.[3]

A new order (No. 546) in respect to women's wages was issued by the Ministry of Munitions on May 8, 1918, which besides consolidating existing orders made certain changes in the rates of pay, usually in the way of an advance over previous rates. Some of the important alterations are as follows:

(a) Higher wages are authorized for work especially dangerous, laborious or responsible.

(b) The principle of differential time rates for time workers and those on systems of payment for results has been abolished.

The percentage over time rates which piece work prices or premium bonus time allowances are required to yield has been altered from 33 1/3 to 25 per cent.

(c) Special rates have been fixed for wood work processes and for aircraft work which yield to the women workers not less than 6d. per hour.[4]

The trade unions have criticized the government for fixing standard rather than minimum rates of wages for women work-

[1] Circular L85, *British Industrial Experience*, vol. 1, pp. 428-432.
[2] Order 893. *Ibid.*, p. 453.
[3] *Christian Science Monitor*, September 6, 1917, quoted in *Monthly Review of U. S. Bureau of Labor Statistics*, October, 1917, p. 83.
[4] *Monthly Labor Review*, U. S. Bureau of Labor Statistics, August, 1918, pp. 160-161.

ers, but the government has defended the practice and claims that experience has justified its adoption. The women workers are for the most part unorganized and advances in wages come to them not through collective bargaining but through a compulsory order.

> If the orders had fixed minimum rates there would have been a tendency for women to agitate that they should be increased on any and every pretext on the principle that having got so much by no effort of their own they should be able to double their emoluments by determined agitation. Moreover, many of the conditions under which women are employed on munitions work must necessarily be of a temporary nature and continue only for the war period. It is of advantage both to employers and employed to divide the work done by women into two broad classes for which both parties know definitely the rate that will be paid.[1]

In spite of the considerable increases which have been made from time to time in the wages of women munition workers the women's organizations claim that the advances in wages lag so far behind the advances in prices that the government standard wages have about the same purchasing power that the minimum rates fixed for the sweated trades had before the war. The increase in the cost of the items entering into the ordinary working man's budget had been about 75 per cent between July, 1914, and June, 1917, so that the average rate for women workers which the Minister of Munitions said in June, 1917, was 25s. would have the same purchasing power as 14s. would have had in 1914. It must be remembered, however, that the steady employment and the overtime worked have meant that the earnings of women have been greater than before the war, even though it be admitted that the overtime is undesirable. It must also be admitted that the rates of pay of women in the controlled establishments are higher than in uncontrolled establishments for the same kinds of work. Recognition of this fact has caused the women's organizations to demand that the government rates be extended to all work on government contracts.[2] Other government departments, it is said, have not been as generous

---

[1] *British Industrial Experience*, vol. 2, p. 1036.
[2] Mary Conyngton, "Women in the Munition Trades," *Monthly Review*, May, 1918, p. 156.

as the Ministry of Munitions in the matter of women's wages, though the Admiralty has generally advanced its rates to the level of the munitions trades. The Post Office Department has made its wage increases in the form of war bonuses and these have been larger for men than for women. The strongest complaints have been made in regard to female clerks working under civil service rules whose weekly wages were only from 20s. to 26s. for clerical work and 30s. for supervisions. The women were also receiving much less than men received for similar work.[1]

In those private industries in which minimum wage rates are fixed by trade boards under the Act of 1909, the minimum rates have been advanced in an effort to meet the increases in the cost of living. Although considerable advances were made by the tailoring, confectionery and tin box boards, it does not appear that the increases had been sufficient to make up for the decreased purchasing power of money.[2] Although the scope of several boards has been widened during the war no new boards have been set up, except the agricultural wages boards provided by the Corn Production Act of August 21, 1917.[3] Although these agricultural boards are to fix minimum wages for women as well as for men the legal requirement that these rates must be such as will yield to the worker an average of at least 25s. a week does not apply to women.

In those trades in which women are employed and in which there are strong labor organizations the efforts of the unions to protect their wage standards have generally led to agreements whereby women substituted for men are to be paid the men's rates. These agreements have been of special importance on the railways and in the cotton, woolen and worsted, china and earthenware, and boot and shoe industries and have improved materially the position of the women workers.[4]

---

[1] Andrews and Hobbs, *op. cit.*, p. 104.
[2] *Ibid.*, pp. 101-102.
[3] As explained later (pages 307-308) legislation has been enacted in 1918 making possible the extension of the trade boards without necessitating Parliament sanction in each case.
[4] Andrews and Hobbs, *op. cit.*, pp. 102-103.

In those trades in which there are neither legal regulations nor trade agreements, the wages of women workers have advanced from time to time because of the growing scarcity of labor, but " there is no reason whatever to suppose that the rates approximate to the rates of the men displaced." [1] The smallest increases in women's wages appear to have been in those trades which employed large numbers of women prior to the war. Here the influence of custom and the natural desire on the part of employers not to spoil the labor market have prevented increases in wages except such as have been necessary to prevent the workers from transferring to the munitions and other trades. Such increases as have been granted have generally taken the form of war bonuses.[2]

REGULATION OF MEN'S WAGES

The problem of the regulation of men's wages has been much simpler than that of women's wages, because of the more limited scope of the regulations.

No regulations of men's wages were authorized by law until after the passage of the Munitions of War (Amendment) Act, 1916. Section 7 of that act empowered the Minister of Munitions " to give directions as to the rate of wages, hours of labor or conditions of employment of semi-skilled and unskilled men employed in any controlled establishment on munitions work, being work of a class which prior to the war was customarily undertaken by skilled labor, or as to the time rates for the manufacture of complete shells and fuses and cartridge cases in any controlled establishment in which such manufacture was not customary prior to the war." All such directions were binding on the owners of such establishments and on the contractors and subcontractors employing labor therein. Prior to the passage of this amendment, the Ministry of Munitions had attempted to control the matter of remuneration of semi-skilled labor, when

---

[1] *The Position of Women after the War*, p. 8.
[2] Andrews and Hobbs, *op. cit.*, p. 105.

substituted for skilled labor, by means of Circular L3 issued in October, 1915, at the same time as Circular L2 dealing with women's wages was put out. Both circulars were prepared by the Central Munitions and Labor Supply Committee and their provisions could in the nature of things only be of an advisory character. After the amendment to the Munitions of War Act these provisions of Circular L3 were made mandatory by the issue of Order 182.[1]

By the terms of this order semi-skilled and unskilled male laborers employed to do the work of skilled labor were to be paid the same time rates, piece prices and premium bonus rates as were customarily paid when the work was performed by skilled labor. These rates were not to be altered unless the means or methods of manufacture were changed, and all overtime, night shift, Sunday labor and holiday allowances were to be paid on the same basis as for skilled laborers. In the case of time ratings for the manufacture of complete shells and fuses and cartridges, where such manufacture was not customarily undertaken by an establishment before the war, the rates were fixed at 10s. below the current district rates for turners, but were not to be lower than 28s. a week, except that the starting rate for inexperienced men might be 26s. for a period not longer than two months. Extra sums were to be paid for setting up, fuse making and shell making machines. This order was not regarded as of great importance as the work of machining shells, fuses and cartridge cases has been done for the most part by women and the other work covered by the order has usually been dealt with by agreement between the unions and employers, for the order was not intended to prevent or discourage collective bargaining. Whenever such an agreement has been made between an employers' federation and a trade union the wages fixed by such agreement become the district rate for this class of work and any of the federated firms which are controlled are free to give effect to the agreement without awaiting the sanction of the Minister.[2] A special tribunal to

[1] *British Industrial Experience,* vol. 1, p. 454.
[2] *Ibid,* vol. 2, p. 1038.

deal with cases in dispute coming within the scope of the order
was constituted in March, 1916, at the same time and having the
same chairman as the tribunal for women's wages. Very few
cases involving men's wages have been referred to it.[1]

Complaints were made by employes in nonfederated controlled establishments and by employers in the federated ones
that they were suffering discriminations as a result of the application of awards raising wages in the federated establishments.
An interview was sought with the Minister of Munitions, who,
after considering the matter, informed the parties on February
26, 1917, that he " was prepared to take such steps as may be
necessary to secure that any award given in the trade in question
shall be applied to nonfederated controlled establishments."
Later this rule was incorporated in the Munitions of War Act,
1917. The movement for the standardization of wages made
rapid progress during the year 1917 and an agreement was
reached between associations of employers and of employes in
the engineering and foundry trades that wages should be settled
by arbitration at four month intervals during the war—in
February, June and October.[2] In this way it was hoped that it
would be possible to adjust wages to the changes in the cost of
living.

In September, 1917, the Minister of Munitions extended to
various engineering and foundry trades in England and Scotland
the terms of an award of the Committee on Production, allowing
a bonus of 3s. per week for men and 1s. 6d. for boys under 18,
these bonuses " to be regarded as war advances intended to
assist in meeting the increased cost of living and are to be
recognized as due to and dependent on the existence of the
abnormal conditions now prevailing in consequence of the
war." [3] Bonuses of 5s. for men and 2s. 6d. for boys were allowed
in several trades in September to date from April 1, 1917.[4] A
bonus of 12½ per cent on earnings was allowed " fully qualified

[1] *British Industrial Experience*, vol. 2, p. 1037.
[2] *Ibid.*, p. 1039.
[3] *Ibid.*, vol. 1, pp. 462-470.
[4] *Ibid.*, pp. 470-473.

skilled engineers and molders " in October, 1917.[1]   The same
allowance was made to " plain time workers in the shipbuilding
and munitions trades " by the War Cabinet towards the close of
1917.[2]   .

A movement which has made considerable progress in Great
Britain during the war, although it has had to meet the opposing
traditions of the trade unions, is the adoption of the system of
payment by results.   The shipbuilding trades have agreed to
accept the principle and the rates of pay are to be fixed by agreements arranged by district conferences of employers and employes.   In many individual establishments the necessity for
increased output has also led to the introduction of various
systems of piece work for different occupations.   The chief
difficulties encountered are said to be (1) the fixing of prices
for piece work and of the time period for premium results; and
(2) the application of payment by results to groups of workers
to whom individual piece work or premium bonus is unsuited.
It was said in the official reports on this subject that the first
difficulty seemed best met by " skilled rate fixing and publicity
as to the methods of wage payment and the changes therein.
The second difficulty, it was said, had been overcome by " the
institution of various kinds of collective or overhead bonuses." [3]
The system of payment by results and the difficulties of adjusting wages under this system in a way satisfactory to the piece
workers themselves and as between piece and time rate workers
was one of the causes of industrial unrest which was reported
on by the commissions appointed in 1917 to deal with that
subject.[4]

Cost of Living

It is impossible on the basis of available information to
present here any accurate comparison of the changes which have
taken place during the war in the wages or earnings of the work-

[1] *British Industrial Experience*, vol. 1, pp. 474-475.
[2] *Labour Gazette*, 1918, p. 6.
[3] *British Industrial Experience*, vol. 2, p. 1039.
[4] See below, chap. ix.

ing classes and of the cost of the commodities which must largely enter into the consumption of the ordinary working man's family. Index numbers are available which show the rate of increase in the prices of food and there is some information concerning the prices of other commodities. Index numbers are lacking which would show the rate of increase in the prices of labor.

The index numbers for the wholesale prices of 47 selected commodities, taking the year 1900 as the basis, represented by the number 100, show an advance from 113.6 for the first seven months of 1914 to 143.8 for the year 1915, 186.5 for 1916 and 242.9 for 1917.[1] On the same basis the index numbers showing retail prices of food, weighted in accordance with the proportionate expenditures in prewar budgets, show an increase up to July 1, 1918, of 114 per cent in the large towns, 106 per cent in the small towns and 110 per cent throughout the kingdom, over the prices for July, 1914.[2]

In spite of very rapid advances in wages during the war, as shown in the early pages of this chapter, it is doubtful whether such advances have been anywhere near equal to the above increases in either wholesale or retail prices. When pay for overtime, Sundays and holidays, besides the greater regularity of employment, are taken into consideration, perhaps the economic situation of the English working man or working woman is not materially worse than it was before the war, but if so, this means that it requires more effort to maintain the same standard of living. As a matter of fact, the old standard is not being maintained, but substitutes have been made for commodities largely consumed before the war. The *Labour Gazette* calls attention to changes in dietary which have been made and says in relation to the above changes in the retail prices of food:

If eggs were omitted from the dietary, margarine substituted for butter and the consumption of sugar and fish reduced to one-half of that prevailing before the war, the general percentage increase between July, 1914, and the 1st of January, 1918, instead of being 106, would be 59.[3]

[1] *Labour Gazette*, 1918, p. 5.
[2] *Ibid.*, p. 266.
[3] *Ibid.*, p. 5. By July 1, 1918, this number would have been 67. *Labour Gazette*, 1918, p. 26.

If this statement is intended to show how a laboring man may be able to modify his diet so as to meet the increase in the cost of food, it may possess interest and value, but if it is presented to indicate that such changes nullify or render of no account actual changes in purchasing power, it is equivalent to saying that a man's standard of living is in no danger of being lowered as long as he is able to practice economies and make use of substitutes.

Of much more significance, as showing that the above figures do not necessarily mean that the advances in food prices have made the position of the working man a precarious one, is the statement in the *Gazette* that rents of working class dwellings are not appreciably higher than before the war and that many other items of expenditure have not advanced, on the average, as much as that for food. The *Gazette* has endeavored to estimate the extent of the increase in the cost of living, taking the working man's family budget as a whole.

The increase from July, 1914, to January 1, 1918, in the cost of all the items ordinarily entering into the working class family expenditure, including food, rent, clothing, fuel and light, etc., may be estimated at between 80 and 85 per cent, taking the same quantities of the various items at each date and eliminating advances arising from increased taxation, and between 85 and 90 per cent, if increases due to taxation are included.[1] By July 1, 1918, the general increase is estimated at between 100 and 105 per cent including taxation and about 7 per cent less "if the amount of increased taxation on commodities is deducted.[2]

In July, 1917, one of the eight commissions appointed by the Prime Minister to investigate the causes of industrial unrest quoted the *Labour Gazette* as authority for the statement that between July, 1914, and June, 1917, the increase in the cost of food amounted to 102 per cent, the increase in the cost of living from 70 to 75 per cent, the increase in the cost of food on "an economical basis" to 70 per cent, while with regard to wages the commission says: "The highest figures put before us only showed an increase in earnings of something like 40 or 50 per cent of prewar rates."[3]

[1] *Labour Gazette*, 1918, p. 5.
[2] *Ibid.*, p. 266.
[3] *Industrial Unrest in Great Britain.* Bulletin No. 237 of the United States Bureau of Labor Statistics, p. 47.

On September 1, 1916, the President of the Board of Trade appointed a departmental committee " to investigate the principal causes which have led to the increase of prices of commodities of general consumption since the beginning of the war, and to recommend such steps, if any, with a view to ameliorating the situation, as appear practicable and expedient, having regard to the necessity of maintaining supplies. The committee made an interim report in about three weeks from the date of its appointment, in which it noted the increases in prices which we have mentioned and, while they admitted that the rates of wages had not kept pace with the increase in prices of food and other necessaries, they concluded that after taking into account greater regularity of employment, additional overtime, night work, etc. :

There is less total distress in the country than in an ordinary year of peace, the majority of the classes which chronically suffer from distress being in unusually regular employment, and that this, together with the higher wages earned by, and greater needs of, so many skilled and unskilled workers employed directly and indirectly in the production of munitions of war, has tended to increase considerably, in some directions, the total demand for food. On the other hand, certain classes normally in regular employment, whose earnings have not risen in the same proportion as the cost of living—for example, the cotton operatives and some classes of day wage workers and laborers—are hard pressed by the rise in prices and actually have to curtail their consumption, even though the pressure of high prices may have been mitigated in some cases by the employment of members of a family in munition works and by the opening of better paid occupations to women.[1]

With reference to the prices of meat, milk and bacon, the only commodities dealt with in this interim report, the committee made various recommendations having to do with the increase of shipping and refrigerating facilities, prohibition of the slaughter of young live stock, increased use of women for milking and dairy work, government or local control over the distribution and prices of meats and milk, and increased economies in the supply of meat to the army.[2] Seven of the twelve members of the committee also signed a memorandum in which they recommended that the government " enlarge its purchases of meat and

[1] Board of Trade, Departmental Committee on Prices. Interim report on meat, milk and bacon. Quoted in *Monthly Review*, January, 1917, p. 51.
[2] *Monthly Review*, January, 1917, p. 55.

bacon from outside sources and, where possible, become the sole purchaser, and should insist upon the purchasing public getting the full benefit of advantageous buying." It was further recommended that a large measure of public control be exercised over home supplies and that reasonable prices be fixed. The action which the government was taking with reference to coal and wool it was thought might well be extended to meat, bacon and milk.[1]

This is not the place to describe the methods by which the British Government has undertaken to exercise control over the production, prices and distribution of foodstuffs in order to meet the needs of both the military forces and the civil population. It suffices to say that control has been exercised in many ways, by stimulating increased production at home, by direct governmental purchases either alone or in cooperation with her allies of imported food supplies, by control of shipping with a view to increasing the importation of food and lessening that of less needed commodities, by prescribing maximum prices of the commodities whose supplies could be controlled, by compulsory rationing of sugar and later of meat, flour and bread, by prescribing methods of manufacture of flour, bread, etc., by encouraging economy in the use of food, by regulating the price and distribution of milk, by limiting the use of grain for the manufacture of alcoholic liquors, by the establishment of meatless days, by the promotion of vegetable gardening and keeping of pigs by cottagers and by licensing the manufacture and sale of food.[2]

The steps taken by the Ministry of Food to carry out the recommendations of the commissions on industrial unrest with regard to the control which the government should exercise over the prices and distribution of food are dealt with in the following chapter.[3] The government has also fixed the price of coal at the pit's mouth[4] and has forbidden any increase in the rent

[1] *Labour Gazette*, 1916, p. 364.
[2] These methods are described in the *Monthly Review of the United States Bureau of Labor Statistics*, March, 1917, pp. 392-407; June, 1917, pp. 928-945, and December, 1917, pp. 100-101.
[3] Pages 264-265. See also *British Industrial Experience*, vol. 2, pp. 1100-1101.
[4] Act of July 25, 1915. *British Industrial Experience*, vol. 1, p. 899.

of small dwelling houses or of the rate of interest on mortgages on such dwellings.[1] While these measures have not prevented a continuation of the rise of prices, especially of food, they do show that the government has seriously concerned itself with the problem and its measures have doubtless provided a more equitable distribution of the supplies available than would have taken place without regulation. Control over the prices of commodities can not well be made effective unless control can be had at the same time of the supply and (or) demand forces. Many of these forces are not under government control or can not be exercised in war times without affecting detrimentally other and more important matters. The real causes for the increase in the prices of food are well stated in the report of Hon. G. N. Barnes, setting forth the steps which the Ministry of Food had taken to comply with the recommendations of the commissions of industrial unrest. " *Why prices are high.*—Increased currency causes an increased demand for goods. If currency is multiplied faster than the supply of commodities, the result is a rise in prices. If the increase of currency is accompanied by an actual falling off in the supply of commodities, the rise will be very marked. Assuming money to mean everything which is accepted in payment for goods, there is probably more money in circulation in the country than ever before, and a great deal of this money is spent in buying food. For various reasons there is actually less food to buy; there is increased consumption by the armies in the field; there is reduced production owing to shortage of labor at home; ships carrying foodstuffs are sunk, and there is a scarcity of available tonnage to bring in more food."[2]

Hours of Labor

We have already shown how employers early in the war began to make use of overtime as a means of increasing production and of making good the shortage of labor caused by the recruiting campaign. We have also noticed that the government felt that

[1] Act of December 23, 1915. *British Industrial Experience,* vol. 1, p. 859.
[2] *Ibid.,* vol. 2, pp. 1101-1102.

the need for munitions was so urgent that it was necessary to relax the laws restricting the hours of employment of women and young persons which had been built up through a long series of years for the purpose of protecting the health and morals of these classes of persons. Since the laws relate only to women and children and since the subject of hours of labor, so far as it relates to these classes of persons, is dealt with in another monograph of this series,[1] it will not be necessary here to review at length the evidence on which the government has acted to restore the legal restrictions which had been so hastily withdrawn in order to meet an emergency. It is sufficient to say that in reimposing this restrictive legislation and in some cases even extending it, the authorities have not been governed by senti-mental considerations or even primarily by considerations affect-ing the health and welfare of the working classes, but the investi-gations which have been made by government order and the regulations which have been imposed, following these investi-gations, have been dictated primarily by the consideration as to what scale of hours is likely to give the largest amount of pro-duction.

At first the reports of the factory inspectors were very op-timistic as to the effect of the partial removal of the restrictions on the hours of labor of women. The patriotism of the workers and their desire to do their part in the prosecution of the war caused them not only to accept willingly enough the extension of the permissible hours of labor, but to work with " a spirit of sustained, untiring effort never seen before and most admirable." The Chief Inspector of Factories and Workshops in his report for 1914,[2] reported that there was " a noticeable absence in all the reports from the inspectors of any evidence of increased sick-ness," and while it was admitted that in some trades it was found necessary to reduce overtime because of the strain imposed, he was able to reach the following conclusion: " Looking at the question as a whole, it is probably safe to say that, whatever may be the future effects of so prolonged a strain, there is at present

[1] Andrews and Hobbs, *op. cit.*
[2] *Ante*, pp. 54-57.

no sign that workers have been injuriously affected." At this time the general order of the Chief Inspector's department permitted overtime for women and boys over 16 of 5 hours a week or 7½ hours in munitions establishments under certain conditions as to meal hours. The orders also permitted women and young persons to be employed at night, a return to a condition which had been abolished by law in 1844 and by international agreement in 1906. The conclusions of the inspectors with regard to the effects of overtime on production at this time were that " while long and even excessive hours can be worked with advantage for short periods, continued overtime, if not kept within proper limits, soon fails in its object and ceases to aid production." [1]

Before many months had passed a change in the character of the reports as to the effects of overtime work is noticeable. Not only the inspectors, but in many cases the employers, were beginning to note a falling off in production and were beginning to question the wisdom of overtime work. More sickness among the operatives was noticeable and even when the employes were not sick they did not present themselves regularly for employment.

The government had not satisfied itself with exempting from the provisions of the factory acts those factories which belonged to the Crown or were engaged on work for the government, but had, under authority of the Defense of the Realm Acts, extended the scope of exemption to " any factory or workshop in which the Secretary of State is satisfied that by reason of the loss of men through enlistment or transference to government service, or of other circumstances arising out of the present war, exemption is necessary to secure the carrying on of work required in the national interest." This increased very greatly the scope of exemption and led to a rush of applications to be allowed to work overtime. It was noticeable, however, said the Chief Inspector,[2] that there was a " marked reduction in the amount of latitude sought and allowed." There were few applications for

[1] Report of Chief Inspector for 1914, p. 60.
[2] Annual Report of Chief Inspector for 1915, p. 8.

permission to work on Sundays and requests for Saturday afternoon work were less common. The limits of overtime allowed
by the general order of the department remained as in the preceding year, with special orders for large munition firms which
allowed somewhat more than the usual amount. Even among
these firms there was a distinct tendency to reduce the hours of
work. Sunday labor had been found particularly unsatisfactory, for it resulted in a loss of time on other days of the
week.[1]

In September, 1915, the Minister of Munitions appointed a
Health of Munition Workers Committee to consider and advise
on questions of industrial fatigue, hours of labor, and other
matters affecting the personal health and physical efficiency of
workers in munition factories and workshops. The Chairman
of the committee was Sir George Newman, M.D., and the other
members of the committee represented not only the medical pro-
fession, but the factory inspector's office, the trade unions and
the employing interests. The committee made its first report in
November, 1915, and has continued to make reports from time
to time during the war. Its conclusions have been reached on
the basis not only of oral testimony from managers, foremen
and workers, but on numerous special studies and investigations,
and its findings have been mainly responsible for modifications
made by the Ministry of Munitions and other departments in
their orders relating to production and to the health and safety
of workers.

The first report (Memorandum 1) related to Sunday labor.
The committee found that " the great majority of the employers
consulted are unfavorably disposed to Sunday labor." They
found that supervision was difficult and imposed a severe strain
on the foremen, that it meant high wages and an unsatisfactory
output and they felt that " the seventh day, as a period of rest,
is good for body and mind." The testimony of trade unionists
showed that though a high rate of wages had made Sunday labor
popular for a time, the men were beginning to feel the need of
more rest and that this need was responsible for much of the lost

[1] Annual Report of Chief Inspector, 1915.

time. The committee concluded that: " The evidence before the committee has led them strongly to hold that if the maximum output is to be secured and maintained for any length of time, a weekly period of rest must be allowed. Except for quite short periods, continuous work, in their view, is a profound mistake and does not pay—output is not increased."

The committee recommended that Sunday labor be confined to sudden emergencies and to repairs, tending furnaces, etc., in which cases the employes should be given a rest day during some other part of the week. Although the committee felt that the need for this relief from Sunday labor was more urgent for " protected " persons than for the adult males, it considered that " the discontinuance of Sunday labor should be of universal application." Furthermore, the committee felt that " the foreman and the higher management even more certainly require definite periods of rest." [1]

An interdepartmental committee was set up late in 1915 by the Home Office, the Admiralty, the Ministry of Munitions and other supply departments to provide for the regulation of the hours of labor on government work. This committee had no statutory power to deal with the hours of labor of adult male labor, but after repeated conferences with employers in the munition industries it secured the discontinuance of Sunday labor in the northeast coast area. This committee found more opposition on the part of employes than on the part of employers to the discontinuance of Sunday labor, owing to the fact that high rates of pay were granted for this work and the claim that the high cost of living had made this work necessary.

The Ministry of Munitions made known its views on the undesirability of Sunday labor by the issuance of Circular L180 and M. M. 10, in which it stated that " both in the interest of the workers and production " a weekly rest period, preferably Sunday, should be given " to all classes of labor, male, female, adult and juvenile " and held that overtime work was more desirable than Sunday labor. Finally in April, 1917, the Min-

[1] *Sunday Labor* (Memorandum No. 1), Bulletin, United States Bureau of Labor Statistics, No. 221, pp. 14-19.

istry of Munitions issued Circular L86, calling for the discontinuance of Sunday labor in all controlled establishments on and after May 1.[1]

In a special report on hours of work issued by the Chief Inspector of Factories in 1917, it is stated in regard to industries in general, not merely munition plants:

> Sunday work has now been reduced to small dimensions; it is stated that experience has proved it to be unprofitable and even harmful, that employers generally and the large majority of the work people have long been converted to this view, and that its sole attraction is that it brings with it increased wages, on which account there has, in certain limited areas, been some opposition to its discontinuance.[2]

The Health of Munition Workers Committee made a report (Memorandum No. 5) in January, 1916, which dealt with hours of work and another report (Memorandum No. 12) in August, 1916, which dealt with output in relation to hours of work. The aim of the committee was stated to be " to ascertain the hours of employment most likely to produce a maximum output over periods of months, or maybe even of years," and its recommendations were made on the expectation that the war would be of long duration. The information collected dealt only with the hours of employment of workers engaged on the production of munitions of war for which the Minister of Munitions was responsible. All classes of workers whose output was measured were on piece work and there were no trade union restrictions upon output. The committee's conclusions as to output briefly stated were:

1. Women on moderately heavy work will not attain a maximum output if they work for more than 60 hours per week, and observations seem to show that an equally good output will be secured in a working week of 56 hours or less.

2. Women on light work apparently reach their maximum productivity in a working week of about 62 hours.

3. For men engaged on very heavy work the maximum output is secured when the hours of work are 56 or less per week.

4. For men engaged in moderately heavy work, the most effective work is secured when the hours are about 60 per week.

[1] Andrews and Hobbs, op. cit., p. 124.
[2] Labour Gazette, 1918, p. 305.

5. For men or youths engaged on light work maximum output is attained only when the hours of work are 70 or more.

6. The best hours of work, suited for peace times, are in every case considerably shorter than those mentioned.[1]

Later investigations made by the same committee and extending over a longer time seem to show that the maximum output can in most cases be secured with hours considerably less than those just given and should be as stated below:

1. Women on moderately heavy work reach maximum productivity at 50 hours per week.

2. Women on light work produced more in a working week of 54.8 hours than in one of 64.9 and in a week of 48.1 hours their output was only 1 per cent less than in the week of 64.9 hours.

3. Men on heavy work of sizing produced 21 per cent more in 51.2 hours per week than in a week of 58.2 hours.

4. Fifteen youths on light labor produced only 3 per cent less output in a week of 54.5 hours than in one of 72.5 hours.[2]

The committee found the following objections to extended overtime:

1. It is liable to impose too severe a strain on the workers.

2. It frequently results in a large amount of lost time.

3. It imposes a very serious strain upon the management, the executive staff, and the foreman, both on account of the actual length of the hours worked and the increased worry and anxiety to maintain output and quality of work.

4. It is liable to curtail unduly the period of rest and sleep available for those who have to travel long distances to and from their work, a matter of special importance in the case of young persons.

5. The fatigue entailed increases the temptation to men to indulge in the consumption of alcohol; they are too tired to eat and seek a stimulant.[3]

While the committee had not found that the strain of long hours had caused any serious breakdown among workers there had been many indications of fatigue and there was medical evidence tending to show that the long hours were making themselves felt on older men and on those suffering from physical

[1] *Output in Relation to Hours of Work* (Memorandum No. 12), Bulletin of United States Bureau of Labor Statistics, No. 221, pp. 31-46.

[2] *Monthly Review of U. S. Bureau of Labor Statistics*, November, 1917, pp. 61 62.

[3] *Hours of Work* (Memorandum No. 5), Bulletin, U. S. Bureau of Labor Statistics, No. 221, p. 21.

infirmity. One thing brought out in this report, as well as in that of the Chief Inspector of Factories, was that the increased pay resulting from overtime had enabled the workers to secure better food and greater material comfort generally and these had helped to counteract the strain of long hours.[1]

The committee shows much sympathy with the 48 hour week so strongly urged by many persons. To make it a success would however require a reorganization in factory management which would be difficult to bring about in war times. The committee recommended that for adult males the average weekly hours (exclusive of meal times) should not exceed 65 to 67. Hours in excess of this should only be worked for short periods and to meet sudden and unexpected circumstances. The overtime should be concentrated within three or four days a week and when overtime is worked there should be no Sunday labor. For women and girls the committee held that " continuous work in excess of the normal legal limit of 60 hours per week ought to be discontinued as soon as practicable." Some reasonable time should be allowed for readjustment. For boys employed to assist adult male workers the committee, " though with great hesitation," recommend that they be allowed to be employed on overtime up to the maximum suggested for men, " but every effort should be made not to work boys under 16 more than 60 hours per week." [2]

The committee recommended day and night shifts in preference to overtime, but did not desire it to be thought that they regarded night work as a good thing. The arguments against it were that it was uneconomical because of the higher rates of pay, supervision was frequently unsatisfactory, conditions of lighting seldom good and workers got less satisfactory sleep in the day time, and the unfamiliar meal hours were likely to derange digestion.[3]

The conclusions of the committees on hours of work were confirmed by the scientific investigations into the nature, causes

[1] Bulletin of U. S. Bur. Labor Stat. 221, p. 21. Annual report of Chief Inspector of Factories, 1915, p. 9.
[2] *Hours of Labor, loc cit.,* pp. 25-26.
[3] *Ibid.,* pp. 26-28.

and results of industrial fatigue made for the Health of Munition Workers Committee and for the British Association for the Advancement of Science [1] and by the reports on sickness and injury (Memorandum No. 10) [2] and on employment of women and girls (Memorandum No. 4) [3] also made for the Health of Munition Workers Committee. There was general agreement that "overtime labor is physiologically and economically extravagant" and that "it frequently fails in achieving its object."

The interdepartmental committee on hours of labor were prompt in making use of the reports and recommendations of the Health of Munition Workers Committee and on September 9, 1916, the Home Office (under which is the Department of Factory Inspection) sent to employers in munition factories a letter regarding the hours of labor of women and children saying that "after due consideration, it has been decided that effect must be given to the main recommendations of the (health of munition workers) committee in this respect as soon as possible." Accompanying the letter was general Order No. 187 "to regulate the hours of work of women and young persons employed in munition factories, including, with certain exceptions all works in the occupation of the Crown and all controlled establishments." [4] The order became effective on October 2, 1916.

This order permitted women and girls to be employed not to exceed 60 hours per week. Boys of 14 (under one plan 16) and over might be employed not to exceed 63 (under one plan 65) hours per week. Several schemes of employment were offered, one of which must be adopted by the employer, for arranging the factory hours. Some of the plans called for a rest period of 24 hours each week and regular intervals for meals were to be provided. Women might work at night if properly supervised by a woman welfare worker or responsible forewoman. Week end volunteer workers might be employed with the sanction of the superintending inspector.

[1] These several reports are summarized in the *Monthly Review of the U. S. Bureau of Labor Statistics*, December, 1916, pp. 97-105.
[2] Bulletin No. 221, U. S. Bureau of Labor Statistics, pp. 61-72.
[3] *Ibid.*, No. 223.
[4] *British Industrial Experience*, vol. 1, pp. 475-483.

Further investigations made by the Health of Munition Workers Committee under newer conditions which have developed show that the earlier recommendations of the committee as to the number of hours that might be worked need to be revised and that " the time is now ripe for a further substantial reduction in the hours of work." [1]   The committee calls attention to the fact that conditions in industry have greatly changed during the war.   Older men and more women and young persons are being employed and they are doing heavier work than formerly. Both employers and workers are coming to recognize the undesirability of the long hours.   " Whereas at the beginning of the war there was a general belief that longer hours necessarily produced larger output, it has now become widely recognized that a 13 or 14 hour day for men and a 12 hour day for women, excepting for quite brief periods, are not profitable from any point of view." [2]   According to the reports of the factory inspectors, there has been a great change for the better in regard to the number of hours worked in all classes of factories since the first year of the war.   " The general tendency has been to restrict the weekly hours of work to an amount very little, if at all, in excess of those allowed under the Factory Act, and to arrange for more elasticity in the daily limits." [3]   The report of the Chief Inspector for 1917 says that the employment of women and young persons for hours in excess of the maximum legal limits of the ordinary provisions of the Factories Act is now rare.[4]

HOLIDAYS

Closely related to the subject of hours of labor is that of holidays. The importance of holidays in the life of the working man or woman has been thoroughly appreciated by the government departments concerned with the production of ships, munitions

[1] Summary of report on weekly hours of employment (Memorandum No. 20) in *Monthly Review of U. S. Bureau of Labor Statistics,* February, 1918, p. 87.
[2] Weekly hours of employment, *loc. cit.,* p. 86.
[3] Report of Chief Inspector of Factories, 1916.
[4] *Labour Gazette,* August, 1918, p. 345.

and other war supplies, but modifications in the practices prevailing in peace times have had to be made to suit war exigencies in this as in other matters.

On July 28, 1916, an order (No. 501) was issued under authority of the Defense of the Realm Acts, which authorized the government to suspend the usual bank holidays whenever the observance of such holidays would " impede or delay the production, repair or transport of war material or of any work necessary for the successful prosecution of the war." [1]   On December 5, 1916, an order (No. 840) was issued which made it legal to require employers to give their employes some other day as a holiday in place of the one which had been omitted by government order within a specified period of time. [2]

Circular L23 issued this year by the Ministry of Munitions states that: " The Minister fully recognizes the necessity for some holiday period both for the health of the work people and also for the overhauling and repair of machinery." It asks that in granting such holidays care be taken to see that the regular output of munitions be not interrupted more than is necessary, and that in so far as it is practicable, all munitions and shipbuilding establishments in the same districts should grant holidays of the same length, at the same time and in accordance with the usual custom of the district. [3]

Order 697, dated July 3, 1917, of the Minister of Munitions required the employers in controlled establishments to observe the custom of the districts or agreements which had been made in regard to the summer holidays, but such holidays when fixed by agreement were not to exceed one week in length unless approved by the Minister. [4]   It has also been found necessary to issue an order (No. 663, September 25, 1916) setting aside certain days as " rest days " in controlled establishments. [5]

[1] *British Industrial Experience*, vol. 1, p. 133.
[2] *Ibid.*, vol. 1, pp. 137, 180-182.
[3] *Ibid.*, p. 298.
[4] *Ibid.*, pp. 298-299.
[5] *Ibid.*, p. 294.

WELFARE WORK

One of the most gratifying results of the industrial trans-
formation in Great Britain during the war has been the growth
of welfare work in both private and public establishments.   A
considerable number of industrial establishments had already
established such departments before the war.   Thirty factories
having such departments sent representatives to a conference at
York in 1913,[1] but progress in this direction was greatly accelerated during the war.   There are at least three reasons for
this rapid development.   (1) The tendency to concentrate war
work in large establishments, where the absence of close personal
relations between employers and employes made some form of
supervision of the workers desirable; (2) the rapid substitution
of women and young persons for men, which meant that employers must find some way of making their factories attractive
working places, and the conditions surrounding the home life
of the workers safe from the standpoint of both health and
morals; (3) the stimulus furnished by the Ministry of Munitions to the owners of controlled establishments.

The first point receives emphasis in the report of the committee appointed by the economic section of the British Association for the Advancement of Science to investigate into outlets for labor after the war.   "One of the tendencies of the
war," says that committee, " is clearly to transfer a more than
normal proportion of the nation's business to large concerns.
Though this has its drawbacks, the balance on account is probably to the advantage of the women who have entered, as far
as the safeguarding of their lives is concerned, and consequently
of that of the men who will return." [2]   Only the larger plants
could well afford the expense of a well organized welfare department, but given a sufficient number of employes the cost of

[1] *Welfare Supervision* (Memorandum No. 2 of the Health of Munition
Workers Committee), Bulletin No. 222 of U. S. Bureau of Labor Statistics,
p. 24.
[2] Draft Interim Report, 1915, p. 6.

welfare supervision need amount to only a few cents per week for each person employed.

The employment of women and young persons in large numbers called attention to the need of furnishing better accommodations for the workers both within and without the factory. Housing accommodations were found to be woefully insufficient in many localities where women were being sought for employment purposes. The absence of good transit facilities only emphasized this need. The necessity for traveling to and from work for long distances and the impossibility of returning home for the noonday meal called attention to the need for industrial canteens and the more delicate human instruments being dealt with when women were employed showed the need of facilities to prevent the increase of illness and broken time. The reports of 'the factory inspectors give illustrations of the improvements which were being made in factories where women were employed. " Instances are given of greater cleanliness, better heating, lighting, ventilation and sanitary accommodation, improved first aid and ambulance arrangements and the provision of protective clothing. In many cases occupiers have provided tea in the afternoon, free of charge for those working overtime, with very beneficial results." [1]

The Ministry of Munitions soon after its establishment began to give serious attention to the question of the welfare of the workers in munition plants. Circular L6 issued by the Ministry in November, 1915, made recommendations for the care of women workers. The Health of Munition Workers Committee appointed by the Minister of Munitions in September, 1915, gave especial attention to the matter of welfare work, issuing no less than six memoranda on the subject between November, 1915, and August, 1916. [2] Some of the recommendations of the committee, like that of establishing industrial canteens, were at once acted upon by the Minister. Finally at the end of January, 1916, a Welfare Department, under the direction of Mr. B. S. Rown-

[1] Annual report of the Chief Inspector of Factories and Workshops, 1916.
[2] These memoranda have been reprinted and published as Bulletin No. 222 (Welfare Work in British Munition Factories) of the U. S. Bureau of Labor Statistics.

tree, a manufacturer well known for his interest in these matters, was established by the Ministry of Munitions to give effect to the recommendations of the Health of Munition Workers Committee's recommendations " with regard to welfare supervision, especially with regard to women." [1]

The general purpose of the Welfare Department of the Ministry of Munitions is stated to have been " to raise the well being of the workers to as high a point as possible in all factories engaged in the manufacture of munitions of war, etc.[2] Not all the welfare work undertaken by the department had to do with the health and comfort of women. The Health of Munition Workers Committee distinctly states in one of its reports[3] that " a suitable system of welfare supervision would be of advantage in munition works where 500 adult males or 100 boys are employed." The Ministry of Munitions recognized this need to the extent of issuing a memorandum to welfare supervisors of boys[4] in March, 1917. In view of the fact, however, that the work of the Welfare Department was limited for the most part to the supervision of the welfare of women and boys and that this subject has been adequately dealt with in another monograph in this series,[5] it will be necessary here only to indicate the scope of work undertaken by the department. The work includes: (a) seeing that clean and wholesome workrooms are provided and that the work is suited to the capacity of the worker; (b) providing adequate facilities for securing nourishing food at reasonable prices, and under restful and wholesome conditions; (c) regulating the hours of work and providing rest periods so as not unduly to tax the workers' strength; (d) seeing that the wages are sufficient to provide for the physical efficiency of the worker and allow a sufficient margin for reasonable recreation; (e) seeing that suitable cloak rooms, lavatories, toilet rooms, overalls, etc., are provided to enable decent standards to be met;

[1] British Industrial Experience, vol. 1, p. 483.
[2] Ibid., vol. 2, p. 1058.
[3] Memorandum No. 2, loc. cit., p. 29.
[4] British Industrial Experience, vol. 1, pp. 493-499.
[5] Andrews and Hobbs, op. cit., chaps. xii and xiii.

(f) endeavoring to reduce the dangers to life and health to a minimum; (g) providing such supervision as is necessary to insure a good standard of behavior among the employes; (h) seeing that the workers are treated with due consideration by foremen and those in authority; (i) providing where necessary for suitable recreation outside of working hours, especially for those working under strain or monotonous work; (j) endeavoring to see that adequate and reasonable transit facilities to and from work are provided; (k) seeing that the housing accommodations, food, etc., provided by the company are good and the price reasonable and supervising lodgings of workers in private homes; (l) giving especial attention to the living conditions and morals of boys and girls employed. Although the Welfare Department concerns itself with all these matters, it does not deal with all of them directly, but refers such matters as hours of labor to the proper government departments and the matter of lodgings to the local advisory committees.[1]

The Welfare Department assists employers to find and to secure training for welfare supervisors. These welfare supervisors assist in hiring workers, keep records of their broken time and rates of pay, investigate complaints by workers, supervise working conditions, canteens, rest rooms, housing and transit facilities and recreation facilities and conditions. The Ministry of Munitions in order to give to owners of controlled establishments the utmost encouragement to carry on welfare work allows the salary of an approved welfare supervisor, the cost of overalls and other necessary equipment to be treated as working expenses and allows the cost of canteens as expenditures out of revenue instead of out of capital, so that it may be taken into account in the limitation of net profits under Part 2 of the Munitions Acts. The cost of cloak rooms, lavatories, etc., is written down to the value of the owner at the end of the period of control.[2]

It is said that the benefits which have resulted from the establishment of the Welfare Department in the saving of time and

---

[1] *British Industrial Experience*, vol. 1, pp. 1058-1059.
[2] *Ibid.*, vol. 1, p. 295; vol. 2, p. 1062.

in the increase of output have been very great. While the work of welfare supervision has been severely criticized and it has often been difficult to get satisfactory supervisors, the work on the whole, at least under the emergency conditions created by the war, seems to have justified itself by its results.[1]

The efforts of the government to introduce welfare work in factories during the war did not stop with the munition industries. On August 3, 1916, the Police, Factories, etc. (Miscellaneous Provisions) Act was adopted, whereby the Home Department was authorized to issue orders to occupiers of factories or workshops to make necessary " arrangements for preparing or heating and taking meals, the supply of protective clothing, ambulance and first aid arrangements, the supply and use of seats in workrooms, facilities for washing, accommodations for clothing, arrangement for supervision of workers," where it appeared to the Secretary that " the conditions and circumstances of employment or the nature of the processes " required special provision to be made for the welfare of workers.[2]

No orders were issued under authority of this act until October, 1917, during which month orders were issued requiring suitable clothing for workers in tin or terne plate factories and for women employes requiring suitable accommodations for caring for clothing, drying clothing if wet, and suitable mess rooms and washing facilities, also requiring wholesome drinking water in all factories employing 25 or more persons and requiring first aid facilities for workers in foundries, metal works, etc.[3]

HOUSING CONDITIONS AND LEGISLATION

The housing situation in Great Britain, which even before the war was so acute that the Prime Minister in 1913 estimated that about 100,000 or 120,000 cottages were needed,[4] became much

[1] See Andrews and Hobbs, *op. cit.*, pp. 138-140.
[2] 6 and 7 Geo. 5, c. 31. See also *British Industrial Experience*, vol. 1, pp. 885-889.
[3] *British Industrial Experience*, vol. 1, pp. 888-895.
[4] L. Magnusson: "War Housing in Great Britain," *Monthly Review of U. S. Bureau of Labor Statistics*, December, 1917, p. 220.

more serious as the war continued and as financial and labor difficulties made the building of houses much more difficult. In 1917 competent persons estimated that 400,000 cottages were required in England and Wales, if the needs of the working classes were to be met.[1] The Housing and Town Planning Acts of 1890 and 1909, which authorized the Local Government Board to furnish financial assistance to municipalities desiring to carry on housing projects, had apparently failed to accomplish their purposes.

After the war had been in progress for some months the movement of work people toward the centers of munition manufacture resulted in great congestion and overcrowding in these communities. Lack of suitable housing accommodation is one of the causes of industrial discontent cited by the commissions appointed to study this subject in 1917. Even before this time, however, Parliament had acted with a view to remedying the situation. At the very outbreak of the war, on August 10, 1914, two acts were passed, one of which authorized the local government board to assist any authorized society which limited its profits to 5 per cent, by making loans to or taking shares in the capital of such societies " or otherwise as they think fit." By the same act the commissioners of works were with the consent of the Treasury given power " to acquire and dispose of land and buildings and to build dwellings, etc." This act was limited to " housing of persons employed by or on behalf of government departments where sufficient dwelling accommodation is not available."

The other act was intended to relieve unemployment in the building trades, which it was supposed would be acute, and was limited in its operation to one year from date of passage.[2] As no considerable unemployment developed, the act was not taken advantage of and does not concern us here.

An amendment to the Defense of the Realm Act was adopted on March 16, 1915, which gave the government power to take possession of any unoccupied land for the purpose of housing

[1] Magnusson, op. cit., p 221.
[2] Both acts are reprinted in British Industrial Experience, vol. 1, pp. 855-858.

workmen employed in connection with the manufacture of war materials, and a later act provided that, in purchasing the land, the government would not take into consideration unearned increments or decrements created since the beginning of the war.[1] It is under the authority of the Defense of the Realm Acts that the Ministry of Munitions, the Army and the Admiralty have assisted in the construction of houses for the working classes. Up to March 37, 1917, the Ministry of Munitions had advanced £3,181,654 for this purpose. The expenditures for the Army and Admiralty have been by comparison insignificant.[2]

The expenditures made by the Ministry of Munitions has fallen under three heads: " (1) direct grants to municipalities and employers, (2) loans to contractors for permanent housing schemes, and (3) direct construction costs for permanent or temporary housing in the neighborhood of national establishments." [3] Most of the work accomplished has been undertaken by the Ministry itself. The Ministry purchases the land and constructs the houses and then makes arrangement with the municipality or some public utility or private concern to take over the property at the expiration of a certain number of years after the war at the value the property then has.

Permanent housing has been undertaken wherever the situation made this possible. Although much temporary housing was necessary, it has not been found satisfactory. " In the long run," says the Ministry, " there can be no doubt that the provision of temporary accommodation is wasteful. There was a saving in the immediate capital expenditure involved, but the great bulk of the money spent would bring no return of any kind." [4]

Temporary housing by the Ministry of Munitions has taken several different forms: (1) cottages, (2) tenements, i.e., barrack-like rows, (3) houses of various types and (4) hotels,

[1] L. Magnusson, *Monthly Review*, December, 1917, p. 224.
[2] L. Magnusson: "Financial Aspects of War Housing in Great Britain," *Monthly Review of U. S. Bureau of Labor Statistics*, June, 1918, p. 201.
[3] *Ibid*, p. 202.
[4] Quoted by Magnusson, *Monthly Review*, etc., June, 1918, p. 203.

i.e, temporary boarding and lodging houses.[1] Of these the most popular were the cottages and separate houses. The hotels it is said were a failure. Many of them were not fully occupied. Although managed by some body like the Y. M. C. A., the workers disliked them because they lacked privacy.[2] The cottages are the only ones from which the receipts from rents have equaled the expenditures, apart from capital.[3]

Besides the work done by government departments under the authority of the Defense of the Realm Acts, work has been carried on by the Local Government Board and the Commissioner of Works under authority of the Acts of 1890, 1909 and 1914. Most of the work has been done by a loan of funds and it is said that "numerous towns have been developed as permament communities under the town planning principles of the Act of 1909."[4] The office of works has itself undertaken extensive construction, especially at the Woolwich Arsenal.[5]

A recent memorandum issued by the advisory housing panel of the Ministry of Reconstruction deals with the emergency created by the cessation of building during the war and estimates that to make up the deficiency it will be necessary to build in the year after the war "250,000 houses, plus an additional 75,000 for each year after 1917 through which the war is continued." In addition, there should be 50,000 houses built in rural districts.

The panel propose that the state should provide the entire cost of construction and should own the houses until prices have reached their normal level, when they should be transformed to the local authorities at prices adjusted to their worth. The local authorities should act as agents of the state in managing the property and collecting the rents.[6]

The government has not stopped with the construction of houses and hotels in its efforts to solve the housing problem. In December, 1915, a law was passed restricting the increase in

[1] Magnusson, *Monthly Review*, etc., June, 1918, p. 204.
[2] Andrews and Hobbs. *op. cit.*, p. 143.
[3] Magnusson, *Monthly Review*, etc., June, 1918, p. 205.
[4] *Ibid.*, December. 1917. p. 226.
[5] *Ibid.*, June, 1918, p. 205.
[6] *Labour Gazette*, 1918, p. 263.

rents and taxes on small houses as already mentioned.[1] The impracticability of building sufficient houses to accommodate all the population of the munition centers led to the passage of the Billeting of Civilians Act of May 24, 1917.[2] A central billeting board makes a survey of housing conditions and, when it finds it to be necessary, civilian workers are billeted upon the civil population in the same way that soldiers are billeted. It is said that " it is possible in some cases to billet a working population equal to or greater than the population disclosed by the census "[3] and that in this way congestion has been relieved even in towns where it was reported that the housing situation was bad.

UNEMPLOYMENT AND ITS RELIEF

At a time when the nation has been exhausting its resources to find sufficient workers to supply its industrial and war needs, it is evident that unemployment would not be a serious problem and such as did exist would be practically unavoidable. We have already discussed the situation as it existed during the first year of the war and have seen that by the middle of 1915 unemployment had reached the lowest level in Great Britain which had been known since statistics on the subject began to be collected. Conditions have not changed for the worse since that time. Generally speaking, the percentage of unemployed among trade unionists has been less than one per cent—for much of the time less than one half of one per cent. The situation in the trades whose members are insured against unemployment under the National Insurance Act (Part 2) has been almost equally favorable. Occasionally, some temporary difficulties in certain industries or areas, such as a shortage of materials, have sent the unemployment curve upward somewhat, but the situation has never been serious and has not called for any extraordinary mode of relief.

[1] See pp. 204-205.
[2] British Industrial Experience, vol. 1, p. 867.
[3] L. Magnusson, Monthly Review, December, 1917, p. 225.

The distress committees set up under the Unemployed Workmen Act, 1915, have almost ceased to function. The low water mark of their activity seems to have been reached in May, 1916, when only 37 people were given relief by them.[1] All the exceptional modes of relieving distress which were adopted by the government or by voluntary agencies at the beginning of the war have been discontinued.

Similar fortunate results indicating individual and social prosperity are shown by the statistics of pauperism. The total number of paupers in England and Wales, which includes casual paupers, paupers in receipt of outdoor medical relief only, lunatics in lunatic asylums and all other classes of paupers, declined from 765,077 at the end of September, 1914, to 596,188 at the end of September, 1917.[2] The decline affected all classes and " apart from inmates of lunatic asylums and paupers in receipt of outdoor medical relief, it may be inferred," says the *Labour Gazette,* " that practically the whole of this decrease is due to the abnormal demand for man-power which set in as a result of the war." [3] In the 35 selected urban areas from which reports are received by the Local Government Board, the number of paupers per 10,000 of the population was only 126 in July, 1918, as compared to 184 in July, 1914.[4]

In one respect, at least, the war has brought increased attention to the subject of unemployment. This has resulted in the extension of the state system of unemployment insurance (Part 2 of the National Insurance Act, 1911) to—

(a) workmen engaged on or in connection with " munitions work," as that term was defined by the Munitions of War Acts, except when excluded by order of the Board of Trade, and

(b) workmen employed in any of the following trades (which are mentioned in the first schedule of the act) whether these workmen are engaged on munitions work or not:

    (1) The manufacture of ammunition, fireworks, and explosives.

    (2) The manufacture of chemicals, including oils, lubricants, soap, candles, paints, colors and varnish.

[1] *Labour Gazette,* 1916, p. 220.
[2] *Ibid.,* 1918, p. 53.
[3] *Ibid.,* 1916, p. 404.
[4] *Ibid.,* 1918, p. 330.

(3) The manufacture of metals and the manufacture or repair of metal goods.

(4) The manufacture of rubber and goods made therefrom.

(5) The manufacture of leather and leather goods.

(6) The manufacture of bricks, cement and artificial stone and other artificial building materials.

(7) Sawmilling, including machine wood work, and the manufacture of wooden cases."

The contributions and rates of benefit under this act are the same as under the principal act. The act is compulsory on employers and employes in the trades mentioned, but exceptions to the compulsory feature may be made by the Board of Trade in the case of those workers who can show that they were employed in munitions work prior to August 4, 1914, or that they were under the age of 18 when they first became employed in the trade.[1]

The act came into force on September 4, 1916. It was to remain in operation for five years from that date or until three years after the end of the war (whichever of those dates may be the later), but the right to receive benefits continues for six months after that date. Just prior to the coming into effect of the act, the Board of Trade issued an exclusive order excluding from the operation of the act practically all classes of munitions workers other than those which might be included in the narrow sense of that term, " the manufacture or repair of arms, ammunition, ships, vessels, vehicles and air craft—intended or adapted for use in war," and of the metals, machines, tools or materials required for the construction of the above.[2] The result has been that fewer workers have been added to the number insured under the principal act than might naturally be supposed. The number of claims for benefits made in July, 1917, under this act were 3,806 as compared to 7,501 made under the principal act.[3]

The extension of the Unemployment Insurance Act to munitions workers was not, of course, due to the present existence of a

[1] 6 and 7 Geo. 5, c. 20. Public General Acts, 1916, pp. 43-45.
[2] *Labour Gazette*, 1916, p. 349.
[3] *Ibid.*, 1917, p. 289.

large amount of unemployment in these trades, but to an uneasiness felt by workers as to the probable effect of a conclusion of peace upon the continuation of employment in these trades. It was probably deemed advisable by the government for another reason, *viz.*, that it would be easier to entice workmen into the munitions trades from the insured trades if they recognized that such a transfer would not cause them to surrender their claims for benefits under the Insurance Act, upon their becoming unemployed. In the early part of 1918, the National Insurance (Unemployment) Act received a further extension, bringing within its scope certain trades not hitherto covered, but the details in regard to this had not come to hand at the time this was written.

DISABLED SOLDIERS [1]

The question of providing for the needs of officers and men who return from the front broken in body or health has been a matter of both public and private concern in Great Britain since the outbreak of the war. The War Pensions Statutory Committee was created in November, 1915, to care for disabled officers and men after they had left the service, including provision for their health, training and employment, and making grants of money when necessary to enable dependents of deceased soldiers to obtain employment.

In December, 1916, a Ministry of Pensions was established and all the work of the statutory committee and that which had been dealt with by other departments along the same line was transferred to the new ministry. The work of the Ministry of Pensions has been along four lines: (1) Providing medical and surgical treatment, including appliances by means of which the disability of the injured man may be reduced; (2) giving functional and technical training, for the purpose of fitting the man for some occupation; (3) finding suitable employment when

[1] The information for this section has been furnished by an article by Mrs. M. A. Gadsby. " Finding Jobs for Great Britain's Disabled Soldiers," in the *Monthly Review of the U. S. Bureau of Labor Statistics,* December, 1917, pp. 650-79.

the man is in condition to accept it; (4) furnishing maintenance for the man and his family while he is receiving his training or is becoming adjusted to his employment.

When the man is discharged from the army or navy, his name and address are sent to the employment office of the district into which the man has gone. The office writes to the man inviting him to register with it in case he wishes its assistance in finding employment. Between May, 1915, and July 13, 1917, 127,300 disabled soldiers and sailors had registered at the employment offices and 59,400 of them had secured employment. The remainder, with few exceptions, were men who had canceled their registrations either because they had found employment by their own efforts or had discovered that their disability was such that they would be unable to accept normal employment.

The Ministry studies carefully the labor market to see that not too many men are reeducated for any particular trade so that they could not all be profitably employed. Local committees are appointed to secure the cooperation of employers, associations and trade unions in determining the occupations in their respective districts in which men are to be employed, the kind of training needed, local provisions for obtaining this training or, if there are no local facilities, the technical institutes or factories throughout the country where it may be secured, the wages to be paid, etc. There are also special investigators who have been appointed to inquire into possible openings in the various trades of the country and the kind of training needed. Elaborate schedules of questions have been drawn up for the purpose of securing detailed information with regard to certain industrial processes and these have been sent to technical schools, factory inspectors, trade union officials, employers, etc., to secure the necessary information. From the information secured from all these sources special pamphlets are issued for various trades telling of the opportunity for using disabled men therein, the previous experience needed, what disabilities would and what ones would not debar a man from the trade in question, etc.

It is said that an employer usually undertakes to find work in his establishment for his former employes if their disability is not too great. Many disabled men, however, are unable to take up their former work and therefore find the services of the Ministry of Pensions of great use.

The British Labor party has come out strongly in favor of securing the best treatment that can be afforded and every appliance that ingenuity can provide or skill suggest in order to restore disabled men for places in industry, and it is stated that as long as there is no diminution in the standard of living and no effort to use the disabled man to defeat the legitimate objects which trade unions have in view, the trade unions desire to assist the disabled in every possible way to secure employment in remunerative work.[1]

[1] G. J. Wardle, M. P.: "British Labor Party and the Disabled." Reprinted from "Recalled to Life" in the *Monthly Review of U. S. Bureau of Labor Statistics*, December, 1917, p. 80.

CHAPTER IX

Industrial Unrest

We have already noticed[1] the increase in the number of strikes which took place during the first half of the year 1915, after the suspension of the industrial truce which marked the early months of the war.

Viewed from the standpoint of prewar conditions, the growth in the number of disputes, as compared with the opening months, was not serious. Only 360 disputes involving 136,636 work people and causing an aggregate loss of 951,000 working days were officially reported for the first six months of 1915, as compared with 663 disputes, involving 361,860 work people and causing a loss of 7,761,800 working days in the corresponding months of 1914, and as compared with 151 disputes, involving 24,979 work people and causing a loss of 147,246 working days during the last half of 1914, which includes five months of actual war.[2]

The seriousness of strikes in war times, is not, however, to be measured by their magnitude but by the extent to which they interfere with the conduct of the war. For this reason the strikes of 1915 gave the government great concern, for the greatest loss in working days and the largest number of work people involved were in the textile, engineering, coal mining and transport trades, those upon which the steady prosecution of the war was most dependent.

The enactment of the Munitions Act on July 2, 1915, marks the adoption of a new policy of the government in regard to the settlement of disputes in the munitions industries—and, under certain conditions, in other industries, viz.—the application of the principle of compulsory arbitration. Judged by immediate

[1] Chapter III, pp. 62-64.
[2] *Labour Gazette*, 1915, pp. 261, 355.

results, this part of the act might well be considered a failure, for the first attempt to enforce it in an important dispute was barren of results and the dispute had to be settled by other means. This dispute occurred in the coal mines of South Wales and Monmouthshire and led to a strike of six days duration which involved, directly and indirectly, 201,401 workers.[1]

THE SOUTH WALES COAL STRIKE

The South Wales coal strike was not entirely due to war conditions. A five year agreement between the South Wales Miners Federation and the mine operators had expired on April 1 and a month earlier the miners had submitted proposals for a new agreement.[2] At the same time the Miners Federation of Great Britain had decided to ask for an advance of twenty per cent in wages in all mines in England, Scotland and Wales to meet the increase in the cost of living. This demand had been, at least partially, met as a result of arbitration by the Prime Minister (Mr. Asquith) in April, whereby there was allowed an advance of wages, varying in the different districts, the exact amounts to be determined by the local conciliation boards. To the South Wales miners, this advance meant an increase of 17½ per cent on the standard wage used as a basis of negotiation. The 20 per cent bonus, if allowed, would have been equivalent to a 32 per cent increase on the standard.

When the South Wales miners pressed for a revision of the five year agreement, the mine operators claimed that their agreement to accept arbitration on the twenty per cent bonus proposal was based on the understanding that nothing more was to be said about the wage agreement. The miners denied that this was any part of the agreement and demanded such a revision of their five year contract as should allow them a further wage increase, operative for three years, and which should provide for the exclusion of nonunion labor from the mines. They had already given on April 1 the required three months' notice of

---

[1] *Labour Gazette*, 1915, p. 299.
[2] *Labour Year Book*, 1916, pp. 74-75.

their intention to suspend work unless a new agreement was entered into.

As the time for the suspension approached and the miners and operators had been unable to agree, the government became concerned as to the effect of a suspension on coal production. Some of the miners engaged on admiralty work had quit work as early as June 18 and the prospect of a failure to agree on the nonunionist issue caused others to quit before the end of June.[1] Government officials took up the negotiations with the miners and the operators where they had broken off and proposed a series of compromises for the war period. These proposals were accepted as a basis of negotiations and the miners agreed to continue work for a fortnight on a day to day contract while negotiations were proceeding. The meaning of some of the government's proposals was not clear, and it was understood that Mr. Runciman, President of the Board of Trade, was to issue an interpretation of them. When this interpretation was issued on July 9, it proved unsatisfactory to the miners, who, on the eleventh, voted to reject the proposed agreement and informed the government that they would accept nothing short of a complete acceptance of their own terms. Unless these demands were granted, they were determined to go on strike on July 14.

Public opinion was generally against the strikers. This much is admitted by the authors of the *Labour Year Book*,[2] who claim that the public was not rightly informed as to the real issues involved. The government now decided to apply to the controversy the arbitration provisions of the Munitions Act, 1915, which had just been adopted. Although coal mining is not among the industries to which the Munitions Acts are generally applicable, under section 3 of the original act the government is empowered by proclamation to extend the arbitration provisions of the act to "a difference arising on work other than munitions work" if "the existence or continuance of the difference is directly or indirectly prejudicial to the manufacture, transport or supply of munitions of war," and if the Minister is

[1] *British Industrial Experience during the War*, vol. 2, p. 982.
[2] See p. 79.

not satisfied " that effective means exist to secure the settlement without stoppage."

Mr. Runciman announced in the House of Commons on July 12 that negotiations with the miners had proved futile and that a proclamation would be issued which would " have the effect of making it an offense to take part in a strike or lockout unless the difference has been reported to the Board of Trade and the Board of Trade has not within 21 days of such report referred it for settlement." [1]

The proclamation itself was issued the following day, but it had no effect in preventing a strike. This took place on July 14. The miners felt that the proclamation was practically a breach of promise on the part of the Minister of Munitions (Mr. Lloyd George). The miners had always been opposed to compulsory arbitration and it was because they understood that compulsory arbitration would be insisted upon by the government that the Miners' Federation had withdrawn from the conference held at the Treasury in March. Later, they had entered into negotiations with Lloyd George to be left out of the scope of the Munitions Bill and had succeeded in securing the insertion of the following clause in section 3 of the act which authorizes the extension of the arbitration provisions to other than the munitions trades: " If, in the case of any industry, the Minister of Munitions is satisfied that effective means exist to secure a settlement without a stoppage of any difference arising on work other than munitions work, no proclamation shall be made under this section with respect to such difference." The government felt that with the miners' announcement of their intention to quit work, " effective means " outside the act no longer existed, while the miners felt that a recognition of the justice of their claims would have avoided the necessity of a strike.

The government had not set up a South Wales munitions tribunal to deal with violations of the act. The penalties provided for engaging in a strike are £5 per day for each individual involved. The government had felt confident that there

[1] *British Industrial Experience*, vol. 2, p. 983.

would be no strike, for the Miners' Federation had given to Mr.
Lloyd George and Mr. Arthur Henderson a pledge that there
would be no strike in the coal fields during the war.[1] The men,
however, had largely drifted away from the leadership of the
executive committee of the Federation, which had advised
against the strike.[2]

The Minister of Munitions now established a general munitions tribunal for Wales and Monmouthshire, but the government decided that it was not expedient to proceed against the
strikers. Negotiations were resumed with the South Wales
Miners' Federation and Messrs. Lloyd George, Runciman and
Henderson went to Cardiff on July 19 and held a conference
with the officials of the union. It was agreed that most of the
demands made by the men should be granted, including a considerable advance in wages. It was further agreed that no action
should be taken by the government against the strikers and that
every effort would be made to maintain and increase the output
of coal. With these concessions, the men resumed work on July
20. The first attempt to extend the operation of the arbitration
provisions of the Munitions Acts to nonmunitions work had
proved a failure. A strike had occurred which had cost, it was
estimated, about £1,500,000 and had reduced the output of coal
by 1,000,000 tons.[3]

Strikes During the War

Another strike involving about 32,000 miners took place in the
South Wales coal fields in August, 1915, caused by dissatisfaction over an interpretation of the agreement of July 30 by Mr.
Runciman. A compromise was soon effected and the men returned to work.[4]

Aside from these two disputes in the coal mining industry,
no strikes of serious importance took place during the latter
half of 1915. Although the record for these months was not

[1] H. L. Gray: *Wartime Control of Industry*, pp. 74-75.
[2] *Ibid.*, p. 75.
[3] *Ibid.*, p. 77.
[4] *British Industrial Experience*, vol. 2, p. 984.

equal to the last six months of 1914, most of the disputes which did occur were in small establishments, involved few workers and were of short duration. The record for the year 1915, considered as a whole, was more favorable than for 1914 or for any year since 1910.[1] It was probably not so much compulsory arbitration under the Munitions Act, as it was a feeling of patriotism and the influence of the war bonuses, which sufficed to keep the workers steadily at their tasks.

The year 1916 presented an even more favorable record than that for 1915,[2] and the record for 1917, while not equal to that of either 1916 or 1915, was better than that of any year of the period immediately preceding the outbreak of the war. The record for the entire war period down to the middle of 1918 is set forth in the following table:[3]

Period Covered	Number of Industrial Disputes	Number of Work people Involved	Aggregate Duration in Working Days of All Disputes in Progress
Last 6 mos., 1914........	151	24,979	147,246
Year of 1915............	706	452,571	3,038,134
Year of 1916............	581	284,396	2,599,800
Year of 1917............	688	820,727	5,513,900
First 6 mos., 1918.......	567	312,750	2,090,800

Several of the disputes which occurred during the years 1916 and 1917 gave the government considerable concern, for they curtailed in a serious manner the production of munitions of war. In March, 1916, there occurred the strike in the engineering trades known as that of the Clyde Workers' Committee. The purpose of this strike was to change the military and industrial policies of the government; to force the repeal of the Munitions of War Acts and the Military Service Acts by holding up war supplies. This strike was in defiance of the agreement made between the leaders of the trade unions and the government and both the strike and the strikers were repudiated by the Amalgamated Society of Engineers. However, the men claimed that

[1] *Labour Gazette*, 1915, p. 355; 1916, p. 6.
[2] *Ibid.*, 1917, p. 7.
[3] *Ibid.*, 1915, p. 355; 1917, pp. 7, 285; 1918, p. 278.

they had not been consulted when this agreement was entered into and that they were not bound by it. They were especially dissatisfied with the arrangements regarding dilution and demanded that shop stewards be allowed to interrupt their work to go into other departments to inspect arrangements for the dilution of labor. The employers objected to this interruption, but were willing to submit the matter to the Clyde commissioners and to give the men's representatives facilities to ascertain what was being done under the dilution scheme.[1] The government acted promptly in the matter of this strike. Under powers conferred by the Defense of the Realm Acts, it proceeded to arrest nine leaders and conveyed them to another part of the kingdom on a charge of delaying the production of munitions in a controlled establishment. Within a week the strike was at an end. After fourteen months the leaders were allowed to return home.[2]

There were few strikes in munitions plants during the remainder of 1916. In June it was found necessary to apply by proclamation Part I of the Munitions Act to a strike of the Liverpool dock laborers,[3] and the same action was taken in October of that year in the case of the Glasgow dock laborers,[4] and in December in the case of the strike of card room and blowing room operatives in the Lancashire cotton mills.[5]

There were few stoppages in the coal mines during 1916. On December 1, 1916, the government took over the control of the coal mines in the South Wales coal fields and on March 1, 1917, it assumed control of all mines in the United Kingdom. This did not put an end to all strikes in the coal fields, however; indeed the number of strikes in coal mines has shown some tendency to increase.[6] In November, 1917, a strike of three days' duration took place in South Wales and Monmouthshire on the part of 2,600 colliery examiners, which threw some 127,000 workers

[1] Gray, op. cit., pp. 48-49.
[2] Ibid., pp. 48-49.
[3] British Industrial Experience, vol. 1, pp. 266-267.
[4] Ibid., pp. 267-268.
[5] Ibid., pp. 268-269.
[6] Labour Gazette, 1917, p. 283.

idle. The strike was over the recognition of the Colliery Examiners Union and was successful.[1] The government has not again attempted to prevent or settle these disputes under the provisions of the Munitions of War Acts, but has made use of the machinery and methods of conciliation which have ordinarily been applied in the cases of disputes arising under private management.

RECENT GOVERNMENT POLICY CONCERNING DISPUTES

On December 22, 1916, Parliament created a Ministry of Labor to take over most of the labor functions being exercised by other departments. One of the first acts of the new Minister was to issue an appeal to the trade unions to give up the practice of striking during the war. The response to this appeal has not been such as he had reason to hope for, as our figures for 1917 clearly show; nevertheless it is said that in response to the efforts of the Minister several large bodies of strikers returned to work. With regard to most of the strikes which have occurred during the war, it must be said that they have been of short duration, frequently lasting only a day or two, and that they do not indicate any intention or desire to embarrass the government in the conduct of the war. It has been said that the prevalence of overtime and Sunday labor, while seldom resented by the workers, who are glad of the extra earnings due to the high rates of pay for such work, has, nevertheless, been the indirect cause of the frequent stoppages. The strain on the nerves of the workers caused by the long hours of work has made them easily irritable and ready to respond to slight provocation.

Recognition of this fact and of the undoubted loyalty of the great mass of the workers and of their desire to assist in the prosecution of the war has led government officials to make relatively little use of their power to prosecute the workers for their participation in strikes, even in the case of munition workers. The penalties provided are looked upon as weapons of last resort and conciliation has generally been regarded as preferable to compulsory arbitration.

[1] *Labour Gazette*, 1917, p. 455.

In the engineering and shipbuilding trades, complaints over pay, leaving certificates, dilution, failure on the part of employers to keep the records of changes in working rules, etc., have been almost continuous and have at times led to disputes of serious proportions. Open defiance of the government, showing itself in the form of called strikes, has perhaps been infrequent, but voluntary cessation of work and other methods of showing dissatisfaction by curtailing production have been resorted to.

In May, 1917, the dissatisfaction in the engineering trades came to a head. Employers were substituting piece work schedules for time schedules and the new rates of remuneration proved unsatisfactory. New machinery was being introduced and laborers were beginning to suspect that it would be impossible ever to carry out the pledges which had been made by employers under Schedule 2 of the Munitions Acts to restore the prewar conditions. Two new subjects of complaint arose about this time: (1) The government found it necessary to withdraw the exemption card agreement which it had made with the Amalgamated Society of Engineers,[1] and which permitted all skilled men of that organization engaged on war work or enrolled as war munitions volunteers, who held exemption cards issued by the society, to escape military service. This withdrawal created great dissatisfaction, although, outside the engineering trades, this singling out of the Amalgamated Society for special privileges had produced dissatisfaction in other unions. (2) The Munitions of War (Amendment) Bill which had been introduced into the House of Commons authorized the dilution of labor on private work. The government had promised in 1915, when the Munitions of War Bill was being prepared, that it would not extend dilution to private work. The need of men for military service was now so great that it asked to be relieved of its promise. Many unions gave their consent, but the Amalgamated Society of Engineers would not do so. When the bill was brought up in the House of Commons, the engineers began to remain away from work and a silent strike

[1] See *ante*, p. —; also *British Industrial Experience*, vol. 1, pp. 324-325.

was being carried on which by the middle of May was causing great embarrassment to the government.

Steps were taken to conciliate the engineers and to make evident to them the need for a change in the government's policy. Certain concessions were offered to them in return for their support. These were:

(a) A promise that when it was necessary to extend dilution to private work, advance notice would be given in the newspapers and three weeks allowed for any protest by any union concerned.

(b) The prohibition of the right to strike would not extend to workers in these establishments.

(c) Dilution of labor in these establishments would at once cease with the close of the war.

(d) Certain concessions were made in regard to standardization of wages, arbitration and the abolition of leaving certificates.[1]

These proposals were not, however, acceptable to the Amalgamated Society of Engineers and they would not agree to dilution on private work. Consequently, when Mr. Winston Churchill became Minister of Munitions, after some further efforts to reach an agreement with the unions, it was decided to omit this part of the scheme from the amendment to the Munitions Acts.

Outside the engineering and shipbuilding trades, the strikes of 1916 and 1917 have not been of a very serious character. Thirty thousand jute workers at Dundee were out on strike for a 15 per cent advance of wages from March 24 to June 8, 1916.[2] Threats of a strike on the railways of the United Kingdom led the government to extend Part I of the Munitions Act, 1915, which pertains to the settlement of industrial disputes, to the railways on August 8, 1917.[3] For the first four months of 1918 the strikes have been numerous, but can not be said to have been very serious or of long duration. They show, however, a disposition on the part of the men to take advantage of the war needs to demand changes favorable to labor, and the needs of employers and the government are such that concessions are usually made.

[1] Gray, op. cit., pp. 51-52.
[2] Labour Gazette, 1917, p. 283.
[3] British Industrial Experience, vol. 1, pp. 269-270.

The rising tide of industrial discontent among the laboring classes, as evidenced by the strike statistics which we have given, did not fail to impress the government officials responsible for the conduct of the war. Desiring to proceed in an intelligent manner to quell this discontent, the government decided in June, 1917, to appoint commissions of inquiry to investigate the causes of industrial unrest and to make recommendations to the government in regard thereto. Before proceeding to discuss the work of these commissions, it is desirable to report briefly the work of an unofficial inquiry into the same subject which had already been made.

BRITISH ASSOCIATION REPORT ON INDUSTRIAL UNREST

The section of economic science and statistics of the British Association for the Advancement of Science, which very early in the war had committees at work investigating industrial and financial phases of the war had a committee investigating the causes of industrial unrest, which made its report early in 1916. This committee was made up of representatives of employers, trade unionists (among whom was Mr. Harry Gosling, President of the Trades Union Congress), economists, such as Charles Booth, Archdeacon Cunningham, Professors Sidney Chapman and E. C. K. Gonner, and other scientifically trained men. The personnel of the committee was such as to make its conclusions of more than ordinary value and the resemblance between its findings and those of the several government commissions, appointed later, lends additional interest to its report. The committee found the principal causes of industrial unrest to be as follows:

1. The desire of work people for a higher standard of living.
2. The desire of work people to exercise a greater control over their lives. and to have some determining voice as to conditions of work.
3. The uncertainty of regular employment.
4. Monotony in employment.
5. Suspicion and want of knowledge of economic conditions.
6. The desire of some employers for more regular and satisfactory labor.
7. The effects of war measures.[1]

[1] Kirkaldy (Editor): *Labor, Finance and the War*, 1916, pp. 21-22.

Some of these causes, it will be noticed at once, have nothing to do with the war, notably number 3, for lack of regular employment certainly could not be a matter of complaint in the middle of 1916. Number 7, on the other hand, relates solely to the war.

1. The committee notes the fact that industrial discontent is coincident with the rise in the cost of living in recent years and that the breakdown of the industrial truce which had prevailed during the early months of the war came at a time when food prices began to show a considerable and steady increase, wages not having risen in equal degree. There is more involved in this question, however, the committee points out, than the mere maintenance of the standard of living. " Work people desire to raise their standard, and this desire has been stimulated by education." The committee admits that this is laudable, but points out that " it is impossible to raise the general standard of living, indefinitely, by raising wages, without at the same time raising the productivity of our industries." [1]

2. The desire of the work people to exercise a greater control over their lives is, the committee declares, a reflex of the extension of the democratic movement from political to industrial life. Disputes over wages, while still most numerous, are not the only ones. Many strikes are now over questions of shop management, discipline and trade union principles. The workers themselves do not seem to have realized the full significance of these demands and in only a few cases have they been definitely formulated by labor groups, but they are likely to play a larger part in the industrial life of the future. Such demands have up to the present time chiefly concerned themselves with restriction of output as a means of protection against speeding up, and reduction of piece rates.

The demand for a recognition of trade unions is partly due to a knowledge that " the more perfect their organization, the more easily will they be able to increase the material benefits which they can obtain for their members," but it is also because

[1] Kirkaldy, *op. cit.*, p. 24.

the "work people believe that the power to control their own lives and the conditions under which they work—*i.e.*, industrial freedom—can only come through a strong and disciplined organization." [1]   In these more important ways and in many minor ways, according to the committee, are workmen showing a tendency to claim " some share of control over the discipline of the workshop." " They are dissatisfied with the status of the wage earner, and call into question the actual relationship that exists in industry today between the different factors concerned. . . . What they aim at is a change in the relationship between employers and work people." [2]

3. " All the work people who have submitted memoranda," says the committee, agree in emphasizing the uncertainty of employment as one of the main causes of industrial unrest. Unemployment insurance has lessened the evil, but the benefits are insufficient for married workers and the majority of workmen are unaffected by the scheme. The committee urges an extension of unemployment insurance, continued efforts to decasualize labor and the establishment of the custom of giving longer notice to those whom it is intended to discharge.

4. Monotony of employment the committee considers as perhaps inevitable under modern conditions of industry, but says that it constitutes " a considerable strain on the nervous system and predisposes the workers to unrest." It points out, however, that monotonous work need not necessarily lead to a monotonous life. Modern town life offers opportunities for pleasure and recreation. What the workers need are opportunities for education, leisure and the material means of obtaining recreation. Inside the factory the monotony may be lessened by brighter and healthier buildings and by a better distribution of rest periods.[3]

5. Suspicion on the part of the workers that they are being exploited is due largely to a want of knowledge of the facts concerning the economic condition of the industry in which they are engaged. The laborers lack the knowledge concern-

---

[1] Kirkaldy, *op. cit.*, p. 26.
[2] *Ibid.*, pp. 26-27.
[3] *Ibid.*, pp. 28-29.

ing market conditions, profits and the commercial and financial position of the industry which might enable them to understand the employers' point of view.

6. The desire of employers for more regular and satisfactory labor represents the employers' point of view in explaining industrial unrest. Employers point to the failure of many men to work regularly and show how this restricts output. They claim that laborers are becoming less reliable and less efficient, that the "least skilled and slowest man employed on the work in question is apt to set the standard for the whole." The committee believes that these conditions could be, at least partially, remedied by the employers regularizing employment as much as possible, discouraging overtime and remembering that laborers are human and should be treated accordingly. To the laborers the committee preaches thrift and forethought.[1]

7. The war measures which the committee finds to be productive of industrial unrest are the restraints imposed by the Munitions Acts and the high speed and long hours of work which produce physical strain and irritation.[2]

The committee's recommendations concerning the changes needed in the organization of industry[3] are far reaching and bear a remarkable resemblance to the plans set forth in March, 1917, by the report of the reconstruction committee appointed by the Prime Minister, generally known as the Whitley report. Possibly the presence of Professor Sidney Chapman on both committees is responsible for this. These recommended changes will be dealt with in the chapter on industrial reconstruction.

INVESTIGATION BY GOVERNMENT COMMISSIONS

The government commissions appointed on June 12, 1917, by the Prime Minister, " to inquire into and report upon industrial unrest and to make recommendations to the government at the earliest practicable date." were eight in number, each covering a

[1] Kirkaldy. *op. cit.*, pp. 29-32.
[2] *Ibid.*, p. 32.
[3] *Ibid.*, pp. 44-50.

distinct geographical section of Great Britain. There were three members of each commission. They started at work almost immediately and worked with such speed that their reports had been received and advance copies placed in the hands of the Prime Minister by July 17. The shortness of the time consumed may have made the inquiry less thorough than would be thought necessary in times of peace, but there is nothing to indicate that different conclusions would have resulted from a more lengthy investigation. Each commission held from 10 to 30 meetings and examined from 100 to 200 witnesses, representing employers, trade unions and other interests concerned, and considered statements in writing submitted by interested parties.

A summary of the various reports was made by Mr. Barnes of the War Cabinet, which covers in a succinct way the principal conclusions and recommendations of the several divisions of the commission. In this summary the following causes of industrial unrest as revealed by the inquiries of the several divisions are set forth:

1. High food prices in relation to wages, and unequal distribution of food.

2. Restriction of personal freedom and, in particular, the effects of the Munitions of War Acts. Workmen have been tied up to particular factories and have been unable to obtain wages in relation to their skill. In many cases the skilled man's wage is less than the wage of the unskilled. Too much centralization in London is reported.

3. Lack of confidence in the government. This is due to the surrender of trade union customs and the feeling that promises as regards their restoration will not be kept. It has been emphasized by the omission to record changes of working conditions under Schedule 2, Article 7, of the Munitions of War Act.

4. Delay in settlement of disputes. In some instances 10 weeks have elapsed without a settlement, and after a strike has taken place, the matter has been put right within a few days.

5. Operation of the Military Service Acts.

6. Lack of housing in certain areas.

7. Restrictions on liquor. This is marked in certain areas.

8. Industrial fatigue.

9. Lack of proper organization among the unions.

10. Lack of commercial sense. This is noticeable in South Wales, where there has been a breakaway from faith in parliamentary representation.

11. Inconsiderate treatment of women, whose wages are sometimes as low as 13s. ($3.16).

12. Delay in granting pensions to soldiers, especially those in class "W" reserves.

13. Raising of the limit of income tax exemption.

14. The Workmen's Compensation Act. The maximum of £1 ($4.87) weekly is now inadequate.[1]

The Barnes summary gives the high prices and unequal distribution of food, the operations of the Munitions of War Acts, including the matter of leaving certificates and the failure to keep a record of the changes in working conditions and the operation of the Military Service Acts as the universal causes of unrest. The want of sufficient housing accommodations, the liquor restrictions and industrial fatigue, it reports as acute causes in certain districts, but not universal causes of unrest. The other causes, it apparently regards as either local in character or having their root in certain psychological conditions. This psychological condition reveals itself first of all in a lack of confidence in the government's promises and in the trade union officials. Many of the causes mentioned are merely manifestations of this psychological condition.

The reports of the several commissions differ greatly in length and in the thoroughness of treatment. The discussion afforded by the commissioners from the southwest area, for instance, is comprised within the limits of seven pages of the U. S. Bureau of Labor Statistics reprint, while that from the commissioners for Wales and Monmouthshire covers eighty-one pages, describes the various industries within the district, the distribution of the population, the growth of industrial combinations, especially in the mining industry, the character and extent of labor organization, and gives a very interesting discussion of the effect of the physical and industrial environment upon the feelings and modes of thought of the inhabitants and shows how this naturally leads to industrial unrest. This report, like several others, concerns itself with the permanent causes of industrial unrest as well as those which have arisen during the war. The permanent causes it divides into economic, social and

[1] *Industrial Unrest in Great Britain.* Bulletin of the U. S. Bureau of Labor Statistics, No. 237, October, 1917, p. 10. All references to this report are to the reprint of the U. S. Bureau of Labor Statistics.

political. Stated briefly, they are: the steady movement to raise
the standard of living, discontent with the housing accommodation and the unwholesome and unattractive environment, and
political propaganda designed to overthrow the capitalist system.[1]
As these causes are, for the most part, independent of the war,
they are not dealt with at length in the Barnes summary and will
not be further considered here. It is to be noted, however, that
they are probably more fundamental causes of industrial discontent than those which have arisen during the war.

Considering the principal causes of industrial unrest in the
order in which they are placed in the Barnes summary, we find
that practically all of them are mentioned in each of the eight
reports, although opinions vary somewhat as to their relative
importance.

HIGH PRICES AND PROFITEERING

1. There is general agreement that the high prices of food, the
failure of wages to advance in equal ratio and a belief that the
high prices are largely due to profiteering and faults in distribution, constitute the chief causes of industrial unrest.[2] Some of
the commissions went so far as to state that if the food problem
could be solved, the other causes of unrest would disappear or
become of minor importance, and in several districts the testimony of witnesses was quoted to the effect that the laborers
would gladly forego any advances in wages which they had
received if food prices could be reduced to the prewar basis.[3]

Agreement among the commissions as to the *cause* of the high
prices was not quite so general. All of them report witnesses as
stating that the high prices are due mainly, if not entirely, to
profiteering. Among the laboring classes this feeling was, as the
West Midland's commissioners said, " both widespread and
dangerous." [4] It was generally felt that the government was
to blame for not having dealt in an effective manner with this
evil. Evidence as to profiteering was generally not given, the

[1] *Industrial Unrest, loc. cit.,* pp. 159-161.
[2] *Ibid.,* pp. 43, 77, 207.
[3] *Ibid.,* pp. 16, 77, 97, 206.
[4] *Ibid.,* p. 98.

opinions as to its existence resting upon the reports of the large
dividends being earned by many industries, upon reports as to
the low cost of meats at the port of importation, upon reports of
the rotting of food at distant points of the kingdom and upon
the personal observation of the witnesses of signs of luxurious
living by employers and their families. Some of the commissions express doubts as to whether any considerable amount of
profiteering has really taken place. Thus the commission for
Wales and Monmouthshire says:

> We are unable to find evidence of any considerable profiteering on the part
> of the retail trade generally, nor do we think . . . that any large part of the
> increase is attributable to excessive freight paid to shipowners. In so far
> as bread is concerned, we have similarly to exonerate bakers, but we were
> unable to obtain any evidence from millers and wholesale grain importers.[1]

Even those commissions that did not accept, unquestioningly,
the charge of profiteering felt obliged to urge that government
action be taken to reduce the cost of food and to stamp out
profiteering in connection with the distribution of food
supplies.[2]

The explanations given by the commissioners themselves of
the increased cost of foods vary greatly and include among other
things, speculation, inflation of the currency, high freight rates,
destruction of ships by submarines, actual shortage of supplies
and faulty systems of distribution.

The remedies suggested are equally diverse. Some of the
commissions propose a limitation of profits of producers, whole-
salers and retailers.[3] Others suggest that the government
stabilize prices and make up any losses to producers or traders
from the public funds.[4] Other suggestions are a greater use of
the cooperative societies and other existing agencies for effecting
a better distribution of food supplies,[5] an immediate reduction
of prices,[6] or, if this be not possible, increasing wages in the

---

[1] *Industrial Unrest*, loc. cit., p. 180.
[2] *Ibid.*, p. 181.
[3] *Ibid.*, pp. 40, 82, 115.
[4] *Ibid.*, pp. 16, 82.
[5] *Ibid.*, p. 45.
[6] *Ibid.*, pp. 103, 192, 208.

lower paid industries in proportion to the increase in the cost of living.[1]

The most elaborate and best considered plan is that suggested by the commission for Wales and Monmouthshire, which provides:

1. All excess profits derivable from the sale and distribution of commodities for home consumption to be appropriated by the state.

2. The purchase by the government, in so far as possible, of all imported food supplies in the country where produced and the conveyance thereof to this country in requisitioned ships.

3. The fixing by the government of the prices to be charged by wholesale dealer, middleman and retailer, respectively, in respect of each article of food sold in this country, as is already done in the case of cheese.

4. War risk insurance on food supplies to be regarded henceforth as ordinary war expenditure, instead of being added to the price of food supplies.

Only one or two of the commissions refer to the difficulties and dangers of price fixing, but they seem to be appreciated by the commission for the southwest area, which says:

The danger of fixing prices for a commodity is, of course, that the supply may cease. The general rule, therefore, should be not to fix prices unless the whole supply is controlled. When this can be done the control should extend from the field of production to the shop counter, and intermediate charges should be limited to a fair remuneration for services rendered.[2]

OPERATION OF MUNITIONS OF WAR ACTS

2. Restrictions of personal freedom, especially those arising from the operation of the Munitions of War Acts, is the second cause of industrial unrest, as given in the Barnes summary. It is closely related to the third and fourth causes, as there given, *viz.*, lack of confidence in the government, and delay in the settlement of disputes, and is not differentiated from them in the discussion by the eight commissions. The three causes, all arising mainly from the operations of the Munitions Acts, will therefore be considered at this point.

It is quite evident from a perusal of the various reports that the rank and file of trade unionists had never accepted the idea that the restrictions imposed upon their personal freedom by the

[1] *Industrial Unrest, loc. cit.*, p. 192.
[2] *Ibid.*, p. 120.

Munitions of War Acts were necessary, and their dissatisfaction with the laws increased, rather than diminished, as time went on. Their dissatisfaction was not alone with the government. One of its most striking manifestations was the distrust which the men had come to have for the trade union executives who had accepted the principles underlying the Munitions Acts and had consented to the incorporation of these principles into legislation. Evidences of this lack of faith in their leaders appear in the reports from nearly every district, but are best set forth in the report of the commissioners for the Yorkshire and East Midlands area, which declares that

> a belief has been engendered in practically all the members of the Amalgamated Society of Engineers and kindred societies we have examined, whether of the advanced or moderate section of thought, that the executive officers of their unions are now powerless to assist them in their present difficulties. . . .
> The result of this apparently universal distrust alike of the trade union executive and of the government departments who act with, and through them, has led to the formation of a vigorous defensive organization for the protection of the workmen inside their own separate workshops, known as the "shop committee" or "rank and file" movement, with shop stewards elected from the workers in every shop.[1]

This organization the commissioners go on to say "threatens to become, in our opinion, a most serious menace to the authority and entire work of the Amalgamated Society of Engineers and other skilled workers' unions."[2]

The subjects of complaints arising from the operation of the Munitions Acts were:

(a) leaving certificates;

(b) the dilution of labor;

(c) failure to record changes of practice as provided under Article 7 of Schedule 2 of the Act of 1915;

(d) inequality of earnings as between skilled and semi-skilled or unskilled labor;

(e) inability or unwillingness to restore prewar conditions;

(f) arbitrary or unsatisfactory action of the munitions tribunals;

(g) delay in securing settlements in matters in controversy when these matters are submitted to the Committee on Production or the Ministry of Munitions.

[1] *Industrial Unrest*, loc. cit., pp. 77-78.
[2] *Ibid.*, p. 78.

(a) Most of the commissions said relatively little concerning the matter of leaving certificates, for while these certificates more than anything else required by the Munitions Acts gave rise to discontent, it was generally understood, while the commissioners were sitting, that the government proposed to modify those sections of the acts which dealt with leaving certificates in such a way as practically to abolish them.

The men felt that to require them to obtain the consent either of their employer or of a munitions tribunal before they could leave their place of employment to obtain work elsewhere, even at higher wages, practically placed them in a condition of industrial servitude. The commissions were practically unanimous in giving their approval to the abolition of the leaving certificates, although some of them stated that employers were fearful of the results on the mobility of labor from the withdrawal of the certificates, and the laborers were apprehensive over the conditions which it was understood would be substituted for the leaving certificates when the latter were withdrawn.

(b) Dilution of labor was complained of much more in some districts than in others. Opposition to it seemed to be slight when the workers were convinced of its necessity. Complaint was made, however, that the workers were not consulted, nor their consent obtained by employers, before attempting dilution, as they apparently felt was called for by the Munitions Acts. Opposition was much stronger to the proposal to extend dilution to private work. The workers claimed that this was a direct violation of the promises made by the government at the time the Munitions Acts were adopted. To extend the plan to commercial undertakings seemed to them merely a method of increasing the profits of private owners. It was the last straw in an accumulation of burdens which had been imposed upon the workers by a government which had refused to listen to their complaints and when complaints to trade union officials were in vain the shop stewards took it upon themselves to call strikes in the spring of 1917 and they found a willing response on the part of thousands of workers.[1]

[1] *Industrial Unrest, loc. cit.*, p. 82.

All the commissions which made recommendations concerning the matter urged that great caution be exercised by the government in extending dilution to private work and that, if it were found necessary to do this, the matter be taken up with the unions—not merely their leaders—and convincing reasons be furnished as to the necessity for this step.

(c) The complaint of failure to record changes of practice on the part of employers, as provided by Article 7 of Schedule 2 of the Munitions Act of 1915, was not general. The commissioners for the northwest area said that "the system of recording in this district seems to be well conceived and carefully carried out."[1] Such complaints as existed were confined to a few trades and were due to a want of knowledge of the methods adopted.

In general it may be said that complaints in regard to this matter were not supported by evidence. They seem to have been merely the outcome of suspicion on the part of the workers that employers were not recording all changes. The acts themselves provided a remedy for any difficulty arising from this source and the government had provided the machinery for its enforcement. Differences of opinion in regard to what constituted a real change of practice might easily arise, but such differences of opinion might be referred to the Ministry of Munitions for its decision in regard to the matter.

(d) The complaint as to inequality of earnings between skilled and semi-skilled or unskilled workers presented a real difficulty for which none of the commissions had a satisfactory solution to propose. The difficulty was largely one of the trade unions' own making. In order to protect the wage standards which the unions had built up before the war, they secured a promise from the government that where semi-skilled or unskilled labor was put on to do the work which had been done by skilled workers before the war the same rates of pay for that work should continue and there should be no reduction in price rates. The consequences were such as could hardly have been foreseen. The splitting up

_____

[1] *Industrial Unrest,* loc. cit., pp. 21-22.

of the processes of work so that they could be done by workers
of little training. and the introduction of improved machinery
enabled these new laborers, working at repetition work and at the
old piece rates, to earn sums undreamed of before the war and
more than was being earned by the skilled worker, usually a
member of the Amalgamated Society of Engineers, who was
working on time rates and was in some cases supervising the
work of these highly paid piece rate workers. The situation in
these trades is eloquently set forth in the report of the commissioners for the West Midlands area:

In the engineering trade £4 ($19.47) a week for a man or woman who
has entered the trade since the war is not an unusual wage; whilst in many
cases the wage reaches £6, £8, and £10 ($29.90, $38.93, and $48.67) a week or
even more, all, be it understood, by workers with no previous experience.
At the same time the tool maker and the gauge maker, both skilled men,
whose skill is the basis on which the machine operates, are still working on
a prewar rate, plus the bonuses and advances received since the war, but,
taking all these into account, are receiving considerably less than the piece
worker.

The result may be imagined. The skilled man with a life's experience
behind him sees a girl or youth, whom perhaps he himself has taught, earning
twice as much as he does. The injury to his self-respect is as great as that
to his pocket. His grievance is aggravated by the fact that the leaving
certificate system prevents him from taking up repetition work himself.
The hard case of these men is recognized by the employer equally with the
workman. Many employers would welcome any scheme whereby a bigger
share of the wages paid went to the tool maker. Their difficulty is that
they are forbidden to take anything from the piece worker and give it to the
day worker, for this would in fact be to reduce piece rates, and unless they
can do this they do not see their way to increase wages.[1]

Although all the commissions had something to say concerning
these inequalities of earnings among operatives, there were few
practicable remedies proposed. To withdraw the prohibition on
reducing piece rates, or to pool the earnings, so that the supervisors and tool makers would receive a larger share than the piece
workers, would subject the government to the charge of having
broken its pledges to the workers. It was proposed that the tool
maker be placed on piece work, but trade unionists and some
employers did not consider this practicable. The one practicable
solution was to grant the supervisor or skilled worker a bonus

[1] *Industrial Unrest, loc. cit.*, p. 96.

on the output of the factory or department, but this meant an increase in the wage bill and naturally was objected to by employers.[1]

(e) Fear on the part of the workers that employers would not carry out their obligations to restore prewar conditions when once the war was over rested in part on mere suspicion of lack of good faith on the part of employers and the government and in part on the impracticability of carrying out such a restoration in view of the changes which were being wrought in industry. This question of the restoration of prewar conditions, said the commissioners from the northwest area, is " probably the question which most exercises the minds of the industrial community —employers as well as employes," [2] and the commissioners from other districts seem almost equally concerned over the matter.[3] Furthermore, the commissioners seem, in some instances, to share the workers' uncertainty as to the practicability of keeping the promises. Some of them, indeed, do not doubt but that the pledges can and will be kept and they express the desire that the government reiterate its promises.[4] Others think that the doubt in the minds of the workers arises from the fact that they see no tangible evidence that the government is making provision for meeting the conditions which will arise after the war.[5] Still others feel that the government should make clear to the men that if variations have to be made these will be made with the assent of the unions.[6]

(f and g) Dissatisfaction with the work of the munitions tribunals and complaints of delay in securing settlements in matters of controversy between employers and employes, whether these matters were referred to the tribunals, to the Committee on Production or to the Ministry of Munitions, were cited by nearly all the commissions as causes of industrial unrest.

In the northeast area " delay in securing arbitration on the

---

[1] *Industrial Unrest, loc. cit.,* pp. 21, 25, 83, 102.
[2] *Ibid.,* p. 24.
[3] *Ibid.,* pp. 109, 118, 179.
[4] *Ibid.,* pp. 25, 56, 83, 121, 180.
[5] *Ibid.,* p. 25.
[6] *Ibid.,* pp. 95, 102, 215.

question of wages " was said to have been one of the causes for
the strike of the engineers in the spring of 1917.[1] Too much
government control in these matters is complained of in the
northwest area, and delay due to the fact that the settlement of
disputes has to be referred to London.[2] In the West Midlands and in the southeastern area the work of the munitions
tribunals is objected to and the men feel humiliated because the
meetings are held in the police court with its " objectionable
criminal atmosphere." [3] Great delay when appeals are taken to
the Committee on Production or the Minister of Munitions is
also complained of in some districts and the ambiguous terms in
which the awards are drawn are a further cause of complaint.[4]

In Wales the commission finds that " delays on the part of the
government in effecting settlements of disputes have proved a
frequent source of irritation and in more than one instance have
led to stoppages of work in industries of national importance." [5]
This commission also claims that the machinery set up to deal
with disputes and claims for advances is too cumbrous, and the
persons selected to deal with these matters are " often entirely
ignorant of the conditions obtaining in the industry affected." [6]

The commission for Scotland reports that workmen and their
representatives find by experience that they get prompt consideration of their grievances only when they threaten to go out
on a strike.[7] Several of the commissions give their approval to
the principles set forth in the report of the reconstruction committee as affording a practicable method of settling industrial
differences.

OPERATION OF MILITARY SERVICE ACTS

3. The operation of the Military Service Acts is the third of
the major causes of industrial unrest as given in the Barnes
summary.

[1] *Industrial Unrest, loc. cit.,* p. 26.
[2] *Ibid.,* pp. 48-49.
[3] *Ibid.,* pp. 93, 112.
[4] *Ibid.,* p. 97.
[5] *Ibid.,* p. 164.
[6] *Ibid.,* pp. 211-212.
[7] *Ibid.,* pp. 164-165.

Complaints are reported by the commissions from all the districts in regard to the matter, but the causes for complaint vary, and a consideration of the several reports shows that much of the discontent was due to a lack of understanding as to the necessity for certain military measures or for a reversal of policies. Nearly all the commissions are careful to state that the great majority of laborers in their district are loyal and that they do not oppose military conscription. Yet all of them assert that the workers are greatly dissatisfied with the operation of the acts. The commission for Scotland probably expresses the opinion held everywhere when it says:

The whole system of the operation of the Military Acts is, in the opinion of the great bulk of the working classes, an exhibition of bungling incompetence, and of exasperating dilatory methods.[1]

The chief causes of complaint are:

(1) Exemption of skilled laborers in certain unions by the trade card scheme. This mode of procedure was objected to by the unions to which it did not apply and by nonunionists, as well. On the other hand, when the trade card scheme was withdrawn, the unions affected, like the Amalgamated Society of Engineers, complained of broken government pledges and also complained that they had been put to great expense in preparation for the issuance of cards which were withdrawn before the system had really gone into operation. At the time the several commissions made their reports, however, the trade card scheme was not causing serious unrest and most of the commissions were of the opinion that its withdrawal was a good thing.

(2) The schedule of protected occupations (M. M. 130) which was substituted for the trade card scheme was criticized for the following reasons:

(a) It gave protection only where a claim for protection was made out and thus threw the burden of proof upon the worker to show that he should be granted exemption.

(b) Those workers who were refused exemption could not understand the reason for the refusal when men in other trades who were bad time keepers or indifferent workers were exempt, merely because they had selected certain occupations which were called "protected trades."

(c) There was more or less confusion in issuing the red and black cards

[1] *Industrial Unrest, loc. cit.*, p. 217.

under the new system, and owing to this confusion and to changing regulations men did not know what was their exact status.

(d) There was complaint that employers in the protected trades undertook to intimidate their men by threatening to release them for military service if they persisted in trade union activities or resented imposition.

(e) The men who had been granted the right of appeal to enlistment complaint committees supposed that they would be heard in person by these committees. Instead it seems to have been the practice to decide the appeal solely on the basis of the statement made by the man on the printed form sent him. The commission for the northwest area says:

"It may be that appeals in many cases are dilatory and frivolous, but it passes our comprehension how any man can claim that he is possessed of a judical instinct acute enough to decide this question merely by reading an official form filled up by an uneducated man." [1]

(f) Skilled men claimed that unskilled men (dilutants) got red cards while they could get only black ones.

(g) Married men claimed that unmarried men were frequently given preference over them.

(3) There were other and perhaps minor causes of complaint in regard to the Military Service Acts, such as objection to the employment in industry of Belgians of military age, complaints that men once rejected were not allowed to settle down with an assurance that they would not again be called up, that men who had fought and been discharged were again called up, that conscientious objectors were not exempt, that businesses built up by an individual were not given due consideratioh, that army officials at times refused to meet trade union officials to discuss grievances of the men, that officers handling recruiting lacked business experience, that medical boards were incompetent and were subjecting men to unfair treatment in their examinations and that skilled men who had passed a trade test and were employed on work of national importance were drafted into labor or work battalions, where they spent months on work which did not require technical training.

Most of these matters the commissions admitted were faults of administration and could be easily remedied. It was suggested by several of the commissions that a great part of the unrest caused by the Military Service Acts could have been

[1] *Industrial Unrest*, loc. cit., pp. 58-59.

avoided if the government had been more open with the public and had made clear the reason for its actions. It was also suggested that the lists of protected occupations needed revision and that the unions which had men in these occupations should be authorized to distribute exemption cards to their members.[1]

LACK OF COORDINATION BETWEEN GOVERNMENT DEPARTMENTS DEALING WITH LABOR

4. The Barnes summary admits that there is general complaint through all the districts that there is " a want of coordination between government departments dealing with labor." [2] An examination of the reports made by the several commissions shows that the chief matters complained of under this heading are as follows:

(1) There are too many departments dealing with labor matters and employers and workmen are often at a loss to know which department to approach when they seek an adjustment of their differences.

(2) Every little detail in regard to industrial relations has to be referred to London.

(3) There is unnecessary delay in taking up and settling disputes.

(4) Contradictory orders and directions are sent out from the different departments.

(5) There is industrial interference by London officials who do not understand local conditions.

The following recommendations are made as to the best method of lessening this confusion and interference.

(1) Employers and workmen should be given more freedom to settle their own differences.

(2) There should be a greater centralization of the government departments dealing with labor and only one recognized channel (the Minister of Labor) for all communications relating

[1] *Industrial Unrest, loc. cit.*, p. 88.
[2] *Ibid.*, p. 11.

to labor. Reference should be made by him to the appropriate department.

(3) High officials of labor and munitions, clothed with authority to settle most differences, should reside in each area, and be ready to visit at a moment's notice localities where unrest appears.

The Barnes summary, while admitting that there may be a want of coordination between the government departments dealing with labor, says that much of what has been said in the reports concerning this matter arises from a lack of a clear understanding of departmental administration. " It seems hardly possible that any single department could during the war carry the whole of the immense problems of the supply departments which have bearing upon the control of labor." [1]

The matters just discussed under the four headings given constitute the universal causes of unrest, reported on by the commissions from all areas. There are in addition to these several other causes which are acute in several districts and which will be briefly discussed here.

BAD HOUSING CONDITIONS

1. The housing conditions are shown to be serious in several areas. The commission for the northwest area made a special report for Barrow in Furness and declared that the situation in that place and the failure of either the government or the municipality to take any practical steps to deal with the matter " has now become a crying scandal." [2]

Barrow is an important munition center in an isolated corner of the northwest of England. It is there that the engineering establishment of Vickers (Ltd.) is located. This plant alone had increased its working population during the war from 16,000 to 35,000, of whom 6,000 are women. Already at the outbreak of the war " there was a well recognized shortage of houses in Barrow." The commissioners give figures which show that

[1] *Industrial Unrest, loc. cit.,* p. 11.
[2] *Ibid.,* p. 67.

whereas in 1913 there were 13,259 houses to accommodate a population of approximately 69,000, at the end of March, 1917, there were only 14,791 houses to hold a population in excess of 85,000. Vickers had supplied nearly half of the additional houses built during the war period.

The commissioners cited instances (1) where nine and even ten people lived in one room, (2) where women had been confined in a room where several other members of the family and a lodger lived, (3) where women expecting confinement were forced to leave their apartments without there being other places to receive them, and other shocking cases of overcrowding. They were very bitter in their criticism of the authorities for having failed to remedy the situation, which was all the more inexcusable when one remembers that under the munitions acts workmen were unable voluntarily to leave employment in a munitions plant to seek employment elsewhere under more favorable circumstances.

In Wales and Monmouth the conditions under which people lived in the mining villages " in sunless houses and in dark back rooms " were shown to be affecting the working capacities of the miners and their dispositions generally.

The workers feel deeply discontented with their housing accommodation and with their unwholesome and unattractive environment generally. The towns and villages are ugly and overcrowded; houses are scarce and rents are increasing, and the surroundings are insanitary and depressing. The scenery is disfigured by unsightly refuse tips, the atmosphere polluted by coal dust and smoke and the rivers spoilt by liquid refuse from works and factories. Facilities for education and recreation are inadequate and opportunities for the wise use of leisure are few.[1]

The situation in this area, it will be noticed, was a matter not of the war's creation but nevertheless deserves consideration as one of the causes responsible for industrial discontent.

In Scotland, the commissioners reported, that they had had " startling revelations of the acute need of houses in industrial centers." It was said that there was immediate need of 100,000 workers' dwellings and that there had been practically no building during the war, and that even before that the need of houses

[1] Industrial Unrest, loc. cit., p. 160.

was sorely felt. The industrial unrest created by this lack of housing accommodations was sufficient to warrant immediate government action.[1]

These were the only areas in which the housing question was dealt with at considerable length, but the commissions from the northeast, the southeast and the southwest areas include the lack of housing accommodations among the causes for industrial unrest.[2]

LIQUOR RESTRICTIONS

The restrictions on the sale and quantity of liquor are said in the Barnes summary to be one of the acute causes of unrest in certain districts. Five of the eight commissions discuss the matter as applicable to their areas. The commissioners from the Yorkshire and the Wales areas do not mention the liquor restrictions and the only mention of them made by the commissioners from Scotland is to say that it is "a remarkable fact" that no complaint was made from any quarter of the liquor restrictions.[3]

In the northeast area the commissioners say that while "the liquor restrictions have not generally led to the creation of industrial unrest," the restrictions on the quantity of beer which can be brewed had led to resentment. The workers believed that beer was an indispensable beverage for men in the so-called "hot" or "heavy" trades. If they were convinced that the restrictions on brewing were necessary in the interests of food conservation, the laborers would accept them with loyal acquiescence, but the belief was prevalent that the food conservation need was being used as an excuse for forcing prohibition, and this the great body of workers opposed. The commissioners also thought that some modifications of the order fixing the evening closing hour at 9 p.m. for licensed premises on the northeast coast might be desirable in the interests of the men who worked overtime.[4]

[1] *Industrial Unrest, loc. cit.,* p. 208.
[2] *Ibid.,* pp. 18, 106, 119.
[3] *Ibid.,* p. 221.
[4] *Ibid.,* pp. 17-18.

In the northwest area the liquor restrictions were said to "contribute to unrest rather than cause it." One employer observed that while the liquor restrictions were perhaps not a cause of unrest, they were "a source of a considerable loss of social temper." The commissioners expressed the opinion that "the schemes of betterment" of temperance reformers "must be kept in their proper place until after the war." They expressed about the same views as the commissioners of the northeast had done in regard to the hours of closing, but said "the more serious cause of unrest" is in regard to "the price of beer and the quality supplied." Government control, in the opinion of the commissioners, should extend to the matter of insisting that the quality of the beer was good and that it was furnished at a reasonable price.[1]

The supplementary report of the commission dealing with the situation at Barrow in Furness laid emphasis on the fact that the early closing hours were causing customers of public houses "to buy bottles of spirits, take them home and consume them too rapidly," which the commissioners felt was especially deplorable in view of the overcrowded houses in Barrow.[2]

The commissioners for the West Midlands area were "frankly amazed at the strength of the objections to the liquor restrictions." Complaints were made in regard to "hours, price and scarcity" and of these the last was "by far the most galling."[3] The commissioners recommended an increase in the supply of beer and a decrease in the price.[4] The same complaints and recommendations are made by the commission for the southwest area.[5]

In London and the southeast area, it is said that "the restriction on the sale of beer and the increase in the price of it has produced hardship, ill feeling and irritation." Inequality in the distribution of supplies was a special grievance here. "In Woolwich, a place to which there is an enormous daily immigration,

[1] *Industrial Unrest, loc. cit.*, pp. 59-60.
[2] *Ibid.*, p. 72.
[3] *Ibid.*, pp. 98-99.
[4] *Ibid.*, p. 103.
[5] *Ibid.*, pp. 118, 120.

public houses are frequently closed for days together on account of want of supplies." [1]

INDUSTRIAL FATIGUE

Industrial fatigue is another acute but not universal cause of unrest, according to the Barnes summary. In one sense, it may be said to underlie all other causes. Every one of the commissions refers to its existence and while few of them place it in the front rank of those causes responsible for industrial unrest, there is plenty of evidence to indicate that it may be a predisposing cause for complaint in regard to other matters.

The workmen are tired and overstrained, and this is not the only result of their work, but is also due to the nervous strain of the war. (Division 4.) [2]

Continued work often carried out under anxieties caused by the war, has tended to cause strain amongst the industrial classes just as it has amongst other classes. (Division 1.) [3]

Men begin to ask themselves whether the sacrifices they are making are really necessary. (Division 2.) [4]

There is ample evidence to show that the continuous labor and duly extended hours during the war have caused a state of nervous exhaustion in large numbers of workers which has made them more susceptible to influences contributing to unrest. (Division 5.) [5]

Considerable evidence was given of industrial fatigue, especially among the classes who have been kept continuously on long hours. (Division 6.) [6]

A condition of nervous strain produced by overwork, uncertainty as to combing out, restrictions on liberty and the like, has also tended to ruffle the tempers of the men and to make them highly sensitive to real and fancied injustice. (Division 7.) [7]

We have not seen any evidence that these (war tension and industrial fatigue) are causes of industrial unrest, although probably they are aggravations of it. (Division 8.) [8]

The workers have been for three years working at high pressure during too long hours and under strenuous workshop conditions never before experienced. They have been denied all opportunities of relaxation and recuperation, and this, too, at a time when there was an ever growing physical weariness and fatigue. There is among some of them a regrettable amount of uncertainty and suspicion as to the aims and objects of the war, the issues

[1] *Industrial Unrest, loc. cit.*, pp. 108-109.
[2] *Ibid.*, p. 99.
[3] *Ibid.*, p. 27.
[4] *Ibid.*, p. 41.
[5] *Ibid.*, p. 106.
[6] *Ibid.*, p. 118.
[7] *Ibid.*, p. 162.
[8] *Ibid.*, p. 221.

of which do not stand out as clearly as they did in the autumn of 1914. The nerves of the men and their families are racked by hard workshop conditions, low and unfair wages in some cases, deficient housing accommodations, war sorrows and bereavements, excessive prices of food, the vagaries of the recruiting officer, and withal by a feeling that their privileges as members of certain trade unions had been given up only to better the condition of others who had not served any apprenticeship to their trades. (Division 3.) [1]

LOCAL AND MINOR CAUSES

Of the local and minor causes of industrial unrest presented in the reports of the several commissions, complaints in regard to the low scale of remuneration of warehouse workers, railway clerks and national health insurance agents and of the conditions of work of railway men and of the failure to carry out the promises to pay women workers the same rates of pay as were given men for the same work are made by the commission for the northwest area.[2] The employment of German prisoners in conjunction with British workmen and the better conditions which they enjoy are subjects of complaint in London and the southeast.[3] Low wages in agriculture and the autocratic management of the dockyards by the Admiralty are dealt with by the commission from the southwest area.[4]

Casual work by dock and wharf laborers, the employment of Chinese labor on British ships while British seamen are unemployed, the unsympathetic attitude of some employers towards trade unions and the refusal of a small section of workers to recognize their obligations to join trade unions, are considered by the commissioners from Wales and Monmouthshire to be among the permanent economic causes of industrial unrest, while the lowering of the income tax basis, the failure to take steps to train and employ men discharged from the army and the navy and the inadequacy of war pensions, separation allowances and workmen's compensation are among those causes for discontent which are due directly to the war.[5] Failure to pay trade union dues,

[1] *Industrial Unrest, loc. cit.*, p. 81.
[2] *Ibid.*, pp. 60-63.
[3] *Ibid.*, p. 109.
[4] *Ibid.*, p. 119
[5] *Ibid.*, pp. 159, 160; 184-186.

competition among unions, the inadequacy of the sum (£5—$24.33) allowed to seamen who lose their kits through a vessel being torpedoed or mined, delays in paying seamen entitled to compensation and lowering of the income tax so as to bring workmen within its range are all made the basis of complaint by Scotch workmen.[1]

GOVERNMENT INSTITUTES IMMEDIATE REFORMS

In spite of these minor differences as to the causes of industrial unrest in the several districts, the thing which most strikes the reader of the reports is the remarkable unanimity among the commissions as to the extent of industrial unrest and the principal causes for its existence. The unanimous character of the reports did not fail to leave its impression upon the government which had instituted the inquiry and steps were at once taken by the appropriate government departments to carry out the recommendations made by the commissions as far as these recommendations were deemed to be of a practicable nature. Within six weeks from the time when Mr. G. N. Barnes, Minister for Labor, had presented the reports of the commissions on industrial unrest to the Prime Minister, he was able to report that progress had been made in the direction of carrying out the recommendations of the commissions along the following lines:[2]

1. *Food Prices and Profiteering.* The Food Controller had formulated a definite scheme for the reduction of prices, the stoppage of profiteering and the regulation of the distribution of essential foods and was on the point of putting the new plan in operation. The plan included the appointment by local authorities of food control committees in every county or metropolitan borough to cooperate with the Food Controller and assist in the administration of his orders and regulations. Maximum prices were to be fixed for certain commodities over the supply of which control could be obtained from producer down to the

[1] *Industrial Unrest, loc. cit.,* pp. 213, 219.
[2] *Christian Science Monitor,* September 26, 1917.

retailer. In some cases the wholesale prices were established by the Food Controller and the retail prices by the local committees. In other cases the retail prices were fixed by the Food Controller, but the committees might grant "temporary and provisional licenses for the charging of retail prices in excess of those specified." In the case of nearly all imported commodities, where the sole control was in the hands of the government, schemes for equitable distribution of the commodities were provided.[1] The general purpose of the orders and regulations was "to do away with profiteering altogether, . . . to limit profits at every step from the producer to the consumer, and at the same time to regulate the supply."[2]

2. *Munitions of War Acts.* The Munitions of War (Amendment) Bill of 1917 had been passed before Mr. Barnes made his report of progress and this amendment contained several provisions intended to lessen the dissatisfaction felt by the laborers with the operation of these acts. It gave the Minister of Munitions the power to abolish the leaving certificates and it was understood that this would be done within a few weeks when certain safeguards had been devised which would prevent the migration of skilled laborers to less skilled but more remunerative occupations. The amendment contained provisions intended to prevent arbitrary changes in piece rates, and a special committee had been appointed to endeavor to correct the situation arising from the discrepancy between skilled time and unskilled piece workers. The amendment act also gave power to the Minister to make awards binding on all employers in the trade —the familiar "common rule," as it is known in Australasia. Mr. Barnes also stated that a committee of trade unionists was being appointed to advise Mr. Winston Churchill, the Minister of Munitions, on industrial questions.[3] The original plan of the government to apply the dilution policy to private work had been abandoned, thus removing another cause for complaint.

3. *The Military Service Acts.* The numerous complaints

[1] *Monthly Review of U. S. Bureau of Labor Statistics*, November, 1917, pp. 91-104.
[2] *Ibid.*, December, 1917, pp. 100-101.
[3] *Christian Science Monitor*, September 26, 1917.

occasioned by the operation of the Military Service Acts, it was thought, would be lessened somewhat by the transference of recruiting to the National Service Commission—a civilian department. This would give an opportunity for a full consideration of the industrial demand for men as well as the military needs and would help to reduce the friction between these two interests which had arisen.

4. *Housing.* Mr. Barnes reported that a far reaching scheme of housing after the war was being undertaken by the Local Government Board through the local authorities. It was hoped that in those communities where the reports of the commissions had shown there was serious need for additional houses, some immediate action would be forthcoming.

5. *Agricultural Wages.* The act fixing a minimum wage for agricultural workers had received the royal assent. The minimum wage fixed by the bill (25s. a week) was that recommended by the commissioners reporting on industrial unrest.

6. *Workmen's Compensation.* The Workmen's Compensation (war addition) Bill, which had been introduced in consequence of representations made by some of the commissioners that the maximum of £1 payable under existing acts was totally inadequate under existing conditions, had become a law. It not only raised the maximum amount payable but also provided for a one quarter increase in the sums payable to those whose earnings were below £2 a week.

7. *Delays in Granting Pensions.* These had been at least partially overcome by recent legislation.

8. *Seamen's Compensation.* The losses to seamen who had served on vessels torpedoed or mined and who had lost their effects were covered by extending the scheme of compensation, which applied to transports and government chartered vessels, to officers and men on all British ships. The maximum amount payable had also been increased.

9. *Relations between Employers and Employed.* The recommendations made by the Reconstruction Committee on Industrial Councils and the setting up of trade constitutions were

being dealt with as rapidly as the importance of the subjects would warrant.[1]

STRIKE IN THE ENGINEERING INDUSTRY

How far these attempts to remedy the industrial situation have satisfied the workers it would be difficult to say. The record of industrial disputes for the latter part of 1917 and the early half of 1918 do not indicate that industrial unrest in Great Britain has been quieted to any considerable degree. Probably the deeper causes can not be reached while the strain of war time continues. How ready the workers in the engineering trades are to respond to real or assumed grievances is shown by the recent (July, 1918) strike caused by the " embargo." This strike in the engineering industry in July, 1918, was due fundamentally to a widespread discontent which has been prevalent for several years in these trades (1) over the extension of dilution, (2) to the failure of the government to make the obligations to restore trade union conditions after the war legally binding on employers, and (3) to the belief that industrial conscription in one guise or another was actually being applied to the engineering industry.

This feeling was intensified and brought to the breaking point by the discovery that the Minister of Munitions (Mr. Winston Churchill) had issued secret orders to certain firms in Coventry and elsewhere, " forbidding them, under drastic penalties, to engage any new or additional skilled men, whilst leaving them free to increase the dilution by taking on semi-skilled men. These orders were apparently to be kept from the workmen's notice. Unfortunately, one firm nailed them up on its gate, and as one of the trade union officials observed immediately ' the fat was in the fire.' To the men it seemed as if the intention was to make it impracticable for any man to change his employers, under penalty not only of loss of income but also of a prompt calling up for the army." [2] The government acted vigorously in the

[1] *Christian Science Monitor*, September 26, 1917.
[2] *New Statesman*, July 27, 1918, p. 325.

matter and gave notice that it intended to call up for military service all men on strike.   Trade union opinion throughout the country on the merits of the strike was divided and after a few days most of the men returned to work.

CHAPTER X

Industrial Reconstruction

None of the warring countries seems to have given more thought to after the war problems than has Great Britain. It is a remark which has been made so often that it has become commonplace that " this will be a different world after the war," but not many people have set themselves deliberately the task of endeavoring to ascertain just how the war is changing industrial relations or in what ways these changes can be controlled so as to insure an improvement in the working and living conditions of the great mass of mankind—the laboring classes.

In all countries in which the carrying out of a political or military program requires the consent and cooperation of the great mass of the people, it is obvious that that program must be one which will appeal to the needs and desires of the laboring classes. The government of Great Britain recognized this fact at the outset and gave organized labor a position in the war councils of the nation and sought the support of the leaders of the trade unions in carrying out its military and industrial program. In spite of wide differences of opinion which have developed between the coalition government and some of the leading trade unionists, and in spite of much industrial discontent, it is only fair to say that the government has never failed for long to receive the support of most of the labor leaders and of the great majority of their followers.

Government Recognition of Labor Demands

The government has, on its part, gone far to recognize the legitimacy of many of the labor demands and of the feeling which has grown up, that in the new industrial order which is to arise at the close of the war, labor is to play a much larger part in the management of industry than most industrial managers or governmental leaders have hitherto been willing to concede to it. A most striking example of this new point of view in government circles is to be found in an informal reply made by Mr. Lloyd George to a deputation sent by the Labor party on Tuesday, March 6, 1917, to present to the Prime Minister a series of resolutions which had been adopted at a party conference held in Manchester the preceding January to discuss "after the war" problems. The significance of this statement lies, of course, in the fact that while it was made in an informal manner and as an expression of a personal opinion, it was made by a man occupying the highest official position in the land and who had been accepted by Parliament as its leader.

After the deputation had presented the resolutions and several members had offered explanations as to their meaning and purposes, the Prime Minister spoke, in part, as follows:

There is no doubt at all that the present war . . . presents an opportunity for the reconstruction of the industrial and economic conditions of this country such as has never been presented in the life of, probably, the world. The whole state of society is more or less molten and you can stamp upon that molten mass almost anything so long as you do so with firmness and determination. . . . I firmly believe that what is known as the after the war settlement is the settlement that will direct the destinies of all classes for some generations to come. The country will be prepared for bigger things immediately after the war than it will be when it begins to resume the normal sort of clash of selfish interests which always comes with the ordinary work-a-day business affairs and concerns of the world. I believe the country will be in a more enthusiastic mood, in a more exalted mood, for the time being—in a greater mood for doing big things; and unless the opportunity is seized immediately after the war, I believe it will pass away, I will not say forever, but it will pass away far beyond either your ken or mine, and perhaps beyond our children's. Therefore, you are doing well in giving your time and thought to considering, and considering deeply, and considering on a bold scale, on a daring scale, what you are going to do after the war.

I am not afraid of the audacity of these proposals. I believe the settlement after the war will succeed in proportion to its audacity. The readier we are to cut away from the past, the better are we likely to succeed. . . . I hope that every class will not be hankering back to prewar conditions. I just drop that as a hint, and I hope the working class will not be the class that will set such an example, because if every class insists on getting back to prewar conditions, then God help this country! I say so in all solemnity.

Therefore, what I should be looking forward to, I am certain, if I could have presumed to have been the adviser of the working classes would be this: I should say to them, "Audacity is the thing for you." Think out new ways; think out new methods; think out even new ways of dealing with old problems. Don't always be thinking of getting back to where you were before the war; get a really new world.[1]

To what extent the Labor party accepted the advice given on such high governmental authority is evident to all who have read the social reconstruction program of the British Labor party.[2] The executive committee of the party in its annual report to the Nottingham Conference itself remarks somewhat dryly apropos this interview:

On that occasion the Prime Minister, after having had an opportunity of considering the series of resolutions referred to, advised the party to "be audacious"! Judging from the comments that have followed the publication of the Report on Reconstruction, a general impression may be gathered that there has been little hesitation in adopting the Prime Minister's advice.[3]

RECONSTRUCTION PROGRAM OF BRITISH ASSOCIATION

The first constructive suggestions of reforms needed in the field of labor did not, however, originate with organized labor— at least not from the laborers alone. During the first year of the war the Economics Section of the British Association for the Advancement of Science set itself the task of studying, somewhat intensively, the economic and financial problems of the war and the way in which the changes in industrial relations caused by the war could be turned to good account in the recasting of industry in the after the war period.

The first year's report [4] of the committees appointed did not present the subject of industrial relations in any notably fresh way. In the published speeches on the promotion of industrial harmony [5] there are some interesting facts growing out of the industrial experience of the various speakers, representing both

[1] Report of the Sixteenth Annual Conference of the Labor Party, p. 169.
[2] *Labor and the New Social Order*.
[3] Report of the Seventeenth Annual Conference of the Labor Party. Nottingham and London. 1918, p. 37.
[4] Kirkaldy (Editor): *Credit, Industry and the War* (London, 1916).
[5] *Ibid.*, pp. 17-67.

employers and employed, and in the final essay[1] by the venerable
Archdeacon of Ely (William Cunningham) there are some hints
as to the direction which state enterprise may take in the future,
but there is nothing in this volume which could be regarded as a
program for the relations between employers and workers.

In the report of the second year,[2] however, we find in the
report of the Committee on Industrial Unrest, sketched in rough
outline, a program for the organization of industry which is of
interest, not only for the suggestions themselves but because it
contains the germs of the later reports of the government's
Reconstruction Committee on joint standing industrial councils
and perhaps of some portion of the program of the British Labor
party.

The membership of this British Association committee was
composed of not only professional economists and social re-
formers, like Professors Kirkaldy, Chapman, Scott and Gonner,
Archdeacon Cunningham, Hon. Charles Booth and Mr. Sidney
Ball, but of prominent employers like Sir Hugh Bell, Sir C. W.
Macara and Mr. Pickup Holden and of trade union leaders like
Hon. C. W. Bowerman and Mr. Harry Gosling. Professor
Chapman is the only member of this committee who was also a
member of the subcommittee of the Reconstruction Committee
which made the report on joint standing industrial councils.
This may or may not be of significance, but perhaps too much
importance should not be attached to the resemblance between
the proposals of the British Association Committee and those
contained in the Whitley report. Simliar plans for the reconstruction of industry seem to have been in the minds of many
persons. They had already found a partial expression in producers' cooperative societies and in the trade agreements made
by the best organized trade unions and the employers' associations in several industries which gave definite recognition to the
rights of trade unions to participate in industrial management,
in so far as the wages and working conditions were affected by
this management.

We have already noted [3] the causes of industrial unrest as they

[1] Chapter V, Economic Problems After the War.
[2] Kirkaldy (Editor) : Labour, Finance and the War, chap. ii.
[3] Chapter IX.

are set forth in this report of the committee of the British Association. The recommendations which the committee makes for the removal, or at least the alleviation, of these causes are as follows: (1) An improvement in the general attitude and outlook of employers and workmen, which could be accomplished, the committee thinks, by frankness on both sides and by a willingness on the part of both employers and workers to discuss industrial matters together, by a better knowledge on both sides of "the fundamental facts and principles of economics," and by having employers consider the collective cost of labor, and not the total amount of wages earned by the workman each week; (2) better machinery for dealing with disputes, calling for a recognition by the state of approved associations of employers and trade unions and of the enforcement of trade agreements, for "permanent joint boards or committees" in each industry, "to consider all matters of common interest to both employers and employed," and of a national joint board, composed of representatives of employers and workers, similar to the industrial council created by the government in 1911, but whose services had never been utilized; (3) a better organization of industry along lines which will presently be shown; and (4) certain postwar arrangements in regard to demobilization, the carrying out of the government's agreements with the trade unions and an effort to forecast commercial and financial development with a view to the determination of a labor program.[1]

The suggestions in regard to industrial boards or committees and of a national joint board to settle industrial disputes bear a close resemblance to those later made by the Reconstruction Committee, but the most interesting suggestions by the British Association committee are found in the section (3) relating to the organization of industry. The committee begins its recommendations under this heading with the advice: "*That the necessity for cooperation between employers and employed be frankly recognized by both parties.*" Calling attention to the interdependence in industry of capital and labor, the committee urges employers to refrain from speeding up production to the point

[1] *Kirkaldy, op. cit.,* pp. 40-52.

where the workers suffer from fatigue, and workers are urged not to restrict output in a way which precludes the attainment of maximum production in the long run. Both sides are urged to cooperate in determining by observation and experiment what is the work limit which yields the highest output with the least fatigue. In many industries it should be possible to obtain " a standard working day and a standard speed for machinery which would be a rough indication of the point at which the industry would attain its maximum long period efficiency." In industries in which work was not standardized and in which " gluts of work alternate with periods of slackness," the problem would be more difficult and an effort should be made to decasualize industry as far as possible. To secure the highest results in production when two or more persons cooperate in producing, there must be an equitable method of sharing the joint product, in order that the different parties concerned shall be satisfied with their share of the product. The committee makes no recommendation on the subjects of a minimum wage or a fixed return on capital because " the conditions in different trades and districts are so varied that it would not be possible to make hard and fast rules on either point." It leaves these matters to be settled by the " local or central joint boards," which it is about to suggest.[1]

The committee's suggestions as to the kind of cooperation between employers and employed in the processes of production are such a departure from the present methods of shop management and so closely resemble the later suggestions made by the committee on reconstruction that it seems best to quote them at length.

The cooperation between work people and managers should go further than the mere distribution of the products of industry. The carrying out of the processes of production, as we have seen, involves a series of cooperative actions which can be accomplished best if the parties concerned work together with full confidence in each other. This spirit can be attained only if all those engaged in industry feel that they have some share in determining the conditions under which the work is carried on. At the present time these arrangements are made by the managers, and, if the work people are

[1] Kirkaldy, *op. cit.*, pp. 44-46.

not satisfied with them, they may attempt to force concessions by with-holding their labor.

How far is it possible for the work people to take part in the organiza-tion? With such things as the marketing of products labor is only indirectly concerned, but with others (*e.g.* workshop arrangements and the speed of machinery) it is directly concerned. Those functions of organization which are concerned with bringing together the different factors of production, determining the proportions of these factors in any enterprise, and bring-ing the product to the consumers, must remain in the hands of the managers. It is important that the most capable persons shall have the management, and the best way of securing this is to leave the system of free enterprise as it exists today.

Variations in the demand for an article, or in the price of raw materials, may involve changes in the kind of machinery, the proportion of machinery used in relation to other factors, and so on. These are questions which are dependent on the judgment of those who are responsible for the higher management, and must, therefore, remain under their control.

There are other branches of organization concerned with the detailed working of factories which might be carried out by cooperation between the workers and the management. They are functions which, in a large factory, are sometimes delegated to works managers and foremen, and concern the precise arrangement as to hours of work, rest periods, working shifts, speed of machinery, the subdivision and grading of labor, discipline, etc. These matters might be determined with the assistance of a committee of workers who know the conditions existing in the factory. Such arrangements could not be left entirely in the hands of the work people without any conditions as to output. A certain minimum output would have to be fixed for each workshop so controlled, and it would be to the interests of the industry and all those engaged in it to increase this output as much as possible. Such a committee would be able to guard against excessive speeding up, and would remove one of the main causes to which restriction of output is attributed. Industry would be likely to gain, not only from the removal of these re-strictions, but also from the more willing cooperation of the workers and the possible saving in the cost of supervision. It is reasonable to expect that fewer foremen and supervisors would be required.[1]

The committee discusses at considerable length the questions which would have to be considered and the possible modifications which would have to be made in industrial arrangements when labor saving machinery is introduced or new processes are adopted which diminish the amount of labor so that both the interests of the workers and those of employers will be protected. The suggestions made by the committee proceed on the assump-tion that both employers and employed are well organized and

[1] Kirkaldy, *op. cit.*, pp. 46-47.

are prepared to carry on collective bargaining. Both the employers and the workers are recommended to organize along the following lines:

1. Associations of one trade in a given district.
2. National associations of each trade.
3. Local federations of trades.
4. National federations of the trades.

The national federations of workers and of employers should elect an industrial council, which should act as a court of appeal in industrial disputes which could not be settled otherwise. Approval by the state should be given to these organizations when they work in accordance with its regulations, and the state would be the protector of the consumers and of the national interest. It is said that "under this system, work people would enjoy all the advantages aimed at by the extreme party such as the Syndicalist, but the dangers and risk inseparable from a revolutionary policy would be avoided." [1]

TRADE UNION AGREEMENT

It was stated above that the views concerning the reorganization of industry did not originate with members of the working classes or, at least, not with them alone. Who, within the membership of the British Association committee on the subject of industrial unrest, was the first to suggest the essential features of the program we have just discussed, we are not informed. Professor Kirkaldy of the University of Birmingham was the Chairman of the committee and seems to have been mainly responsible for the form in which the proposals are set forth, though he tells us that within the committee the points on which the members were in agreement were " infinitely more important than those on which there was some difference of opinion." [2] We must now hasten to add that if the " intellectuals " first gave coherent expression to the new views concerning industrial organization, which must doubtless have been taking shape in the minds of many men even in the years antedating the war, another

[1] Kirkaldy, *op. cit.*, pp. 47-50.
[2] *Ibid.*, preface, p. iv.

expression of the same views comes from trade union circles so soon following the completion of the British Association Committee's report that it shows that its author had either for some time held the same views as those expressed by the committee or was so well prepared mentally to accept them when they were first presented that he quickly made them his own.

Mr. Harry Gosling, who was President of the British Trades Union Congress in 1916, and the following year was President of the Transport Workers' Federation, was one of the members of this British Association Committee on Industrial Unrest, where he either imbibed the new ideas concerning labor participation in industrial management, or, more likely, helped to develop them. At any rate in his inaugural address at the Trades Union Congress, held at Birmingham in September, 1916, we find him, after stating the labor problems which are likely to come up for solution at the close of the war, giving expression to the longings of the working man in the following words:

> Would it not be possible for the employers in this country, on the conclusion of peace, when we have rid ourselves of the restrictive legislation to which we have submitted for war purposes, to agree to put their business on a new footing by admitting the workmen to some participation, not in profits, but in control?
>
> We workmen do not ask that we should be admitted to any share in what is essentially the employer's own business, that is, in those matters which do not concern us directly in the industry or employment in which we may be engaged. We do not seek to sit on the board of directors, or to interfere with the buying of materials, or with the selling of the product. But in the daily management of the employment in which we spend our working lives, in the atmosphere and under the conditions in which we have to work, in the hours of beginning and ending work, in the conditions of remuneration, and even in the manners and practices of the foreman with whom we have to be in contact, in all these matters we feel that we, as workmen, have a right to a voice—even to an equal voice—with the management itself. Believe me, we shall never get any lasting industrial peace except on the lines of democracy.[1]

That such a plan for the reorganization of industry after the war had not yet formed the subject of deliberation by national gatherings of the laboring classes seems evident from the fact

[1] Report of Proceedings of the Birmingham Trades Union Congress, 1916, p. 61. The same views are expressed in the author's pamphlet, " Peace: How to Get and Keep It," p. 10.

that we find no mention of any such a plan in the after the war resolutions adopted at the Manchester conference of the Labor party in January, 1917, which resolutions were subsequently presented to the Prime Minister, as already noted.   The only reference to the control of industry in these resolutions has reference to industries which have been or may be nationalized. The resolution dealing with this matter states that " no schemes for the nationalization of industry can be accepted as satisfactory which do not provide for their effective control by the workers in those industries." [1]

Other discussions of after the war problems which took place about this time show that the idea of a fundamental change in the relations between employers and employed had not yet taken possession of the minds of either group in such a way as to lead to a definite formulation of a program for the democratic control of industry.   In January, 1917, a conference was held in London between representatives of capital and labor which was presided over by the Right Hon. Frederick Huth Jackson, President of the Bankers' Institute, to consider after the war problems, at which it was agreed that Parliament should be urged to establish a board whose functions it should be " to regulate and supervise (a) the reinstatement in civil employment of the present forces; (b) the settlement in normal employment of civilian workers now in government or controlled establishments; (c) any general redistribution of labor arising out of the war.[2]   It is at once obvious that these resolutions, dealing only with the subjects of demobilization and the redistribution of labor, are

---

[1] Report of the Sixteenth Annual Conference of the Labor Party, 1918, p. 123.   The executive committee of the Labor party in presenting the report of its subcommittee entitled *Labour and the New Social Order*, which has been so widely circulated and has created such a sensation because of its radical and far seeing plan of reconstruction, declared that this documnt had been " based on resolutions adopted by previous conferences, particularly the series passed by the Manchester Conference in 1917." (" Report of the Seventeenth Annual Conference of the Labor Party." Nottingham and London, 1918, p. 37.)   While this is doubtless true of many of the proposals found in this justly famous document, it should be noted that the demand for democratic control of industry which finds expression therein does not call for such a cooperative control of industry as is proposed by the Reconstruction Committee of the War Cabinet.

[2] *Monthly Review of United States Bureau of Labor Statistics*, March, 1917, p. 479.

much narrower in scope than the recommendations of the British Association committee and could hardly have influenced the government to set forth a program for the reorganization of industry. They may have exerted some influence in leading the government to appoint a committee to consider the subject of industrial reconstruction, though there is no evidence to support this view.

REPORT OF THE RECONSTRUCTION COMMITTEE

Prior to the formation of the present government, the subject of reconstruction had been dealt with by Ministers of the Crown who were members of the Cabinet—the so-called Cabinet Committee. After the new government took office this arrangement continued for a time and various subjects were dealt with and reports were made thereon by subcommittees appointed for this purpose.[1] Among these subcommittees was one called the Subcommittee on Relations between Employers and Employed, of which the Right Hon. J. H. Whitley, M.P., was the Chairman.

This subcommittee was asked:

1. To make and consider suggestions for securing a permanent improvement in the relations between employers and workmen.
2. To recommend means for securing that industrial conditions affecting the relations between employers and workmen shall be systematically reviewed by those concerned, with a view to improving conditions in the future.[2]

This committee issued an interim report on the subject of joint standing industrial councils on March 8, 1917.

In this first report the committee dealt only with the problem of how to secure "permanently improved relations between employers and employed in the main industries of the country, in which there exist representative organizations on both sides." It was felt that the circumstances of the times, when industry had been forced to a temporary reorganization to meet war needs, which would in turn necessitate another readjustment when the

[1] The War Cabinet Report for the Year 1917, p. 199.
[2] Interim Report of Subcommittee, etc. Reprinted in Bulletin 237. U. S. Bureau of Labor Statistics, p. 229. (Parliamentary Paper. Cd. 8606.)

war was over, offered a great opportunity to secure that the cooperation between employers and employed which the war had brought about should not only continue but should be strengthened. The committee did not hesitate to express the opinion that "any proposals put forward should offer to work people the means of attaining improved conditions of employment and a higher standard of comfort generally, and involve the enlistment of their active and continuous cooperation in the promotion of industry." In order to provide the means of securing this cooperation between employers and employed the committee recommended that the government "should propose without delay to the various associations of employers and employed the formation of joint standing industrial councils in the several industries where they do not already exist, composed of representatives of employers and employed, regard being paid to the various sections of the industry and the various classes of labor engaged."

Among the matters to which these councils should give their early attention are questions of demobilization and how the government guarantee and the undertakings of employers to restore the trade union rules and customs suspended during the war are to be met. The committee recognized that in some cases employes as well as employers would not desire to have the old rules and customs restored, but it insisted that any new arrangements to be made must not only have the acquiescence of the unions but must be the joint work of employers and employed.

To complete the work of organization of any industry, it is not sufficient to have only this national industrial council.

What is needed is a triple organization—in the workshops, the districts, and nationally. All three organizations should proceed on a common principle and the committee offered the following proposals to be laid before the national industrial councils:

(a) That district councils, representative of the trade unions and of the Employers' Association in the industry, should be created or developed out of the existing machinery for negotiation in the various trades.

 (b) That works committees, representative of the management and of the workers employed, should be instituted in particular works to act in close cooperation with the district and national machinery.

The design for these committees should be a matter for agreement between the trade unions and the employers' associations in each industry, for only in this way could their support for such a scheme be secured. " The object is to secure cooperation by granting to work people a greater share in the consideration of matters affecting their industry and this can only be achieved by keeping employers and work people in constant touch."

 While admitting that the respective functions of works committees, district councils and the national councils would have to be determined in accordance with conditions which had grown up in each industry, the committee made mention of the following questions which, it thought, might well be dealt with by the national council or be allocated by it to the district councils or works committees:

 1. The better utilization of the practical knowledge and experience of the work people.

 2. Means for securing to the work people a greater share in and responsibility for the determination and observance of the conditions under which their work is carried on.

 3. The settlement of the general principles governing the conditions of employment, including the methods of fixing, paying and readjusting wages, having regard to the need for securing to the work people a share in the increased prosperity of the industry.

 4. The establishment of regular methods of negotiation for issues arising between employers and work people, with a view both to the prevention of differences and to their better adjustment when they appear.

 5. Means of insuring to the work people the greatest possible security of earnings and employment, without undue restriction upon change of occupation or employer.

 6. Methods of fixing and adjusting earnings, piece work prices, etc., and of dealing with the many difficulties which arise with regard to the method and amount of payment apart from the fixing of general standard rates, which are already covered by paragraph 3.

 7. Technical education and training.

 8. Industrial research and the full utilization of its results.

 9. The provision of facilities for the full consideration and utilization of inventions and improvements designed by work people, and for the adequate safeguarding of the rights of the designers of such improvements.

10. Improvements of processes, machinery and organization and appropriate questions relating to management and the examination of industrial experiments, with special reference to cooperation in carrying new ideas into effect and full consideration of the work people's point of view in relation to them.

11. Proposed legislation affecting the industry.

A careful comparison between this plan for industrial councils and the plan for industrial organization presented in 1916 by the committee of the British Association for the Advancement of Science will show that they are, in essentials, the same plan. The Whitley report makes the plan somewhat more definite than that set forth by the British Association committee, but the general resemblance between the two programs can not help but cause speculation as to whether or not they did not have a common origin in the brain of some one individual.

The Whitley report urges the government to put the proposals made by the committee before the employers' and work people's associations in the well organized trades and to request them to adopt the proposals with the aid of such assistance as the government can give while it acts only in an advisory capacity. To those persons who feared that the combination of employers and employes through the medium of these industrial councils might lead to the sacrifice of the interests of the community, the committee expressed the opinion that the councils would have regard for the national interest. If they did not, the state, which " never parts with its inherent overriding power," could intervene. The committee repeated its statement that the plan presented was only intended for " industries in which there are responsible associations of employers and work people which can claim to be fairly representative." A later report was promised for trades not so well organized, but the committee gave it as its considered opinion " that an essential condition of securing a permanent improvement in the relations between employers and employed is that there should be adequate organization on the part of both employers and work people."

DISCUSSION OF THE WHITLEY REPORT

The reception which the Whitley report has received from employers as well as from employes is remarkable in view of the somewhat radical character of the recommendations which, if adopted, would change fundamentally the prevailing character of the wage system. The report of the committee was made in March, 1917, but was not made public for several months. Meanwhile, the eight commissions appointed to consider the causes of and remedies for industrial unrest had been appointed and had begun their work. They were asked to inquire of the parties which appeared before them their opinion concerning the value of the recommendations of the Whitley committee and the desirability of putting the plan therein proposed into operation. The Right Hon. George N. Barnes, who presented the summary of the reports of the commissions, said that the reports of the commissions bore " a striking testimony to the value of the proposals made in the report of the subcommittee of the Reconstruction Committee, dealing with the relations of employers and employed," and that, " broadly speaking, the principles laid down appear to have met with general approval." [1]

Taking up the reports of the commissions in each of the various divisions, we find the following responses to the proposals of the Reconstruction Committee:

Division 1—Northeast Area. The commissioners advocate the establishment of shop committees to represent the men and to confer with representatives of the employers " for the discussion of questions affecting labor as they may arise in the shops." They express themselves as " thoroughly in accord with the underlying principles " of the report of the Reconstruction Committee on industrial councils. In their own particular area, they feel some doubt " as to whether in view of the existing machinery for the settlement of disputes and the discussion of policy affecting the regulation of labor, there would not be

[1] *Industrial Unrest in Great Britain*, Bureau of Labor Statistics of U. S. Department of Labor. Bulletin 237, p. 12.

considerable danger that the setting up of new machinery might impair the usefulness of that which now exists." In any case they caution against making the machinery too elaborate.[1]

Division 2—Northwest Area. The support of the recommendations of the Reconstruction Committee by the commissioners of this area are very cordial. These recommendations fall in line with suggestions which the commissioners make as to the need of decentralized control of industry by the government. The commissioners assert that " what is wanted in industry is a reconstruction of ideas, and both capital and labor have got to meet together and carry on the machinery of industry on the principle that they must be ready to reject all prospects of gain which involve loss to others."[2] They state that they have been much impressed by the report of the Reconstruction Committee and have placed the proposals before important deputations of employers and workers and have asked their opinion of them. " Although they all expressed a natural desire to consider them more fully, yet the principle at the bottom of them was received with cordial approval. This principle, which seems to us to be a statesmanlike proposal of the best method of dealing with unrest . . . is exactly what is wanted in this area to allay many causes of industrial unrest."[3]

The commissioners urge the importance of presenting the proposals to conferences of the leaders of trade unions and of employers' federations, to see " how the program of the Reconstruction Committee can best be made a living fact." In doing so they suggest that the proposal for works committees be presented and discussed before that for district councils is taken up.

The man at the bench is not greatly interested in district councils, and national industrial councils are to him as far removed from his ambition as the House of Lords, but the shop or works committee is another thing altogether, and this we think should be put right in the front when any endeavor is made to explain the scheme to the working man. We know this by experience, because we have tried to explain the scheme in the "order of going in" assigned to the various councils by the Reconstruction Committee.

[1] *Industrial Unrest in Great Britain, loc. cit.,* pp. 28-29.
[2] *Ibid.,* p. 55.
[3] *Ibid.*

When we approached the matter by describing national councils first, the working man was not interested, as, indeed, why should he be? But when we began to describe the scheme, starting in the shop and gradually by a natural evolution blossoming out into district councils and finally national councils, he got a real grip of what we were telling him, and seemed to think there was a lot in it, and that it was a practical business affair touching his daily life which he would like to take a hand in . . . We can conceive no better method of impressing the people that the government is in earnest in helping to allay industrial unrest than by asking representative bodies of men and employers to start a national mission to the country to explain to working men that in the future handling of labor the workers themselves are to be part and parcel of industrial control.[1]

The commissioners discuss briefly the question of the restoration of prewar conditions and observe that labor leaders in that area desire that the government's promises be " kept in the spirit and not in the letter."

After the war we have abundant evidence that the real hope of the best workers of this area is not a restoration of prewar conditions, but a far, far better thing. As a modern social reformer writes: " We want life raised to a higher level, and while the keenness of our sufferings and the height of our exaltation are still with us, the larger vision prevails," and what they are waiting for here is that someone should announce, from the housetops that this is what the government is ready to carry out with the power of the nation at their back. We have been face to face with men and women who are working for their country, and if the right message comes from those in authority, we can assure the government that they are ready to cooperate with them in bringing about a better condition of things in the industrial world.[2]

Division 3—Yorkshire and East Midlands Area. The commissioners in this area do not refer directly to the proposals of the Reconstruction Committee, but they doubtless have them in mind when they say that many of the men have expressed a willingness to cooperate with the management in establishing some system for the betterment of the industry and when they urge "the immediate introduction and setting up of workshop committees, composed of equal numbers of workers and of the management, the workers being elected by those employed in each works, for the consideration of questions affecting the

[1] *Industrial Unrest*, etc., loc. cit., p. 56.
[2] *Ibid.*, p. 57.

industry." They also provide for reference of matters which can not be settled by local agreement to district councils and if need be to national councils.[1] In this area the plan of a " shop committee," or rank and file movement, with shop stewards elected by the workers in each shop, had already developed in the engineering industry and the commissioners were inclined to view this movement with favor and their recommendations of workshop committees seem to have had in view the extension and further development of this mode of organization.[2]

Division 4—West Midlands Area. The commissioners in this area state that there was a sharp conflict of opinion among witnesses as to the desirability of shop committees. Some felt that both the trade union authority and the employer's authority would be weakened by such committees. The commissioners made no recommendations, but they said that "the weight of evidence on both sides is against the change." On the other hand they favor organization of both employers and employed as " the best security for industrial peace." Of the Whitley report they had this to say:

We express a general approval of that report. We are also impressed with the advantages in large works of frequent meetings between men and their employers, not merely managers or foremen. This takes place in several works where men, either through a shop committee or otherwise, have regular and frequent opportunities of meeting a partner, if the business is carried on by a firm, or a director, if by a limited company. This excellent practice should be made universal; it brings employers and employed into touch, gives a chance of settling incipient grievances, and affords the employed some say as to the conditions under which they work.[3]

Division 5—London and Southeastern Area. There is no specific reference to the Whitley report by the commissioners in this area, though they call attention to the shop steward movement, which they think is likely to lead to revolutionary activities " unless some satisfactory arrangement be made for representation of the work people in shop negotiations." [4]

[1] *Industrial Unrest, loc. cit.,* p. 83.
[2] *Ibid.,* pp. 78, 81.
[3] *Ibid.,* p. 101.
[4] *Ibid.,* p. 111.

Division 6—Southwest Area. The commissioners in this area content themselves with stating that: " The general principle of the Whitley report, which we endorse, is acceptable to employers and workers," and with a commendation of the Ministry of Munitions for establishing workshop committees on the lines recommended in the Whitley report in munition factories. They recommended that the same steps be taken in the Admiralty dockyards, the railway shops, and where possible in all controlled establishments. District councils in the munitions areas are also recommended.[1]

Division 7—Wales and Monmouthshire. The commissioners for this area discuss at much length the proposals of the Whitley committee, the " main principles " of which they " gladly adopt." They say that they had invited opinions from witnesses in regard to these proposals and "quite a large number " of them, representing both employers and employed, "declared themselves in favor of the principles underlying the recommendations." The representatives of both the North Wales Coal Owners Association and of the South Wales Coal Owners Association, so far as they had had opportunity to discuss the matter, favored the plan of industrial councils and even regarded it as essential that some experiment on the lines of the Whitley report be tried. Although the South Wales Miners' Federation had not yet sent in an expression of opinion in regard to the proposals, resolutions from the South Wales Branch of the National Association of Colliery Managers were received, which, while throwing some doubt on the practicability of some of the proposals, expressed the opinion that the joint councils were the best means of securing better relations between employers and employed and called attention to the fact that the coal mining industry was already so highly organized that the machinery for working of the joint scheme could easily be set up.

There was, said the commissioners, " one striking exception " to the general endorsement of the proposals of the Whitley report. The owner of a large steel and tin plate works expressed the opinion that the industrial councils would be used as a means

[1] *Industrial Unrest, loc. cit.,* p. 121.

of manufacturing grievances on the part of the men's representatives. To this the commissioners pertinently reply:

> We think on the whole that this view is probably governed too largely by the idea that like the conciliation boards the main function of these councils would be to consider grievances. The report, itself, however, makes it sufficiently clear that other questions should bulk far more largely among the duties of such councils, and that in so far as wages, for instance, are concerned the councils should limit themselves to the consideration of general principles rather than the actual fixing of definite rates.
>
> We are ourselves of opinion that the machinery of the proposed threefold councils—works committees, district councils, national councils—would provide the means for the developing of the policy we have already advocated of identifying the worker more closely with the control of his particular industry.[1]

The commissioners are particularly desirous that the works committees should have jurisdiction over the discharge of employes and over the appointment and dismissal of "all colliery firemen, examiners and deputies."[2]

Division 8—Scotland. The commissioners from this area deal very briefly with the proposals of the Reconstruction Committee, but they say that the plan suggested "met with general approval." "None of the organizations represented had had time to study it minutely or to consult upon it, but without committing themselves to details, the principle of the report of the Reconstruction Committee was favorably received."[3]

The Ministry of Labor, besides asking the commissions on industrial unrest to make inquiries concerning the attitude of employers and working men towards the proposals of the Committee on Reconstruction, in July, 1917, addressed a circular letter to the principal employers' associations and trade unions asking for their views on the proposals made in the Whitley report. In October the Minister stated that replies had been received from a large number of employers' organizations and trade unions and that they generally favored the adoption of the proposals.[4] Although no compilation of these replies has so

---

[1] *Industrial Unrest*, etc., *loc. cit.*, pp. 172-175.
[2] *Ibid.*, p. 175.
[3] *Ibid.*, p. 219.
[4] Industrial Reports, published by the Ministry of Labor, No. 1, p. 2.

far, as is here known, been published, various expressions of opinion by employers and labor organizations have been made public. It might naturally be expected that labor organizations would generally approve the underlying principles of the plan, since they call for a much larger participation by labor in industrial management than employers have usually been willing to concede. What is most surprising is the cordial reception which the plan seems generally to have received from employers.

The Federation of British Industries, meeting in the summer of 1917, after giving full consideration to the Whitley report, gave its approval to the plan. It is worthy of note that the federation expressed the opinion that in order to insure efficient production after the war it will be necessary to have the cooperation of labor, and that laborers will have the right to demand improved conditions of employment, a higher standard of comfort and an opportunity to appreciate the true interests of the trade in which they are engaged. The federation believes the best results of such cooperation can only be secured when complete organizations of employers as well as employes exist in each trade. If any considerable number of either employers or employes remain outside their respective organizations, it becomes almost impossible to have security for agreements arrived at. The federation considers this point so important that it favors government recognition and standing of organizations of employers and work people, but it desires no interference by the government in the creation of the proposed organization.

In the constitution of the national industrial councils the federation favors centralization of policy and decentralization of administration. The basis of the scheme should be the trade councils of employers and employes, that is, each trade or section of an industry should form a council representative of the employers' organization and of the trade or section of an industry. District councils, it believes, will be chiefly useful in acting as a court of arbitration in the case of any industrial dispute in the trade in the district which arises out of the conditions peculiar to that district.

The federation thinks the works committees should be entirely voluntary in the case of each individual firm, and not in any way officially constituted. The functions of these committees, it thinks, should be limited to reporting to, or receiving from, the management complaints regarding breaches of any agreements which may have been made between the employers and the work people.

It may be said at once that any such limited scope of the work of the works committees would be far from meeting the wishes of the representatives of the working classes who have interested themselves in this plan. Their chief interest in the scheme comes from the promise that through these workshop committees labor can share in the management of industry, in so far as the relations between labor and management are concerned.

The Federation of British Industries would go further than the creation of national industrial councils. There should also be a superior body of representatives of employers and employes in each group of trades which might be called councils of industry and, crowning the entire scheme, a national industrial council, made up of representatives of all industries. These councils could serve among other purposes as courts of appeal from the trade councils where employers and employes in such councils could not agree. The federation also believes that some of the questions dealt with in the Whitley report should be considered, first of all, by the national industrial council and that the final decision in all matters of general policy should rest with the same body after opportunities for criticism had been given to the councils of industry and the trade councils.[1]

If surprise be felt by the reader at the apparently cordial support which British employers have given to the report of the Reconstruction Committee, which implies such far reaching consequences in the relations between employers and employes, a partial explanation for this liberal attitude of employers may be found in the fear which has apparently developed during the war of extended government ownership and management of industry, unless some plan for continued private ownership be

[1] Abstract of report of the British Federation of Industries, as given in the *Christian Science Monitor*, September 22, 1917.

adopted which shall be mutually satisfactory to capital and labor. In the above account of the suggestions offered by the British Federation of Industries, it will be remembered that the view was strongly urged that there should be government recognition of organizations of employers and work people, but no interference with their plan of cooperation. This is only one hint of an underlying feeling on the part of employers which finds more complete expression in a leading article in *The Economist* of December 1, 1917. This journal, it will be recognized, is peculiarly the representative of the financial and commercial classes in Great Britain and therefore may be expected to voice the conservative point of view. After giving its endorsement to the principle of the Whitley report, this article proceeds to contrast the workings of such a scheme for the reorganization of industry with those which it believes to be inherent in any system of government ownership and management, which latter plan it condemns in the following words:

Out of all this clash between government departments on the one hand, and of employers and workmen on the other, much good will arise, though we shall have to pay pretty heavily for it. In the minds both of employers and workmen of all classes is growing up a profound dislike of all government interference, and a not less profound determination to get quit of it at the first opportunity. We have all had a painful lesson in state socialism and it stinks in our nostrils. The old demand of socialist orators that the government should nationalize this, that and the other is moribund, if not dead. What all classes now want, and want so badly that their hearts ache for it, is to complete the war in a manner satisfactory to the Allies, and to get rid of the government control of industry. Both employers and workmen want to try a new system of self-government, and to evolve a method of working which will give to all producers a harmony of interest. Nothing has so greatly stimulated this common desire for cooperation as the experience of working under government control during the past two years, and specially during the last year when departments, commissions and committees have multiplied so rapidly for the confounding of honest, unhappy men who understand their work and want to be allowed to get on with it. When the war ends there will be a reaction towards independence from control which may carry us too far in the opposite direction, but it will be as healthy as the present system is unhealthy.

THE GOVERNMENT ADOPTS THE WHITLEY RECOMMENDATIONS

Expression of opinions favorable to the Committee of Reconstruction's plan for joint standing industrial councils had been so general that by October 20, 1917, the Minister of Labor was ready to announce that the War Cabinet had decided to adopt the Whitley report as " part of the policy which they hope to see carried into effect in the field of industrial reconstruction." The Minister felt it necessary to attempt to quiet certain fears which had been expressed by some persons who had examined the report and to explain why the government felt it desirable that employers and employes should put the plan into operation in the well organized industries. As to the fears which had been expressed, the Minister said : (1) That this plan did not contemplate any extension of state interference in industry. " The formation and constitution of the councils must be principally the work of the industries themselves." When formed they would elect their own officers and determine their own functions and procedure. (2) That the adoption of the plan did not mean that it should be applied without modification to each industry. " Each industry must adapt the proposals made in the report as may seem most suitable to its own needs." In some industries works committees might be regarded as unnecessary. In some industries the functions assigned to district councils might be more important than in others. (3) That " it should be made clear that representation on the industrial councils is intended to be on the basis of existing organizations among employers and workmen in each industry," although the councils when formed might grant representation to any new bodies which had come into existence and which might be entitled to representation. (4) That the scheme was not intended to promote compulsory arbitration.[1]

The reasons why the government was " anxious to see indus-

[1] Industrial Reports of the Ministry of Labor, No. 1, pp. 1-3.

trial councils established as soon as possible in the organized trades," the Minister gave as follows:

(1) The experience of the war had shown the need for frequent consultation between the government and the chosen representatives of employers and workmen in the industries most affected by war conditions, and it was desirable to have clearly recognized who were the proper and duly constituted parties to consult. The problems which would arise during the period of transition and reconstruction would be no less difficult than those which had arisen during the war and the government would need the advice of the industrial authorities.

There are a number of such questions on which the government will need the united and considered opinion of each large industry, such as the demobilization of the forces, the resettlement of munition workers in civil industries, apprenticeship (especially when interrupted by war service), the training and employment of disabled soldiers, and the control of raw materials.

(2) It would further be necessary to insure a settlement of the "more permanent questions which have caused differences between employers and employed in the past, on such a basis as to prevent the occurrence of disputes and of serious stoppages in the difficult period during which the problems just referred to will have to be solved." The Minister stated that the government desired it to be understood that "the councils will be recognized as the official standing consultative committees to the government on all future questions affecting the industries which they represent," and he closed by urging that the representative organizations of employers and employes come together in the organized trades and prepare for the reconstruction period by creating these councils.[1]

THE MINISTRY OF RECONSTRUCTION

The general approval which the report of the Reconstruction Committee received was doubtless partly responsible for the decision of the government to organize a special department to deal with problems bound to arise and to demand urgent attention on the conclusion of peace. On August 21, 1917, Parlia-

[1] Industrial Reports of the Ministry of Labor, No. 1, pp. 3-6.

.ment enacted " the New Ministries Act, 1917, which, with a view to promoting the work of organization and development after the termination of the present war," provided for the appointment of a Minister of Reconstruction. The office was to cease to exist two years after the conclusion of the war. The work assigned to the new Ministry is best shown by quoting the following paragraph from Section 2 of the act creating the ministry:

It shall be the duty of the Minister of Reconstruction to consider and advise upon the problems which may arise out of the present war and may have to be dealt with upon its termination, and for the purposes aforesaid to institute and conduct such inquiries, prepare such schemes, and make such recommendations as he thinks fit, and the Minister of Reconstruction shall, for the purposes aforesaid, have such powers and duties of any government department or authority, which have been conferred by or under any statute, as His Majesty may by order in council authorize the Minister to exercise or perform concurrently with, or in consultation with, the government department or authority concerned.[1]

Since the creation of the new ministry the subcommittee on relations between employers and employed of the Committee on Reconstruction has been continued as the Committee on the Relations between Employers and Employed of the Ministry of Reconstruction. Dr. Christopher Addison, who had been the Minister of Munitions, was appointed as the Minister of Reconstruction. On October 24, 1917, the new Minister made an address in which he set forth in a general way the problems which the new department had to meet. He mentioned in particular the unemployment problem, the competition which would take place at the close of the war among the nations to secure the raw materials needed, the need for cooperation among the traders to help the government and the need for increased productivity which could only come through better cooperation between capital and labor, better conditions of life, better training and better industrial methods. He commended the proposals of the Whitley report and urged employers and workers to get together and " form some machinery for the settlement of differences." The Minister

[1] *British Industrial Experience*, vol. 1, p. 902.

also called attention to the need of improved housing conditions, to satisfy which called for the cooperation of local governments.[1]

The work of the new Ministry is by no means confined to the attempted solution of labor problems, as the foregoing remarks would show, and as is shown even better by the list of commissions and committees which had been appointed by the new Ministry during the year 1917. These include not only committees on demobilization, labor and employment and housing, but also committees and commissions dealing with various aspects of trade development, finance, raw materials, coal and power, intelligence, scientific and industrial research, agriculture and forestry, public administration, education, aliens, legal interpretation and other matters.[2]

Second Report on Industrial Councils

A second report on joint standing industrial councils by the Committee on the Relations between Employers and Employed was made in October, 1917. The first report had dealt only with those industries in which organizations of employers and employed were well established and in which industries, therefore, the machinery for establishing industrial councils could easily be set up. Besides these industries, which the committee treats as Group A, it is recognized that there are two other industrial groups—" Group B, comprising those industries in which, either as regards employers and employed, or both, the degree of organization, while considerable, is less marked than in Group A," and " Group C, consisting of industries in which organization is so imperfect, either as regards employers or employed, or both, that no associations can be said adequately to represent those engaged in the industry."

For the industries in Group B, the committee favors the application of the proposals made in its first report whenever an examination by the Ministry of Labor, in consultation with the

[1] *British Industrial Experience,* vol. 2, pp. 1106-1107.
[2] A list of commissions and committees set up to deal with questions which will arise at the close of the war. Ministry of Reconstruction. London, 1918.

association concerned, shows that the organizations are sufficiently well developed to permit of the application of these proposals. In such industries, however, whenever it is proposed to form a national industrial council one or two official representatives should assist in the initiation of the council and should continue to sit with it in an advisory capacity, without a vote, until the organization within the industry is so complete as no longer to make his presence and advice necessary. Some Group B industries might be so situated as to make district councils unnecessary, though a national council was formed; others might require district councils with or without a national council. Though not directly stated, it is apparently the intention of the committee that works committees should be set up in all establishments in Group B industries where they do not already exist.

Industries in Group C, because of their lack of organization of employers and workers, are not yet ready for either national or district councils or for the sort of deliberation and agreements which take place in these councils. For such industries the committee recommends the application of the machinery of the Trade Boards Act, "pending the development of such degree of organization as would render feasible the establishment of a national council or district council." The committee favors such modifications of the Trade Boards Act as will empower the boards to deal "not only with minimum rates of wages but with hours of labor and questions cognate to wages and hours." Where an industry in Group C becomes sufficiently organized to permit of the establishment of industrial or district councils, the committee recommends that the trade board in that industry bring the matter to the attention of the Minister of Labor, in order that the steps necessary to the establishment of such councils may be taken.

In any industry in Group A or B which has sections or areas in which there is not adequate organization to make participation in the industrial councils practicable, the committee recommends that the national industrial council in that trade apply for an order which shall either institute a trade board for that section of the industry or authorize the industrial council itself to act as a trade board under the act, and the committee recommends legislation which shall give to the Minister of Labor the power to issue such an order. This would bring the entire trade up to the standard of minimum conditions which had been agreed upon by the industrial council. In this way the committee believes that " most of the chief industries of the country could be brought under one or other of the schemes contained in this and the preceding report. There would then be broadly two classes of industries in the country—industries with industrial councils and industries with trade boards." [1]

Works Committees

In the report which we have just summarized, the Committee on Relations between Employers and Employed does not deal with the question of works committees in industries in Group C, but in a supplementary report, made at the same time, it deals with the whole question of works committees. We have already noticed that in the reports of the Commissions on Industrial Unrest, it was stated that the employes consulted showed especial interest in that part of the committee's report which had to do with works committees. The committee itself regards the works committees as " an essential part of the scheme of organization," which it has suggested and it does not hesitate to say that the successful development and utilization of such committees is of equal importance with the commercial and scientific efficiency of the business. It believes that one of the partners or directors of every business should " devote a substantial part of his time and thought to the good working and development of such a committee."

The peculiar function of the works committee is to establish and maintain a system of cooperation between employers and employed in the individual establishment in matters affecting the daily life and comfort of the employes and the efficiency of the business. Such a committee would not concern itself with such

[1] Ministry of Reconstruction, *Second Report on Joint Standing Industrial Councils.* London, 1918.

questions as the rates of wages and the hours of work, for these are matters to be dealt with by district or national councils. Works committees need not all be alike in form, but should conform to the particular circumstances of the trade. The committee emphasizes the statement that such committees must not be regarded as in any way a substitute for, or an interference with, trade unionism. On the contrary the complete success of these committees depends upon the degree and efficiency of organization in the trade. This seems to be the nearest to which the committee comes to answering the question which it had raised in the second report, *viz.*, whether or not works committees could be organized and made use of in industries in Group C.[1] In its supplementary report the committee recommended to employers and employed that they should study the experience which had already been had, both before and during the war, with works committees, and stated that on its recommendation the Ministry of Labor had issued a memorandum on such experience for the benefit of employers and work people.

This report [2] by the Minister of Labor was made public in March, 1918. It is outside the scope of this work to deal fully with this report, which shows what was the extent and what were the functions of works committees which had come into existence in various establishments before and during the war. It may be stated, however, that while such committees, existing under a great variety of names, had long been known in various industries, usually as a part of the machinery of trade unionism, the war was largely responsible for bringing them into existence in the engineering trades, where there had taken place " such a change in both the form and function of workshop organization that the discussion of the general idea of works committees may be said to have developed out of those conditions." [3]

Not one condition but a variety of conditions had been responsible for this war time development of works committees. An

[1] Ministry of Reconstruction, *Supplementary Report on Works Committees*. London, 1918.
[2] *Report of an Inquiry into Works Committees made by the Minister of Labor.* Industrial Reports, No. 2. London, 1918.
[3] *Works Committees*, Industrial Reports, No. 2, p. 3.

embryonic system of shop stewards, acting originally for their trade unions, had in some cases developed into an organization which had gained in strength and prestige as the power of the trade union officials had declined, due to the loss of the right to strike. The introduction of dilution had also presented many questions of detail which required the establishment of dilution committees in many establishments, with which committees of workers the management conferred in its endeavor to answer these questions. So also methods of remuneration, time keeping, welfare work, war charity and other causes had been at times and in various places responsible for the growth of an organization within an industrial establishment which had developed into a genuine works committee, if it had succeeded in securing the confidence of both the workers and the management.[1]

It appears from this report that of the existing works committees there are few on which the management has direct representation. Most of them have only representatives of the workers. Sometimes there are separate committees for the skilled and for the unskilled workers. Separate committees to represent the women workers are rare, but they frequently have representation of some sort on the committee. Where the majority of the men in any establishment are unionists, the tendency is to place only union men on the committee. The size of the committees in existence varies from 12 to more than 30.[2] The report urges strongly that where works committees exist and are recognized and dealt with by the management, those who represent the management on the committee, if it be a joint committee, or who meet the committee, if they are not members, should belong to the highest rank and should include the works manager or, if there be one, the labor superintendent, and one or more of the directors. Both sides are likely to gain by this direct contact between the management and the workers.[3]

The functions of the works committees vary even more than do their types. The rule is almost invariable that their functions are consultative rather than executive:

[1] *Works Committees*, loc. cit., pp. 9-13.
[2] *Ibid.*, pp. 14-20.
[3] *Ibid.*, pp. 25-26.

Usually a works committee can bring matters before the management and discuss them with the management; it can press its views about these matters on the management; in the last resort, it can induce the trade union organization to call a strike. But the works committee can not, usually, as such carry its views into action, or insure that they shall be carried into action by any direct machinery. The management has the executive power, and unless the management is impressed by the representations of the members of the committee, or by the sanction which lies behind them, those representations will not lead to executive action.[1]

The works committees, therefore, present grievances of the workers to the management. Their right to do so is recognized by the management and usually the management welcomes the cooperation of the works committee in attempting to adjust these grievances. The committee does not consider district rates of wages, hours of work or other general conditions common to the district or to the industry as a whole. On the other hand, it does consider and present individual complaints about wages and piece rates. It considers with the management the interpretation of awards and orders and the conditions of work within the establishment. In some cases it has made suggestions as to economies in the running of machinery, has improved time keeping and discipline. The extent to which dilution was to be introduced has been dealt with by some committees and the works committee has been permitted by the management to suggest alternatives to dilution which have been adopted. It seems generally to be admitted that the works committee should be consulted in regard to dismissal of employes and in the matter of reducing the working force in dull seasons. Some employers are willing to take up with the works committee the selection of the foremen.

On the whole, the impression which one gains from the survey of the field covered by such works committees as have come into existence in Great Britain prior to or during the war is that these committees have not yet in most cases come to participate in the management of industrial establishments, to the extent favored by the Committee on the Relations between Employers and Employed of the Ministry of Reconstruction. They have

---

[1] *Works Committees, loc. cit.*, p. 27.

usually come into existence on the initiative of the workers and in engineering establishments, at least, to represent the workers' point of view in ways which could no longer be adequately represented by the trade unions. The employer has, therefore, not usually been directly represented on these committees and while he has tolerated, perhaps even welcomed, their assistance, owing to the necessities of the labor situation, there still remains much to be done before it can be said that works committees can be regarded as a necessary and well recognized part of the machinery of industrial management.[1]

The relations of the works committees with the trade unions can not be said to be definitely settled. Generally speaking, it may be said that the closer these committees are to the management the farther removed are they from the trade unions and *vice versa*, though this is clearly not the desire or intention of the Whitley committee. A certain suspicion of the works committee seems to have been developed among the leaders of unionism, due to the fact that these committees have developed rapidly during the war to deal with questions with which the unions could not deal because of their agreements with the government, which had been translated into legislation. On the whole, however, there seems to be no idea of a permanent hostility between the works committees and the trade unions. " General questions of district or national conditions are left to the trade unions, while the works committee deals with either the detailed application of these general rules within the works or with questions entirely peculiar to the works." [2]

Difficulties arise, of course, where there are several, or even many, unions represented in the same establishment or where the

---

[1] Mr. G. D. H. Cole, "Recent Developments in the British Labor Movement," *American Economic Review*, September, 1918, who speaks of the Whitley report as an "unsatisfactory tribute" to the demands of labor and as being "the offer of a partial and limited joint control by employers and trade union representatives," appears to think that the shop stewards movement which has grown up during the war in the engineering industry is a much more democratic movement than the plan favored by the Whitley report. But if the conclusions of the Ministry of Labor report on works committees are to be relied upon, the influence exercised on industrial management by existing works committees is less than that favored by the Whitley report.

[2] *Works Committees, loc. cit.*, p. 39.

skilled men are organized into unions and the unskilled are not, but these matters are capable of adjustment and, on the whole, it is possible that the development of works committees will strengthen rather than weaken the trade union movement.

CONCILIATION AND ARBITRATION

The mention by the Whitley committee of the subjects of arbitration and conciliation in its earlier reports and the erroneous impression which had been left upon some people that the industrial councils were intended mainly to provide new machinery for settling industrial disputes led the committee at the end of January, 1918, to issue a special report on conciliation and arbitration, in which its views on these subjects were set forth at some length.

The committee is opposed to any system of compulsory arbitration. Full of significance is the following sentence: " The experience of compulsory arbitration during the war has shown that it is not a successful method of avoiding strikes, and in normal times it would undoubtedly prove even less successful." The committee is not even in favor of any scheme " which compulsorily prevents strikes or lockouts pending inquiry," but it does favor agreements between the parties which provide that the matter in dispute shall be left to arbitration, and it favors arrangements in the organized trades " for holding an inquiry before recourse to the extreme measures." It also favors giving to the Ministry of Labor power " to hold a full inquiry when satisfied that it was desirable, without prejudice to the power of the disputing parties to declare a strike or lockout before or during the progress of the inquiry." The position of the committee may therefore be summed up in the statement, voluntary or compulsory investigation and publicity without compulsory arbitration. The committee believes that the machinery for the conciliatory adjustment of disputes which already exists in the important trades of the country is on the whole satisfactory and will continue after the war, as before, to achieve success in most instances, especially as the various conciliation and arbitration boards may become merged in or correlated to the joint industrial councils.

The committee believes that the state might, however, go farther than it had gone in times of peace in furnishing the machinery for voluntary arbitration of disputes, and in reviewing the war experience it reports that, of the various tribunals set up by the government to settle disputes under the Munitions of War Acts, the Committee on Production, consisting of three independent persons appointed by the government, had settled the majority of disputes referred to arbitration during the war, other than those affecting the wages of women on munitions work. The committee therefore concludes:

> For these reasons it would appear desirable that there should be a standing arbitration council on the lines of the present temporary Committee on Production to which differences of general principles and differences affecting whole industries or large sections of industries may be referred in cases where the parties have failed to come to an agreement through their ordinary procedure, and wish to refer the differences to arbitration.
>
> Such tribunal should include in its membership persons who have practical experience and knowledge of industry, and who are acquainted with the respective standpoints of employers and work people.

The committee generally favors a tribunal of three persons, but recognizes that there are cases where a single arbitrator may be preferable for hearing local disputes, etc. It also suggests that in order that there may be coordination of decisions by the local arbitrators, the department which appoints the arbitrators should circulate among them the awards and decisions of the standing arbitration council.[1]

The Government Takes Steps to Establish Industrial Councils

Having satisfied itself that the proposals of the Whitley committee as to joint standing industrial councils generally met with the approval of employers' associations and the trade unions, the

[1] Ministry of Reconstruction, *Report on Conciliation and Arbitration*. London, 1918. This report is reprinted in the *Monthly Labor Review* of the U. S. Bureau of Labor Statistics, August, 1918, pp. 237-240.

British Government announced its own acceptance of the recommendations of the committee's report as far as they called for action on its part and on October 20, 1917, the Minister of Labor announced that " the government desires it to be understood that the councils will be recognized as the official standing consultative committees to the government on all future questions affecting the industries which they represent, and that they will be the normal channel through which the opinion and experience of an industry will be sought on all questions with which the industry is concerned." [1]   In order that a council should be entitled to this recognition, however, it must satisfy the Minister of Labor that it was so constituted as to be truly representative of the industry.   The government has set forth at some length what functions it thinks such councils should exercise and has made suggestions as to the form of the constitution of a joint industrial council.[2] It has also expressed the hope that the establishment of such councils will " make unnecessary a large amount of ' governmental interference,' which is at present unavoidable, and substitute for it a real measure of ' self-government ' in industry." [3]

That the government is in earnest in its desire to see the industrial councils established in private industries is evidenced by the report of the representative of the United States Bureau of Labor Statistics in England to the effect that the public interest in the Whitley report is probably greater than in any one reconstruction scheme and that the Minister of Labor is " almost daily attending meetings arranged to enable him to meet associations of employers and work people in a given trade at the same time." [4]
Nearly every trade in the United Kingdom had the question of establishing industrial councils under consideration and up to the beginning of August, 1918, the pottery trade, the building trades, gold, silver and kindred trades, rubber manufacturing, the silk industry, the furniture trade, the manufacture of watches, had all organized joint industrial councils which had held their first

[1] Quoted in the *Monthly Labor Review*, vol. 7, p. 76.
[2] *Ibid.*, pp. 76-79.
[3] *Ibid.*, p. 28.
[4] *Ibid.*, p. 80.

meetings. Twenty-one other industries are mentioned " in which considerable progress has been made towards the formation of joint industrial councils," and " inquiries with regard to the formation of joint industrial councils are now proceeding in some thirty other industries and the ministry of reconstruction have formed interim reconstruction committees for about twenty other industries which may, in some cases, develop into joint industrial councils.[1]

It thus appears that the movement for joint industrial councils is making rapid headway in private industries. The government has been criticized for not having set an example to employers and showing its faith by its works, by setting up industrial councils in its own industries. It has been urged that this be done especially in the Post Office, and the Assistant Postmaster General said in the House of Commons on June 12, 1918, that this proposal would come before the Cabinet in a short time.[2]

INDUSTRIAL COUNCILS AND TRADE BOARDS

Having announced its acceptance of the proposals of the first report on joint standing industrial councils, the government in June, 1918, took up the proposals of the second report and in a joint memorandum of the Minister of Reconstruction and the Minister of Labor set forth its policy with reference to industries in Groups B and C, as dealt with in that report. The announcement was made that it had not been found possible, from the administrative point of view, to adopt the whole of the recommendations contained in the second report, but that the modifications which it had been necessary to make did not affect the principles underlying the committee's reports.

The modifications which it had been found necessary to make were as follows:

(1) It was decided to recognize one type of industrial council only and not to attach official representatives to the council, except on the application of the industrial council itself. The

[1] *Labour Gazette*, 1918. p. 308.
[2] *Monthly Labor Review*, vol. 7, p. 80.

government thus departed from the plan of the committee to recognize the existence of some industries in which industrial organization of employers and employed was only partially developed and which would therefore require official guidance to organize industrial councils. The memorandum says in regard to the distinction in industrial organization which the committee sought to draw: " The only clear distinction is between industries which are sufficiently organized to justify the formation of a joint industrial council and those which are not sufficiently organized," and in regard to the proposal for official advisers, it said: " It is fundamental to the idea of a joint industrial council that it is a voluntary body set up by the industry itself, acting as an independent body and entirely free from state control."

(2) The committee's proposals in regard to industries not having an organization sufficiently developed to warrant the immediate establishment of an industrial council, that trade boards should be continued or established, and that these should, with the approval of the Ministry of Labor be enabled to formulate a scheme for an industrial council, were regarded as impracticable owing to " the wide differences in the purpose and structure of the two types of bodies." The memorandum points out at some length the fundamental differences between the two bodies which may be briefly set forth as follows: (a) A joint industrial council is voluntary in its character; a trade board is a statutory body established by the Minister of Labor. (b) An industrial council is able within wide limits to determine its own functions; a trade board has as its primary function the determination of minimum rates of wages. (c) An industrial council is self-supporting and will receive no monetary aid from the government; a trade board's expenses are defrayed out of public money. (d) An industrial council is composed entirely of representatives of the employers' associations and trade unions in the industry; a trade board includes not only representatives from the industry but appointed members unconnected with the trade. (e) An industrial council exercises direct influence only over the organizations represented upon it; a trade board is not based on

existing organizations of employers and employed, but covers the whole of the trade. The memorandum says that in view of these distinctions in function and purpose between industrial councils and trade boards "it is possible that both a joint industrial council and a trade board may be necessary within the same industry."[1] While this may be possible, this certainly would not harmonize with the avowed purpose of industrial councils which were intended to provide a democratic method of industrial control, without interference by the state.

The discussion of the resemblances and differences between industrial councils and trade boards and a realization of the fact that some industries were not provided for by other schemes may have influenced Parliament somewhat in its decision to amend the Trade Boards Act, 1909, in such a way as to provide for a considerable extension of that mode of industrial regulation. The reasons which prompted the legislation of 1918 are thus stated by the *Labour Gazette*:[2]

In view of the dislocation of industry which it is apprehended may occur after the war, there is reason to fear that the problem of inadequate wages for unskilled and unorganized workers, particularly women, may be rendered exceptionally acute. On the one hand there are a large number of women who have left such occupations as dressmaking in order to work in munition works and other war industries; and on the other hand large numbers of women have entered occupations which were formerly confined to men. The first class will tend to try to find work in their old trades when the demand for war material slackens, with keen competition for employment in these trades as a result; and the second class will in many cases be driven to compete for employment with the returning soldiers. In both cases the competition for employment may reduce wages to an unduly low level, unless precautionary measures are taken.

The success of the Trade Boards Act, 1909, seemed assured, but there was need of making such change in the act as should make it unnecessary to secure a parliamentary order before trade boards could be established in new trades. Under the new act the Minister of Labor can bring a trade within the scope of the principal act by means of a special order, although Parliament may later annul this special order. The Minister of Labor may

[1] *Industrial Councils and Trade Boards.* Memorandum by the Minister of Reconstruction and the Minister of Labor. London, 1918.
[2] 1918, p. 307.

also extend the Act of 1909 to "any trade in which on account
of defective organization wages are unduly low, or there is
reason to apprehend an undue fall in wages when the special war
conditions have passed." Under the new act, a rate fixed by
a trade board may be brought into full operation within three
months after it has been proposed by a trade board, instead of
nine months as under the Act of 1909. The recommendation
of the Whitley report that trade boards be allowed to make
recommendations to government departments with respect to
industrial conditions in their trades was also incorporated in the
new act.[1]

RECONSTRUCTION PROGRAM OF THE BRITISH LABOR PARTY

This chapter would be incomplete if it did not discuss, at least
briefly, some of the demands in the reconstruction program of
the British Labor party which has been given wide publicity
under the title of *Labour and the New Social Order*. Although
it is not the function of this monograph to discuss platforms of
any political party, the circumstances under which this document
has appeared, as well as the substance of the proposals themselves
and the forceful, yet dignified way in which Labor has set forth
its after the war aims, justifies us in departing from the usual
rule, especially in so far as the labor planks in the program are
concerned.

The British Labor party, which was formed in 1900 and in
that year had a total membership of 375,931, has had a remarkable growth, especially during the period of the war. In 1917
the total membership, made up of trade union members and
members of socialist societies, with a few members from other
organizations, was given as 2,465,131. The cooperation between
the party and the parliamentary committee of the Trades Union
Congress has become very marked. Furthermore, within the last
year it has appeared that the Labor party is likely to receive
strong support from members of the cooperative societies which
have through their cooperative congress steadily refused in the
past to engage in political activities. Owing to the adoption by .

[1] *Labour Gazette*, 1918, p. 308.

the government of the policy of taxing cooperative dividends as though they were profits, in the face of strong protest from the cooperative societies, an emergency conference of the cooperative movement in London in October, 1917, decided, practically unanimously, to take up political activity. The executive committee of the Labor party and the parliamentary committee of the Trades Union Congress invited the new political committee of the cooperative movement to confer with them in regard to a common program, and this invitation was accepted. It seems likely, therefore, that in seeking to carry out its new program the Labor party can count on considerable support from the cooperative movement.

The executive committee of the Labor party appointed late in 1917 a special subcommittee to consider and report upon the subject of reconstruction after the war. This subcommittee had, by the beginning of 1918, prepared the report entitled *Labour and the New Social Order*,[1] which having received the sanction of the executive committee was published and circulated widely. It was presented to the Nottingham conference of the party in January, 1918, and was by resolution referred by the conference to all the constituent organizations of the party for their consideration prior to being taken up by the conference in June.[2]

The report [3] begins by a recognition of the fact that the world is standing on the threshold of a new era and that, if civilization itself it not about to perish, at least the basis of the existing social order—" the individualistic system of capitalistic production "—has received its death blow. The Labor party, it goes on to say, " will certainly lend no hand to its revival." What the report attempts to do is to lay out the plans for the new social structure which it is hoped will take the place of the one doomed to destruction. The four pillars of the house which the Labor

[1] Mr. G. D. H. Cole says: "This memorandum bears in every line the evidence that it was written by no less a person than Mr. Sidney Webb." ("Recent Developments in the British Labor Movement" in *American Economic Review*, September, 1918, p. 496.)

[2] *Report of the Seventeenth Annual Conference of the Labor Party*, Nottingham and London, 1918, pp. 37, 116.

[3] In the following abstract I have taken the report as published as a supplement to *The New Republic* for February 16, 1918.

party proposes to erect, "resting upon the common foundation of the democratic control of society in all its activities," it names as follows:

(a) The universal enforcement of the national minimum;
(b) The democratic control of industry;
(c) The revolution in national finance; and
(d) The surplus wealth for the common good.

By a national minimum the authors of the program mean " the securing to every member of the community, in good times and bad alike (and not only to the strong and able, the well born or the fortunate) of all the requisites of healthy life and worthy citizenship." The means by which this is to be guaranteed is by legislation. Much legislation having this purpose in view is already on the statute books—such as the Factory, Mines, Railways, Shops, Merchant Shipping and Truck Acts, the Public Health, Housing and Education Acts, and the Minimum Wage Act, and to this legislation Labor has given its support. These laws, it was said, need considerable improvement and extension and especially a better administration and Labor promises to bring this about. In this connection it is said : " [A] minimum of not less than 30s. per week (which will need revision according to the level of prices) ought to be the very lowest statutory base line for the least skilled adult workers, men or women, in any occupation, in all parts of the United Kingdom."

In the matter of demobilization of the troops and the munition workers the demands of the party are " unhesitating and uncompromising." There must be no discharge or dismissal without guarantee of employment and this employment must be such as accords with the capacity of the employe. The labor to be first released is that most urgently required for the revival of peace production, and to prevent any congestion of the market. The obligation to find suitable employment in productive work rests upon the government and must not be regarded as a matter for private charity.

The policy of the Labor Party in this matter is to make the utmost use of the trade unions, and, equally for the brain workers, of the various professional associations. In view of the fact that, in any trade, the best organization for placing men in situations is a national trade union having local branches throughout the kingdom, every soldier should be allowed, if he chooses, to have a duplicate of his industrial discharge notice sent, one month before the date fixed for his discharge, to the secretary of the trade union to which he belongs or wishes to belong.

The program admits that, apart from the trade unions, " the government must, of course, avail itself of some such public machinery as that of the employment exchange," but it is insisted that until the exchanges are reformed and placed under the supervision and control of a joint committee of employers and trade unionists in equal numbers, they can not hope to command the support of the organized labor movement.

Government responsibility, according to the program, will not end with securing employment for the demobilized soldiers and discharged munition workers. " The government has pledged itself to restore the trade union conditions and ' prewar practices ' of the workshop, which the trade unions patriotically gave up at the direct request of the government itself, and this solemn pledge must be fulfilled, of course, in the spirit as well as in the letter." The program also holds that it is the duty of the government " to take all necessary steps to prevent the standard rates of wages in any trade or occupation, whatsoever, from suffering any reduction, relatively to the contemporary cost of living." Private employers should be informed that an attempt to lower wages will mean industrial strife.

Unemployment must be guarded against.

It is now known that the government can, if it chooses, arrange the public works and the orders of national departments and local authorities in such a way as to maintain the aggregate demand for labor in the whole kingdom (including that of capitalist employers) approximately at a uniform level from year to year; and it is therefore a primary obligation of the government to prevent any considerable or widespread fluctuations in the total numbers employed in times of good or bad trade.

The government, it is urged, should prepare, at once, to carry out a scheme of public works either directly or through the local authorities, and among the undertakings which might well be adopted the following are mentioned : new houses in cities, country and mining districts, schools, training and technical colleges, roads, light, railways, unification and reorganization of the railway and canal system, afforestation, reclamation of land, port and harbor improvements, cooperative small holdings in land. It is also suggested that in order to relieve any pressure from an overstocked labor market, the school leaving age should be raised to sixteen, the number of scholarships and bursaries for secondary and higher education should be increased, the hours of labor of young people should be reduced even below eight hours a week and the hours of adult labor should be reduced to not more than forty-eight per week. The extension of unemployment insurance on the basis of the out of work benefits provided by the trade unions is demanded and the resumption of the government subvention which was withdrawn in 1915—" one of the least excusable of the war economies" —is demanded immediately after the war ceases and it should be increased to at least half the amount spent in out of work benefits.

In setting forth its proposals for the democratic control of industry, it should be noted that the program makes no reference to the Reconstruction Committee's scheme for industrial councils, although this should not be interpreted as an evidence of unfriendliness to that plan. After stating its support of complete adult suffrage, equal rights for both sexes, abolition of the House of Lords, and shorter Parliaments, the program stated that the Labor party, unlike the Conservative and Liberal parties, " insists on democracy in industry as well as in government."

It demands the progressive elimination from the control of industry of the private capitalist, individual or joint stock; and the setting free of all who work, whether by hand or by brain, for the service of the community, and of the community only. And the Labor party refuses absolutely to believe that the British people will permanently tolerate any reconstruction or perpetuation of the disorganization, waste and inefficiency involved in the abandonment of British industry to a jostling crowd of separate private employers, with their minds bent, not on the service of the community, but— by the very law of their being—only on the utmost possible profiteering. What the nation needs is undoubtedly a great bound onward in its aggregate productivity. But this can not be secured merely by pressing the manual workers to more strenuous toil, or even by encouraging the " Captains of Industry" to a less wasteful organization of their several enterprises on a profit making basis. What the Labor party looks to is a genuinely scientific reorganization of the nation's industry, no longer deflected by individual profiteering, on the basis of the common ownership of the means of production; the equitable sharing of the proceeds among all who participate in any capacity and only among these, and the adoption, in particular services and occupations, of those systems and methods of administration and control that may be found in practice best to promote the public interest.

The paragraph just quoted seems at first glance to be a reiteration of the position of the state socialists, but a more careful study of the statement, especially when taken in connection with other parts of the program, seems to warrant the belief that while the industrial program is socialistic, it is not necessarily state socialism which is demanded. Municipal ownership of the means of production of public enterprises in accordance with the Fabian socialists' plan is elsewhere declared to be in accordance with their program. Furthermore, it is by no means certain that they would not accept as coming within their plan, the cooperative ownership of most industrial enterprises by the workers employed therein. There is furthermore no demand for the abolition of interest or even of private profits. Only profiteering is condemned.

The party program does, however, demand the nationalization of the great public utilities, the railroads, canals and even the great steamship lines. Furthermore, it lays great emphasis on the advantages which will come from cheap power, light and heating when the coal mines and the sources of electric power are nationalized. Nor does its program of nationalization stop at these great industries. Life insurance must be made a government function in order to put an end to the " profit making industrial insurance companies, which now so tyrannously exploit the people with their wasteful house to house industrial life assurance."

The Labor party would promote temperance reform by taking the manufacture and retailing of liquor out of the hands of those " who find profit in promoting the utmost possible consumption." Having created a government liquor monopoly the party would grant local option with regard to its sale or prohibition and the regulation of the traffic.

Municipal socialism should extend not only to the municipal public service industries, such as water, gas, electricity and the tramways, but should include housing and town planning, public libraries, the organization of recreation, and the coal and milk industries, where these are not organized by a cooperative society.

The program would have the experience gained during the war by the government in its assumption of the control of the importation of " wheat, wool, metals and other commodities " and its control of the " shipping, woolen, leather, clothing, boot and shoe, milling, baking, butchering and other industries put to good use by keeping these indispensable industries out of the hands of the monopolist trusts.   The centralized purchase of raw material and the public rationing of this material to the several establishments, the public accounting and auditing to stop waste and put an end to the " mechanical inefficiency of the more backward firms " are advantages which ought not to be surrendered.   Price fixing for standardized products should continue.

This question of the retail prices of household commodities is emphatically the most practical of all political issues to the woman elector. . . . It is, so the Labor party holds, just as much the function of government, and just as necessary a part of the democratic regulation of industry, to safeguard the interests of the community as a whole, and those of all grades and sections of private consumers in the matter of prices, as it is by the Factory and Trade Board Acts to protect the rights of the wage earning producers in the matter of wages, hours of labor and sanitation.

The Labor party's financial program calls for the " direct taxation of incomes above the necessary cost of family maintenance, and, for the requisite effort to pay off the national debt, to the direct taxation of private fortunes both during life and at death." It favors progressive taxation on a scale of graduation " rising from a penny in the pound on the smallest assessable income up to sixteen or even nineteen shillings in the pound on the highest income of the millionaires."   The death duties should be regraduated and greatly increased and in this connection it is said :

We need, in fact, completely to reverse our point of view, and to rearrange the whole taxation of inheritance from the standpoint of asking what is the maximum amount that any rich man should be permitted at death to divert, by his will, from the national exchequer which should normally be the heir to all private riches in excess of a quite moderate amount by way of family provision.

But the most radical of all the financial proposals—and yet it is one which has had the support of other than radicals—is the demand that the national debt be promptly paid off by means of a special capital levy, chargeable like the death duties on all property at "rates very steeply graduated so as to take only a small contribution from the little people and a very much larger percentage from the millionaires."

The fourth pillar of the house which Labor proposes to erect is the appropriation to the common good of the economic surplus—"the riches of our mines, the rental value of the lands superior to the margin of cultivation, the extra profits of the fortunate capitalists, even the material outcome of scientific discoveries"—which has hitherto gone to individual proprietors and then been devoted very largely to "senseless luxury." This surplus is to be appropriated by nationalization, municipalization and by steeply graduated taxation, and is to be used for public provision for the sick and infirm, for the aged and those disabled by accident, for education, recreation, public improvements of all kinds, and for greatly increased provisions for scientific investigation and original research in every branch of knowledge, and for music, literature and fine art. It is this insistence upon the importance of education and the advancement of culture which shows the effect of the inclusion of the "intellectuals" within the Labor party and which doubtless accounts in large part for the quality of its leadership.

Other items in the program of the Labor party are a repudiation of the imperialism that seeks to dominate other races, local autonomy for the various parts of the British Empire and democratic self-government wherever possible. The party favors an "imperial council representing all constituents of the Britannic alliance," but only to make recommendations for the simultaneous consideration of the autonomous local legislatures. The party objects to an "economic war" and seeks "no increase of territory." It stands for a universal league of nations and for the settlement of all international disputes by an international council of nations. Some of these political aims are set forth at greater length in the *War Aims of the British Labour Party,* an equally notable document published within a few weeks of the issue of this program.

As already mentioned this draft report on reconstruction entitled *Labour and the New Social Order* was referred for consideration to the June, 1918, conference of the party. The *Resolutions on Reconstruction* [1] which were there adopted differ widely in their wording from the more stately language of the earlier document, yet there is much in common in the substance of the two proposals. The later platform is more specific in regard to many points and less so in regard to others. It is less radical in its financial program. There is no demand for a levy on capital and no insistence that the national debt shall be paid off. The demands for graduated taxation are not so extreme and little is said about the distribution of the social surplus. On the other hand, more is said about political and constitutional reforms, including home rule for Ireland, and especial attention is given to the political and economic emancipation of women. As one might naturally expect the demands for the promotion of scientific investigation and for the application of scientific methods to the solution of social and economic problems, which in the earlier program made so strong an appeal to the "intellectuals," found little expression in a document written mainly by trade unionists.

What chance for adoption in the near future these various proposals of the British Labor party have calls for a power of political prophecy which is not claimed by the present writer. It seems to be generally admitted that if a general election comes in the near future before the war ends, the Labor party is not likely to receive a plurality of the votes cast. On the other hand, the party has undoubtedly gained rapidly in strength and if the Coalition finds itself continued as the party in charge of the government, it may well be that the Liberal element will be willing to accede to important Labor demands in return for support of the

[1] These resolutions are given in *The Survey,* August 3, 1918, pp. 500-504.

government program. Nor do the demands made by the Labor party seem so radical as they would have seemed to a nation which has not found itself compelled to accept a degree of socialistic control which would have seemed to most people unthinkable before the war. To the extent to which governmental regulation has succeeded, there will be a disposition to continue it. The movement for the betterment of the living conditions of the masses of the people, which had made such a good beginning in Great Britain in the years immediately preceding the war, has certainly not been weakened by what has taken place during the progress of the war.

REPORT OF COMMITTEE ON ADULT EDUCATION

The program of the British Labor party is not the only document which has been issued which calls attention to the need of industrial and social reforms in Great Britain in order that the mass of the people may share in the opportunities for a well rounded life which industrial progress and the widening of intellectual interests have presented. The Adult Education Committee (under the chairmanship of the Master of Baliol), Ministry of Reconstruction, has made an interesting report entitled *Industrial and Social Conditions in Relation to Adult Education,* which deserves consideration in any discussion of reconstruction.

The committee found that it was impossible to consider adult education apart from the social and industrial conditions which determine largely the educational opportunities as well as the interests and general outlook of men and women. The committee is convinced that there is a wide demand among adults for an education which is of a nonvocational character and it believes that it is not only the wish for fuller personal development, but primarily the social purpose which inspires this desire for education. The grave problems with which the country will be confronted at the close of the war and the complexity of the social organization make it imperative that this demand for education be met.

The greatest obstacle to meeting it the committee finds to be the long hours of work. It is interesting to know that the committee favors a working day of eight hours or less even though experience should not prove that this shorter working period is the one most productive from the employer's standpoint. " If the desire for maximum output can not be realized without robbing the human being of his opportunities for full participation in the organized life of society and its educational facilities, they (the committee) would unhesitatingly give preference to the satisfaction of the claims of the human being." But if shorter hours of work are to be looked at from this standpoint, it is obvious that the situation is not improved by the practice of overtime employment of which the committee, accordingly, disapproves. It also is opposed to night work, which is not only detrimental to the worker, but disrupts ordinary household arrangements and prevents the use of leisure time for the women as well as for the men.

As to how far monotonous work is a detriment to adult education, the committee feels uncertain. There are some who argue that work which requires no intellectual application leaves the mind of the worker free for reflection on subjects which interest him, while others contend that monotonous work dulls the mind and destroys initiative and intellectual interests. The committee concludes that monotonous work is probably bad for young workers, but that work people who already possess wide interests may not be greatly harmed by monotonous work if the hours of labor be not excessive. For heavy work, the hours of labor should be shortened to much less than eight and mechanical devices should be employed wherever possible.

Unemployment, the committee says, results in physical and mental deterioration and it, therefore, believes the worker should be guaranteed some reasonable security of livelihood, either by such a reorganization of industry as will prevent fluctuations in employment or, where this is impossible, by insurance.

The committee lays much stress on the importance of holidays.

If a reasonable holiday without stoppage of pay were provided, it would have a beneficial effect upon the national life. Not only would those who had definite intellectual interests be able in much larger numbers than at present to pursue them at summer schools, vacation courses, etc., but others would be provided with increased opportunities for travel and the pursuit of those things which make for enlargement of the mind, while the gain to the public health would certainly be considerable.

Attention is also called to the unsatisfactory condition of the housing of the working classes. This is a matter which is closely related to the subject of the committee's consideration because as the committee says: " Housing is admitted to be essentially a woman's question, and the extent to which women will be able to play their part in public affairs is recognized [as dependent] in no small measure on an adequate scheme of housing reform." And in this connection, it is remarked that the scarcity of domestic servants will make it important that houses be designed with a view to convenience and fitted with labor saving devices, if women are to have sufficient freedom from domestic duties to share in intellectual opportunities.

The committee says that in making its report, it has approached the matters dealt with from " the human rather than the economic point of view," although it does not understand that there is any antagonism between the two. " Material progress is of value only in so far as it assists towards the realization of human possibilities." [1]

Government Plans for Demobilization

In regard to one matter whose urgency was emphasized by the Labor party program, important steps have already been taken by the government. This is the formulation of plans for the demobilization of the military and naval forces and of the munition workers. Early in the present year (1918) the Minister of Labor established a committee to be known as the Labor Resettlement Committee, made up of employers and trade unionists in equal numbers, and on March 12, at the first meeting of the committee, the Minister set forth the work which he expected this committee to perform. He told them that he desired from them not only

[1] *Industrial and social conditions.* Abstract of the report by the Adult Education Committee of the Ministry of Reconstruction in the *Labour Gazette,* 1918, pp. 347-348.

advice in regard to the plans to be adopted but assistance with the administrative work which his department would have to carry.[1]   The Minister called attention to the two sets of questions with which the committee would have to deal: first, the resettlement of sailors and soldiers to civil life, and secondly the resettlement of those who had been engaged in war industries.   He said that in regard to the first class a subcommittee of the Reconstruction Committee had examined the matter with great care and he asked that this report be given careful consideration.   Another committee appointed by the Ministry of Reconstruction was considering the case of the civil workers, which the Minister regarded as a more difficult question even than that of the soldiers and sailors.

Among the subjects with which the committee would have to deal, the Minister said, would be the arrangements for providing out of work pay for ex-service men and others who were unemployed.   As regards ex-service men, the government had already proposed to give a month's furlough with full pay and allowance, to be followed by a free policy of insurance against unemployment, valid for a year.   The amount of the benefits had not yet been determined, but it was proposed that it should be possible to draw benefits up to a total of twenty weeks in the year. The majority of the civil war workers, he said, were already insured against unemployment, but the rate of benefit (7s. a week) would have to be increased.   Another question for consideration was the machinery to be used in carrying out demobilization and securing employment.   The government, he said, had decided that the employment exchanges would have to be used for they constituted the only national organization capable of coping with the problem.   The services of other agencies would have to be called on to assist them, especially local committees of employers and employes.   Arrangements had already been made for these local advisory committees and some of the committees were already at work.   The Minister hoped that through the cooperation of these committees, the exchanges would ascertain the demand for labor in their respective dis-

[1] *Labour Gazette*, 1918, pp. 92-93.

tricts and secure the cooperation of the local trade unions in meeting it.

The Minister further called attention to the fact that for resettlement to succeed, the prosperity of the industries must be assured and there was a need to classify the various trades of the country according to their national importance and the immediate prospects of employment which they offered. This required information concerning raw materials, financial facilities and employment in all the principal industries. There were questions concerning the reinstatement of soldiers, sailors and munition workers in the industries from which they had gone, the question of apprenticeship and the training of disabled men. The Minister expressed the hope that very substantial assistance in solving these problems would come from the joint industrial councils which were being set up in various industries.

A committee of the Board of Trade had early in 1916 made a report on the settlement of discharged soldiers and sailors on the land in England and Wales, at which they had arrived at the conclusion that there would be a considerable demand for ex-service men in agriculture at the close of the war, not only to take the place of those who had been killed and permanently disabled but to produce the larger amount of food which it is generally estimated the nation is likely to wish to produce rather than to depend to such a large extent as in the past on foreign sources of supply. The two obstacles which the committee found in the way of attracting soldiers and sailors to the land were the low wages and the lack of suitable housing facilities.[1] The first of these obstacles seems likely to be removed by the establishment of the agricultural wages boards; the second is receiving the attention of the Committee on Housing of the Ministry of Reconstruction.

In his address to the newly formed Resettlement Committee the Minister of Labor referred to two investigations which had already been made, one by the subcommittee of the Reconstruction Committee into the matter of the resettlement of sailors and soldiers to civil life and the other with regard to the

[1] *Labour Gazette*, 1916, pp. 238-239.

munition workers. The reports of the work of the first named committee have not been received in this country, but the " first (interim) report of the Civil War Workers' Committee " has been summarized in the *Labour Gazette*.[1] The recommendations of the committee, briefly stated, are as follows: (a) The government should lend its assistance to assist munition and other workers discharged on the termination of hostilities to return to their former occupations. (b) The machinery used for demobilization and subsequent reemployment should be the employment exchanges working with the Labor Resettlement Committee and the local advisory committees of the Ministry of Labor. (c) The advice of industries as a whole should be sought through the joint industrial councils where they exist and in other cases through the temporary trade committees being set up by the Ministry of Reconstruction, the Board of Trade and the Ministry of Labor, acting jointly. (d) " As soon as there is a reasonable prospect of peace, the local advisory committees and the employment exchanges should take steps to ascertain where workers are likely to be required immediately on the termination of the war and what the demands of individual factories are likely to be." (e) " The registration of individual war workers should be undertaken with a view to facilitating their return to their former employment or finding fresh employment for them." This scheme should be under the Ministry of Labor, cooperating with the trade unions. (f) On government contract work, munition workers should receive a fortnight's notice or a fortnight's pay in lieu of notice. (g) The departments concerned should encourage government departments, public or semi-public bodies and private employers to place postwar contracts in advance, the contracts being arranged, if need be, at provisional prices, to be adjusted later according to revised estimates of the cost of labor, materials, etc. The same steps should be taken by the department of overseas trade. (h) The government, before the end of the war, should have ready further schemes to meet the possibility of any local or general unemployment which may prove to be more than temporary.

[1] " Demobilization of Civil War Workers," 1918, p. 307.

The statement is made by the Minister of Reconstruction that action is being taken in connection with some of these matters. Others will have to be considered by the government in relation to other allied questions of reconstruction.

The Ministry of Reconstruction has made public the report of the committee appointed to consider the resettlement of officers. In accordance with the recommendations of this committee, the Ministry of Labor has established an Appointments Department intended "to provide advice and assistance to officers and others requiring professional and business appointments on their return to civil life. Two committees of this department have been provided, one dealing with appointments and the other with training. On the Appointment Committee will be representatives of the principal professional and business organizations. Local committees similarly constituted will be provided. The Training Committee will be an interdepartmental committee jointly appointed by the Ministry of Labor, the Board of Education and other departments, and the chairman will be nominated by the Board of Education. The universities and other educational organizations and representatives of commerce and industry will be asked to cooperate. "It has been arranged that every officer shall be provided with information as to the facilities for obtaining appointments by the department, which will therefore be in a position to bring to the notice of employers, who may have vacancies to fill, particulars of candidates from every part of the kingdom." Those candidates who have not the necessary training will be furnished with facilities for obtaining this by the Training Committee. No fees are charged either to employers or to candidates for the work of securing positions.[1] This, of course, does not apply to the work of training, which is to be done by existing schools and other agencies.

LABOR READJUSTMENTS IN THE PRINCIPAL INDUSTRIES

Besides the work being done by the departments and committees already mentioned, brief mention should be made of the

[1] *Labour Gazette*, 1918, p. 175.

inquiries conducted by the departmental committees appointed by
the Board of Trade during the year 1916 to consider the position of various industries after the war, particularly with reference to conditions which might exist to hamper the success of
the industry in question when peace had been restored, and to
suggest remedies, if any, for such conditions. These committees
made their report in 1918.[1]

The committee on the textile trades reported that British labor
was peculiarly efficient in these industries, that the output per
person was probably higher than anywhere else in the world,
except perhaps the United States, that there was little restriction
of output " of an habitual or organized kind, owing largely to
the fact that piece work is almost universal." The committee
found evidence of interference by means of trade union and
shop rules with maximum output in the subsidiary processes of
the textile trades. To do away with these restrictions the committee urged that the government as well as associations of employers and employed endeavor to bring about a complete understanding between labor and capital " on the basis of mutual interest, confidence and good feeling."

In the iron and steel trades the committee found labor relations
to be on a better footing in those industries in which both sides
are organized to carry on collective bargaining, but such organization is far from complete. A multiplicity of unions has created
confusion and the committee favors bringing all labor under the
authority of a single trade union and that in the trade agreements
unskilled labor be provided for. Piece and tonnage rates are
favored, for they tend to interest the worker in his work and
also lessen the danger of restriction of output. The committee
favors the eight hour day in works running continuously
throughout the week.

In the engineering trades employers were nearly unanimous
in their complaints that the trade union rules resulted in a
restriction of output below that which represents a reasonable
day's work and that they compelled employers to class as skilled

[1] Summaries of their reports are found in the *Labour Gazette* for August,
1918, pp. 306-307.

work that which in fact was unskilled. The committee believed that both allegations were well founded. The committee favored the establishment of piece rates or a bonus system on time rates. It considered that "in the future it will be all important that output should be encouraged to its maximum," but that the laborers must be convinced that to do this will not result in the cutting down of their best earnings. The committee felt that when peace returns it must be recognized that much work hitherto regarded as skilled must be considered to be within the scope of unskilled men and women and that where female labor can be suitably utilized no trade union rules should hamper its employment. Automatic and other machinery must be freely used.

In the electrical trades the committee found a need of a better understanding between employers and employed, to put an end to arbitrary restrictions of output and to the use of labor saving machinery. There are also needed improved working conditions in factories and better housing. In the shipping and shipbuilding industries the committee said little about labor conditions, but concurred with witnesses "that foreign competition after the war can not be regarded with equanimity, unless employers and employed cooperate efficiently in producing the maximum output at a reasonable price."

In the coal mining industry statistics of output showed that "since 1906 there has been a decline in the yearly output per person employed at the mines." The committee considered this a very serious matter and as affecting the country's competitive power in many directions. It thought that any policy involving restriction of output should be abandoned and that the worker "should have security that if he increases his output he shall not suffer for it by any arbitrary treatment of wage rates." As a step towards securing fuller cooperation between employers and employes the committee favored the establishment by mutual consent in every mining district of joint disputes committees of employers and employes, to whom should be referred all differences which the parties at the individual collieries could not settle between themselves.

It would be folly to attempt to predict to what extent the proposals for reform in labor and working conditions which have been briefly surveyed in this chapter will be adopted in the years following the war and, if adopted, to what degree they will be successful. No doubt here, as in so many other fields of human endeavor, compromise will be the rule. It is enough to know that discussion has begun and is taking place on the basis of an understanding by all parties that the prewar conditions in industry (reference is not here to the agreement to restore trade union customs) can never, and should never, be restored. That the industrial society of the future will be established on the basis of a larger participation by the laboring classes in the management and development of industrial enterprises and of better living and working conditions than have hitherto prevailed seems a safe prediction. That on the part of labor there must be a realization of the fact that any permanent reforms in this direction mean that high wages and good working conditions are dependent on large output and an economical use of materials and machinery is a proposition which requires no demonstration.

There is one labor problem connected with reconstruction in Great Britain which has caused much speculation, but concerning which there is, for obvious reasons, little accurate information—that is the problem of the future of women in industry. Our review of the effects of the war in causing increased employment of women has shown that up to January, 1918, the war had caused an addition of 1,446,000 women in remunerative occupations, outside domestic service and small retail establishments. How many of these women will remain in industry at the close of the war? How far will their remaining make difficult the return of men into gainful occupations?

As no satisfactory answer can be given to either question at this time, all that we shall attempt to do is to call attention to certain phases of the problem which may serve to indicate the way to, at least, a partial solution. (1) Many of the women now engaged in industry will voluntarily leave it at the close of the war. Marriage, or at least the establishment of a home, has been postponed in many cases until the end of the war and will not long be postponed after the war is over and the soldier has returned to industry. Those women (probably not many in number) who have entered industry not from necessity but purely from patriotic reasons and have continued therein until the close of the war, will also, in most cases, forsake their present occupations. (2) Many women, especially among the munition workers, who had been employed in peace time industries but who, during the war, transferred to war time industries, will return to their old occupations as soon as the change in industrial demand makes this possible. (3) Some women who were formerly employed in domestic service or in small retail establishments or who were engaged in remunerative work in their homes will return to these occupations. The number who do so will depend not only on their own inclinations but also on the extent to which the war has left the wealthy and the middle classes capable of maintaining domestic establishments with hired servants to perform the work. (4) Where women have found employment in financial, commercial and professional occupations suited to their strength and capacity, they will be retained in most instances, if they desire to remain. No agreement with the trade unions stands in the way of their retention and probably, in most instances, employers have discovered that women can be secured at lower rates of pay than would be demanded by men for similar work. (5) In industrial establishments where employers have not entered into an understanding with the government and the trade unions to restore the prewar conditions, including the reemployment of the former employes, and women have been employed on work suited to their strength and capacity, there seems to be no reason why such women will not be retained, in most instances, unless the men in the plants are strongly organized and make the matter of reengaging the former employes in their old positions an issue. (6) While in certain establishments, especially those engaged in engineering work, the understanding with the trade unions exists and will be kept, if necessary, by the insistence of the government, yet it must be remembered that new work will be undertaken and new machinery has been introduced which can be utilized to perform this work. Genuine differences of opinion will naturally arise as to the correct interpretation of the agreement to restore pre-war conditions. It is inconceivable that some of these differences will not be resolved in favor of the employer and of the retention of the women who have been employed to operate the new machines. (7) Finally, it must be remembered that many of the men formerly employed will never return to industry. They have given their lives on the battlefield or are physically incapacitated for their former work. There must also be added to this list those who will desire to migrate to the colonies or to other countries or to engage in new enterprises.

While the above categories do not dispose of all the women who have been called into gainful pursuits during the war, it is impossible to measure quantitatively the problem which the country will have to meet of reincorporating into industry the returned soldiers and sailors and of caring, at the same time, for the women who desire to retain their present positions or others equally remunerative. Much will depend upon the women themselves, the opposition which they will make to their being replaced, their organization into trade unions and their use of their new political power—the suffrage. To some extent, it will also depend on the attitude of the men's unions, their willingness to accept women as members and to make the women's cause their own.

INDEX

Addison, Christopher, 294
Adult Education Committee—*see* Education, Committee on Adult
Agriculture: Workmen's Compensation Act extended to, 10; wages, 25, 188; wage boards, 196; low wages a cause of industrial unrest, 263; minimum wage proposed, 14; established, 266; women in, 166, 168
Amalgamated Society of Engineers: Clyde strike in 1915, 65-67, 74; in 1916, 235-236; supplemental agreement to Treasury Conference, 91; agreement with government as to exemptions, 129; agreement withdrawn, 238, 255; dilution of labor on private work, 238, 230
Amalgamated Society of Railway Servants, 9
Arbitration: compulsory, 76, 85, 230; arbitration tribunal for women workers, 100, 189, 190, 191, 193; powers of Board of Trade, 109; awards not subject to appeal, 110; Arbitration Act, 1889, 111; provisions of Munitions Act, 111; settlement of wages, 199; Whitley report on, 302-303
Army reserve munitions workers, 105, 126, 130
Askwith, Sir George, 65
Atkin, Sir Richard, 89
Aves, Ernest, 13

Balfour, Arthur James, 4, 9
Barnes, G. N., 205, 244, 245, 264, 265, 283
Barrow, Eng., housing conditions, 258-259
Belgian refugees, government efforts to furnish work for, 44-48
Beveridge, W. H., 97
Billeting of Civilians Act, 1917, 224
Board of Trade—*see* Trade, Board of
Bonus—*see* Wages
Booth, Charles, 4, 240
British Association for the Advancement of Science: report on industrial unrest, 240-243; reconstruction program, 271; membership of Reconstruction Committee, 272; recommendations to alleviate industrial unrest, 273-276; cooperation between employers and employed, 274-275; organization recommended, 276
British Labor party—*see* Labor party

Central Labor Supply Committee, 181
Central Munitions Labor Supply Committee, 142, 192
Chamberlain, Austen, 8
Chamberlain, Neville, 130
Chapman, Sidney, 240, 243
Churchill, Winston, 13, 148
Civil War Workers' Committee: recommendations for employment of demobilized munitions workers, 322

Clerical and Commercial Employment Committee, 147
Clyde strike: in 1915, 65-67, 74; in 1916, 235-236
Clyde Workers Committee, 235-236
Coal mining industry, labor readjustment, 325
Cole, G. D. H., 32, 78, 79
Compensation—*see* Seamen's compensation; Workmen's compensation
Conciliation and arbitration, Whitley report on, 302-303
Conscription, industrial: not provided for, 94, 96; volunteer plan as alternative, 96, 126; objection to, 124; a reality, 138-139
Conscription, military, 128
Controlled establishments: 90-94; restrictions on employment, 88; profits to be limited, 91; wages, 88, 91, 92, 100, 188, 189, 191-195; effect of munitions amendment, 1917, 92; provisions of act, 100; under regulations of Minister of Munitions, 93; number in 1917, 93-94; percentage of women in, 93; Sunday labor discontinued, 123; rules of dilution, 182-183; records of changes from prewar conditions, 183; hours of labor, 213; holidays, 215; welfare work, 216, 217
Corn Production Act, 1917, 196
Cost of living: changes in, 24-25; percentage increase, 25; rents, 25, 202, 204; savings deposits, 26; reentry of women in industry, 71, 72; relation of wages to, 64, 194, 200-202; report of committee investigating, 203-204; steps taken by Food Ministry, 204-205
Cunningham, Archdeacon, 240

Defense of the Realm Consolidation Act: amendment, 74-75; powers under, 76, 221-222; orders under, 207, 215; Defense of the Realm Regulations, 120, 131
Demobilization: government plans, 319-323; recommendations of Civil War Workers Committee, 322; resettlement of officers, 323
Dilution of labor: 140-184; substitution of women for men, 54, 72, 140, 144-158, 159, 160-168, 178-180, 192, 196, 197; substitutes for skilled labor, 73-74, 96-97, 129, 130, 139, 140, 156, 157, 158, 192, 193, 198; scarcity of male substitutes, 143-144; substitutes in clerical and commercial occupations, 147, 148, 150; trade union restrictions on, 92, 140; opposition of trades unions, 96, 141-142, 163, 180-181; recommendations of Munitions Labor Supply Committee, 97; Treasury agreement, 96-97, 140, 141; dilution necessary, 126; gov-

ernment assists in, 142-143; urges further dilution, 158-160; female labor available early in war, 144-147; industrial training for women, 154-155; by agreement with unions, 163; statistics of extension of employment of women, 168-171; table, 169; sources of supply, women workers, 171-175; mobility of women's labor, 175-178; records of departures from prewar practices, 181-184; rules for controlled establishments, 182-183; extension to private work opposed by Amalgamated Society of Engineers, 238, 239; a cause of industrial unrest, 250-251
Disputes—*see* Trades disputes
Distress committees: work of, 27, 225; appointment of special committee, 42; report, 42-43; care of Belgian refugees, 44-48
Drink problem—*see* Liquor problem

Economist, The, 291
Education, Committee on Adult: report, 317-319
Electrical trades, labor readjustment, 325
Elswick works dispute, 70
Emergency grants, 49-52; table, 51
Emigration in relation to employment, 57-58
Employers' associations, 29
Employers' liability, 10
Employment: irregular, cause of pauperism, 7; in textile trades, 23; Central Committee on Women's Employment, 43; not to be given Belgian refugees of military age, 45; situation first year of war, 54; disabled soldiers and sailors, 55-57, 227-229; committee on methods appointed, 56; report, 56-57; effect of Workmen's Compensation Act, 57; restoration of prewar conditions, 78, 87, 92, 93, 94, 97, 183, 253, 311; of women, 98-100, 111; percentage, 146; extension of employment during war, table, 160; unskilled labor, 98-100; leaving certificates, 102, 103, 104, 105, 249, 250; Labor Party program, demobilized soldiers and munitions workers, 310-311, 322; German prisoners with British workmen, 262. *See also* Unemployment
Employment exchanges—*see* Labor exchanges
Engineering Employers' Federation, 68
Engineering trades: disagreement in, 68-71; controlled establishments, 90-94; Clyde strike in 1915, 65-67, 74; in 1916, 325-326; strike in engineering industry, 1918, 267-268; labor readjustment, 324
Engineers, Amalgamated Society of—*see* Amalgamated Society of Engineers
English industry and labor at outbreak of war, 22-31
Enlistments: restricting from essential industries, 115-119; table, number and percentage, 117
Essential industries: national service scheme, 130-135; list by Director General of National Service, 131; protected occupations list, 134-135; list of certified occupations, 136; women in, 171
Excess profits, 69, 76, 91, 93

Exemptions: under military service acts, 127-130; canceled, 134-135; men entitled to, 136; complaints, 255
Exports, value of, 23-24

Factories Department: overtime, 120-121; rule for protected class of labor, 122; report on hours of work, 1917, 210
Farwell, Justice, decision in Taff Vale Railway strike case, 9
Federation of British Industries, discussion on Whitley report, 289
Food, Ministry of, 204-205
Fyfe, Thomas Alexander, 87, 103

Garrod, H. W., 162
Geddes, Sir Austin, 137
Gladstone, William E., 4
Glasgow dock laborers' strike, 236
Gonner, E. C. K., 240
Gosling, Harry, 240, 277
Government: efforts to relieve distress due to unemployment, 42, 44; to furnish work to Belgian refugees, 44-48; plans criticised, 48; emergency grants, 49-52; relief of disabled soldiers and sailors, 55-57; investigation of industrial unrest, 243-246; reforms to relieve, 264-267; lack of coordination between departments dealing with labor, 257-258; recommendations for improving, 257-258; recognition of labor demands, 269-271

Hatch, Sir Ernest, 44
Health of Munitions Workers Committee, 121, 208, 210, 213, 214, 218
Henderson, Arthur, 77, 88, 234
Holidays: economic value, 214-215, 318-319; labor, 191, 198
Hours of labor: 31, 205-214; government control, 92, 99, 100; overtime, 120-123; scale of hours giving largest amount of production, 206; report of Health of Munitions Workers Committee, 208, 210, 211-213, 214; regulation on government work, 209; special report Factories Inspector, 210; interdepartmental committee's action in regard to, 213; long hours opposed by Adult Education Committee, 318. *See also* Holidays; Sunday labor
Housing problem: contributory cause of pauperism, 6; reform acts to relieve overcrowding, 15-16; supplemented by Finance Act, 1910, 16-17; conditions and legislation, 220-224; estimated needs, 1917, 221; temporary housing, 222-223; government ownership proposed, 223; Billeting of Civilians Act, 224; as cause of industrial unrest, 258-260; government scheme to relieve, 266; Adult Education Committee's report, 319
Housing and Town Planning Acts, 15-16, 221

Immigration in relation to employment conditions, 57-58
Imports, value of, 23
Industrial and Social Conditions in Relation to Adult Education, 317-319
Industrial councils: recommended by British Association, 276; 1st Whitley report on, 279-282; 2d Whitley report on, 295-297; modifications on recommendations, 305-307; resemblances and differences to trade boards, 306-307

Industrial disputes—*see* Trades disputes
Industrial organizations—*see* Trades unions
Industrial panic and readjustment, 32-67.
 See also Reconstruction
Industrial training for women, 154-155
Industrial unrest: payment by results, a
 cause of, 200; disputes during 1914-
 1915, 230, 235; South Wales coal strike,
 231-234; strikes during the war, 234-
 237; recent government policy concerning disputes, 237-240; British Association report on, 240-243; investigation by
 government commissions, 243-246; summaries of causes, 240-243, 244-246; high
 prices and profiteering, 246-248; operation of Munitions of War Acts, 248-
 254, of Military Service Acts, 254-257;
 housing conditions, 258-260; liquor restrictions, 260-262; fatigue, 208, 211,
 262-263; local and minor causes, 263-
 264; government reforms to relieve, 264-
 267
Industry and labor at outbreak of war, 22
Iron and steel trades, labor readjustment,
 324

Jackson, Frederick Huth, 278

Kirkaldy, Adam Willis, 276

Labor exchanges: Labor Exchanges Act,
 1909, 7; registers compared 1913, 1914,
 34, 41; employment for refugees, 46,
 47-48; policy to protect British labor,
 46; providing substitutes, 130, 135-136;
 list of trades for guidance of, 131;
 placements of volunteers, 133; cooperation with National Service Department,
 138; skilled vacancies filled, 144; number on registers 1914, 145, 174; tables,
 145, 147; disabled soldiers and sailors,
 228
Labor laws and legislation: liberal labor
 measures, 4; Trades Disputes Act, 8-10;
 Workmen's compensation, 10-11; old age
 pensions, 11-13; minimum wage, 13-15;
 Housing of the Working Classes Act,
 1890, 15; Housing, Town Planning Act,
 1909, 15-16; supplemented by Finance
 Act, 1910, 16-17; Labor Exchange Act,
 1909, 17; National Insurance Act, 1911,
 (part 2) unemployment, 18-19; (part 1)
 health insurance, 19-20. *See also* Defense of the Realm Consolidation Act;
 Munitions of War Acts
Labor, Ministry of, 177, 237
Labor organizations—*see* Trades unions
Labor party: 37, formation, 4; Munitions
 of War Act, 87; favors aiding disabled
 soldiers and sailors, 229; growth, 308;
 cooperation with Trades Union Congress,
 308-309; reconstruction program, 308-
 317; universal enforcement of national
 minimum, 310-312; restoration of prewar conditions of trade unions, 311; nationalization of great public utilities,
 313; democratic control of industry, 312-
 314; municipal socialism, 313-314; government control of certain commodities,
 314; price fixing for standardized products, 314; financial program, 314-315;
 surplus wealth for the common good,
 315; political aims, 315-316; later program of June, 1918, 316-317; informal
 reply of Prime Minister to Manchester
 resolutions, 270-271

Labor readjustments—*see* Readjustments;
 Reconstruction
Labor Resettlement Committee, 320-322
Labour and the New Social Order, 308-
 317
Labour Gazette, 52, 54, 61, 186, 187, 322
Labour in War Time, 32
Labour Year Book, 62, 69
Lancashire cotton mills strike, 236
Leaving certificates, 102-105, 249, 250
Liberal party, 4
Liquor problem: lost time due to drink,
 81-83; restrictions as cause of industrial
 unrest, 260-262; program of Labor
 party, 313
Liverpool dock laborers' strike, 236
Lloyd George, David, 14, 16, 75, 76, 77,
 78, 81, 83, 84, 94, 130, 140, 141,
 142, 152, 191, 270

Macarthur, Mary, 97
Macassey, Lyndon, 100
Military Service Acts: industrial exemptions under, 127-130; complaints arising from operation of act, 254-257; exemption of skilled laborers, 255; schedule
 of protected occupations, 255-256; minor
 causes of complaint, 256-257; recruiting transferred to the National Service
 Commission to relieve complaint, 265-
 266
Minimum wage: legislation, 13-15; for
 men, 188; women, 191; private industries, 196; agriculture, 266; program of
 Labor party, 310
Mobility of labor: 94, 139; restrictions on,
 101-105; leaving certificates, 102-105
Munitions, Ministry of: creation and policy, 84-85; munitions bill passed, July 2,
 1915, 85; provisions regulating controlled establishments, 91-93; powers,
 88, 99, 100, 104, 180; exemption certificates, 103; regulation of employment
 of released army men, 106; arbitration
 tribunals, 110, 111; lends women demonstrator-operatives, 158; expenditures,
 222; temporary housing, 222, 223;
 Welfare Department established, 217;
 scope of work, 218, 219, 220; Central
 Labor Supply Committee to advise, 181;
 recording changes prewar practice, 182;
 orders affecting wages, 189, 190-192,
 193, 194, 196, 197, 198, 199; hours of
 labor, 213; holidays, 215
Munitions of War Acts: 67; Act of 1915,
 70, 79, 86, 97, 111, 141, 162, 180;
 criticized, 86; abstract of provisions, 87-
 89; meaning of "munitions work," 89-
 90; dilution of labor, 97, 141, 250-251;
 extended to private work, 183, 238, 239;
 amendment abandoned, 184, 239; restrictions on mobility of labor, 101-102;
 penalties provided by act, 108-109;
 wage regulation, 188; settlement of disputes, 109-112, 230; operation of act,
 248-254; complaints arising from, 249;
 leaving certificates, 250; failure to record changes of practice, 251; inequality
 of earnings as between skilled and unskilled, 251-252; inability or unwillingness to restore prewar conditions, 253;
 arbitrary or unsatisfactory action of munitions tribunals and delay in securing
 settlements, 253-254; amendments of
 act, 1916, 86, 98, 99, 108, 111, 162,

189, 190, 197; amendments of act, 1917, 86, 92, 100, 112, 199, 265

Munitions trades: war bonus, 60; profits limited, 69, 91; acceleration of production, 75, 76; local munitions committees, 79; proposals before conference of trade unions leaders representing, 85; controlled establishments, 88, 90-94, 100, 140; wage regulation, 189-190; of women, 190-197; of men, 197-200; changes in wages, 185, 194; meaning of munitions work, 89-90; munitions volunteers 94-96, 104, 124, 126, 213; as alternative for conscription, 96; government orders relating to skilled labor, 98; army reserve munitions workers, 105, 106, 118, 126; overtime, 122, 123, 208; appeals for volunteers, 124, 126; compulsory registration, 126-127; restricted occupations and essential industries, 131; release of workers for military and naval service, 134; women in, 152-154, 160-162; table of numbers and proportion, 161; sources of supply of women workers, 171, 172, 175; recruited from non-industrial areas, 177; training classes for workers, 155, 157, 158; replacement of men by women, 178, 179; orders relating to health and efficiency of workers, 208; to hours of labor, 213; to holidays, 215; welfare work, 216, 217; Welfare Department, 217, 218; housing conditions in munitions centers, 221; unemployment insurance, 226-227; employment of demobilized workers, 322

Munitions tribunals: 103, 104; general, 106; local, 107; provisions of amended munitions act, 1916, 108, 109

Murray, Sir George, 56

National Insurance Act, part 2, unemployment, 7, 35, 49; part 1, health insurance, 19-20; emergency grants under, 49-52

National Labor Advisory Committee, 84, 181

National Registration Act, 1915, 126-127

National service: compulsory registration, 126-127; government scheme, 130-134; reasons for failure, 132; efforts to amend scheme, 132-134; 'new plan, 136-188; appeal for volunteers, 131; number enrolled and placed, 133; outline for enrolling, 137, 138; Ministry of National Service, 131, 132, 133; report of select committee on national expenditure, 133; employment exchanges, 135-136; industrial conscription, 138-139

National Service Department, 133, 134-136

National Service, Ministry of, 131, 132, 138

Newman, Sir George, 208

Occupations: essential industries, 130-135; list of restricted, 131; list of protected, 134-135; list of certified, 136; table, analysis prewar occupations of women workers, 173

Old age pensions: beginning of agitation, 11; law enacted August 1, 1908, 12; provisions of act, 12; advance estimate of number applying, 12; additional allowance during war, 12-18

Overtime work: 98; acts regulating, 119-120; orders permitting, 120, 122, 123; rates for, 191; holiday work, 191; rate of pay, 198; effect on women, 205, 206, 207; Sunday labor, 191, 208, 209, 210, 212; overtime preferable to, 209; strain counteracted by increased pay, 212; objections to, 211; overtime should be concentrated, 212; economically extravagant, 213; opposed by Adult Education Committee, 318

Panic: effect of war on industry, 32; advance of retail prices, 32-33; growth of unemployment, 33-35; methods of public relief, 35-36; trade disturbances less widespread than feared, 42. See also Readjustment; Reconstruction

Pauperism: tendency and public expenditures, 4; causes, 5-7; reduction, 26-27; percentage August, 1914, 35-36; results shown by statistics, 225

Payment by results, 92, 200

Pensions: delays in granting, 266. See also Old age pensions

Pensions, Ministry of, 1916, 227

Poor Law Commission: report quoted, 4; appointed, 4-5; findings and recommendations, 5-8; services of investigation and report, 8

Poor laws, administration and history, 5

Police, Factories, etc., (Miscellaneous Provisions) Act, 220

Prewar conditions of employment, restoration of—see Employment

Prices: wholesale, 24; retail, 24, 31, 32; changes in, 59, 60-62; table of percentages "above normal," 61; of food, 62; cause of industrial unrest, 246; government plans to reform, 264-265

Production: value of imports, 23; value of exports, 23-24; employers and trades unions attempt to agree to program, 67, 68-70; reports of Committee on Production, 71-74; legislation to aid and increase, 74, 88, 92-93; effects of overtime, 206, 207, 208; output in relation to hours of labor, 209, 210, 211

Production, Committee on: appointment, 65; orders resumption of work in Clyde shipyards, 65-66; reports, 71; 1st, "irregular time keeping," 71; 2d, "shells and fuses and avoidance of stoppage of work," 71-72; 3d, demarcation of work, 73-74; 4th, Clyde strike, 65-67, 74; named tribunal to settle strikes, 74; to arbitrate labor disputes, Treasury agreement, 76; work, 1915, 79, 80, 81; recommendations, foundation Munitions of War Acts, 86; awards of war bonuses, etc., 188; right to review wage rate of women, 194; award of bonus extended, 199

Profiteering: cause of industrial unrest, 246-248; government plans to reform, 264-265

Profits, excess, 69, 76, 91, 93

Prosperity: tests applied to working classes, 25-26

Protected occupations list, 134-135

Public utilities nationalization, 313

Railway Servants, Amalgamated Society of —see Amalgamated Society of Railway Servants

Readjustment: reduction of trades disputes, 36-38; recovery of employment conditions, 38-41; in women's trades, 41-42; government efforts to relieve distress due to unemployment, 42-44; special committee appointed, 42; report, 42-44; work for Belgian refugees, 44-48; special committee to investigate conditions, etc., 44; report, 44-48; criticism of governments' plans, 48-49; program of Workers' National Committee, 48-49; emergency grants, 49-52; industrial transfers of women, 52-54; disappearance of unemployment, 54-55; relief of disabled soldiers and sailors, 55-57; report of Local Government Boards' Committee upon methods of employment, 55-57; emigration and immigration, 57-58; changes in wage rates, 58-60; in prices, 60-62; resumption of strikes, 62-67; labor readjustment investigations, 324-325; women in industry, 326-328. See also Reconstruction

Reconstruction: memorandum of advisory housing panel, 223; government recognition of labor demands, 269-271; program of British Association, 271-276; trade union agreement, 276-279; report of Reconstruction Committee, 279-282; discussion of, 283-291; recommendations adopted, 292-293; Ministry of Reconstruction created, 293-294; work of, 294-295; 2d report on industrial councils, 295-297; works committees, 297-302; conciliation and arbitration, 302-303; government takes steps to establish industrial councils, 303-305; industrial councils and trade boards, 305-308; program of Labor party, 308-317; report of Committee on Adult Education, 317-319; government plans for demobilization, 319-323; labor readjustments, 323-325; Board of Trade investigations, 324-325; women, 326-328

Reconstruction Committee on Industrial Councils, 266
Reconstruction, Ministry of, 223
Relations between Employers and Employed Committee, 294. See also Whitley report
Relief work: unemployment, 17; methods of public, 35; government efforts to relieve distress, 42-44; work for Belgian refugees, 44-48; criticism of government plans, 48-49; emergency grants, 49-52; relief of soldiers and sailors, 55-57
Rents, 25, 202, 204
Road Board, 42; efforts for unemployed, 43-44
Rowntree, B. S., 4, 217
Runciman, Walter, 75, 76, 77, 232, 233, 234

Sailors—see Soldiers and sailors
Salisbury, Lord, 4
Samuel, Herbert, 42
Science, British Association for the Advancement of—see British Association for the Advancement of Science
Seamen's compensation, 266
Shortage of labor: early in the war, 113-114; of female labor, 164, 174; overtime work as cure, 119-126; effect on wages, 188; cost of living, 205

Skilled labor: wages, 25; government orders affecting, 98; in demand, 102; substitutions for, 129, 140, 143, 144, 153-154, 156, 157, 158; withdrawn from army and enlistment restricted, 118-119; exemptions, 129; safeguarding, 184
Social legislation, 3-21; findings and recommendations of Poor Law Commission, 5-8; effect upon problems of the war, 20-21
Soldiers and sailors: relief of disabled, 55-57, 227-229; pensions, 229, 266; released from army as munitions workers, 105; employment and reeducation, 228; resettlement in civil life, 321; settlement on land, 321
South Wales coal strike, 231-234
Strikes: Taff Vale Railway strike, 9; percentage of workers involved, 1911-1913, 30; recrudescence of, 62-64; Clyde strike, 65-67, 74; avoidance of stoppages, 72, 74, 76; government can not prevent, 84; prohibition of, 109-112; methods for settling, 109-110; arbitration, 110-111; engineering trades, 129; "silent strike," 184; South Wales coal strike, 231-234; strikes during the war, 234-237; Lancashire cotton mills strike, 236; Glasgow dock laborers' strike, 236; Liverpool dock laborers' strike, 236
Sunday work, 191, 208, 200, 210, 212
Supply and distribution of labor: transfers of women workers, 52-54, 115, 175, 176, 177, 178; obtaining labor, 69; shortage, 54; early in the war, 113-114; overtime work cure for, 119-126; transfers through employment exchanges, 114-115; government efforts to prevent enlistments from essential industries, 115; compulsory registration for industrial purposes, 126; industrial exemptions from military service, 127-130; national service scheme, 130-134; protected occupations list, 134-135; national service and employment exchanges, 135-136; new national service plan, 136-138; industrial conscription, 138-139; Central Labor Supply Committee, 181

Taff Vale Railway strike, 9
Tennant, H. J., 69
Textile trades, labor readjustment, 324
Time keeping, report Committee on Production, 71
Trade, Board of: settlement of strikes, etc., 109, 110, 111, 112; estimates as to enlistments from various trades, 117; appeal to women for war service, 124; exemptions to classes of workers, 129; propaganda for women in farm work, 167; number receiving war bonus or increased wages, 1915, 186; munitions workers excluded from unemployment insurance, 226; report on settlement of soldiers and sailors on land, 321; labor readjustment investigations, 324-325
Trade Boards Act, 1909, 14; amendment of 1918, 307-308
Trades boards, resemblances and differences to industrial councils, 306-307
Trades disputes: industrial disputes, 20-31; reduction in trade disputes, 36-38; industrial truce due to the war, 37; settlement 62, 112, 113; increase of, 62-63; table, 80; serious phase of increase,

80; during 1914 and 1915, 230; recent government policy concerning, 237-240. *See also* Arbitration; Strikes

Trades Disputes Act, 1906, 8-10

Trades unions: legalized, 9; provisions, Trades Disputes Act, 10; labor and industrial organizations, 27-29; increase in female membership, 28; trade union movement, 27-29; strength at outbreak of war, 28; formation of Triple Alliance, 1914, 28-29; relations with organizations of employers, 29; relation to industrial disputes, 30-31; government emergency grants, 49-52; applications for, 51; table, 51; government and the trade unions, 68-85; disagreement in engineering trades, 68-71; speech of H. J. Tennant in House of Commons urging relaxation of rules, 69; recommendations of Productions Committee, 71-74; restrictive rules affecting production, 71-72; stoppage of work, 72; contractor's undertaking in behalf of, 72; demarcation of work, 73; utilization of semiskilled and unskilled labor, 73-74; Treasury conference to consider output of munitions, 75; proposed agreement submitted to, 76; endorsed by unions, 77; Treasury agreement, 78, 84, 86, 91, 92, 140, 141, 142, 162, 180, 181; administration of agreement, 79-81; membership not cause for discharge, 112; skilled craftsmen exempted from military service, 129; resistance to industrial conscription, 130; attitude toward dilution of labor, 141-142, 156, 157, 163, 180-181; oppose dilution, 141-142, 180-181; oppose women for skilled work, 156, 157; allow the substitution of women for men, 163; wage rates, 189, 196; affecting women, 191, 192, 193, 194, 195; agreements, 198; oppose systems of payments by results, 200; Sunday labor, 208, 209, 210; small percentage of unemployed, 224; disabled soldiers and sailors, 220; attitude toward labor participation in industrial management, 276-279; relation of works committees to, 301-302; restoration of prewar conditions, 311. *See also* Arbitration; Strikes; Trades disputes

Trades Unions Congress, 141, 308-309

Treasury Conference: formation and purpose, 75; proposals for submission, 76; endorsed by trades unions, 77; text of amended agreement, 78; press and public favorable to, 78; agreement, 84, 92, 140, 141-142, 162, 180; administration of, 79-81; supplemental agreement, 91

Triple Alliance of Trade Unions, 28-29

Unemployed Workmen's Act 1915, 225

Unemployment: statistics, 22-23; work of distress committees, 26; table, 27; growth, 33-35; war office memorandum to contractors, 36; recovery of employment conditions, 38-41; percentage table, insured trades, 38; trades working on war material, 39; effect of military service, 40; recovery in women's trades, 41-42; percentage table, 42; work of Road Board, 43-44; efforts to find work for Belgian refugees, 44-48; criticism of government plans, 48-49; emergency grants, 49-52; disappearance of, 54;

numbers on registers, employment exchanges, 1914-1917, 145-146; among women, 154; unemployment and its relief, 35-36, 42-44, 55, 221, 224-227; extension of state insurance, 225-226; means of guarding against, 311-312; report of Committee on Adult Education, 318. *See also* Employment

Unskilled labor, 98-100.

Wages: low, contributory cause of pauperism, 7; Trade Boards Act, 1909, 7; trades unions disputes over, 80; changes in, 24-25, 58-59; relation to cost of living, 31; decrease in earnings, 34-35; adjustment of, 79; "war wages," 80; women and unskilled labor, 98-100; wages of men affect supply of female labor, 53; changes in rate, 58-59; war bonus, 59-60, 63, 64, 196, 199, 200; regulation by Minister of Munitions, 100; skilled workmen released from army, 118; war work volunteers, 138; extent of increases, 185-188; fluctuation, 186, 187; attract women to industry, 172; regulation, 188-190; of women's, 190-197; of men's, 197-200; overtime, 191; Sunday, 191, 208, 209, 210; holiday, 191; standardization, 199; payment by results, 200; agriculture, 266; low, a cause of industrial unrest, 263

War Aims of the British Labour Party, 316

War bonus—*see* Wages

War munitions volunteers, 94-96, 104, 124, 126

War Office memorandum to contractors on unemployment, 36

War Pensions Statutory Committee, 1915, 227

War work—*see* National service

Welfare work, 216-220

Whitley, J. H., 279

Whitley report: 248; 1st report on industrial councils and works committees, 279-282; discussions by Northeast area, 283-284; Northwest area, 284-285; Yorkshire and East Midlands area, 285-286; West Midlands area, 286; London and Southeastern area, 286; Southwest area, 287; Wales and Monmouthshire, 287-288; Scotland, 288; approval of Federation of British Industries, 289; extract from *The Economist*, 291; recommendations adopted by government, 292-293; 2d report on industrial councils, 295-297; works committees, 297-298; conciliation and arbitration, 302-303

Women: increased membership in trades unions, 28; women's trades, 41-42; Central Committee on Women's Employment constituted, 43; improved conditions, industrial transfers, 52-54; employment and remuneration, 98-100; arbitration tribunal for, 100; munitions tribunals, 100; appeal to register for war service, 124, 125; number enrolled, 133; protected occupations, 134, 135; in clerical and commercial occupations, 147-151; labor available early in war, 144-147; substitution for men, 54, 72, 140, 141, 144-158, 178-180; increased employment in ordinary lines, 151-152; in munitions trades, 72, 152-154; industrial training, 154-155; substituted for skilled labor,

96-97, 156-158; number and proportion in munitions work, 160-162; in non-munitions work, 162-166; in agriculture, 166-168, 175; statistics of employment, 168-171; table, 169; sources of supply for workers, 171-175; mobility of labor, 175-178; wages, 92, 99, 187, 189, 190-197; hours of labor, 99, 206, 207, 210, 211, 212, 213, 214; overtime, 120, 201, 212; welfare work, 216-220; housing problem as related to, 319; rates of pay not equal to men's cause of industrial unrest, 197, 263; readjustment in industry, 326-328

Workers' National Committee, 48, 49

"Workman" and "workmen" defined, 90

Workmen's Compensation Act, 1909, 10, 57, 266

Works committees: reports on, by Committee on Relations between Employers and Employed, 281-282, 297-298; by Minister of Labor, 298; functions, 299-301; relations to trade unions, 301-302